Mosaic of Fire

Mosaic of Fire

The Work of Lola Ridge, Evelyn Scott, Charlotte Wilder, *and* Kay Boyle

Caroline Maun

The University of South Carolina Press

Published by the University of South Carolina Press
Columbia, South Carolina 29208

www.sc.edu/uscpress

Manufactured in the United States of America

21 20 19 18 17 16 15 14 13 12
10 9 8 7 6 5 4 3 2 1

Library of Congress Cataloging-in-Publication Data
Maun, Caroline C., 1968–
Mosaic of fire : the work of Lola Ridge, Evelyn Scott,
Charlotte Wilder, and Kay Boyle / Caroline Maun.
p. cm.
Includes bibliographical references and index.
ISBN 978-1-61117-086-3 (cloth : alk. paper)
1. American poetry—Women authors—History
and criticism. 2. American poetry—New York (State)—
New York—History and criticism. 3. Greenwich Village
(New York, N.Y.)—Intellectual life—20th century. I. Title.
PS151.M38 2012
811.009'9287—dc23
2012011196

This book is dedicated to
Laurette Marie Lévesque Maun
(1931–2010)
and Dorothy McInnis Scura
(1933–2009)

CONTENTS

ACKNOWLEDGMENTS

This book was born out of my interest in the Evelyn Scott archives, introduced to me by Robert Welker (1924–2008), Professor Emeritus of English at the University of Alabama in Huntsville. Welker wrote a 1958 dissertation on Scott, and at her death in 1963 he received many of her effects from her widower, British novelist John Metcalfe. Welker stored papers he received after Evelyn Scott's death in a carriage house at his home in the Twickenham district of Huntsville, Alabama, and when I completed research for my Ph.D., he donated them to the University of Tennessee Libraries, Special Collections, where they are open for research. It was at that carriage house in Huntsville that I first was introduced to Scott and her circle. Reading their surviving letters, I was struck by the level of engagement she shared with her closest female friends.

My subsequent inquiries led me to other library archives. I am grateful to librarians at the New York Public Library, the Morris Library at Southern Illinois University in Carbondale, and the State Library of New South Wales. I extend particular thanks to Bill Eigelsbach, University of Tennessee Libraries, Special Collections; Diane Ducharme and Naomi Saito of the Beinecke Rare Book and Manuscript Library, Yale University; Lynda Leahy of the Schlesinger Library, Radcliffe Institute for Advanced Study, Harvard University; Leslie Fields at the Mount Holyoke College Archives and Special Collections; Richard Workman of the Harry Ransom Humanities Research Center, University of Texas at Austin; and Zephorene Stickney of the Marion B. Gebbie Archives and Special Collections at Madeline Clark Wallace Library, Wheaton College. Karen Kukil of the William Allan Neilson Library, Smith College, extended outstanding hospitality. I also thank scholars Thomas Austenfeld, John E. Bassett, Michele Leggott, Sandra Spanier, and Mary Wheeling White for information and encouragement.

Those responsible for the Ridge, Scott, Wilder, and Boyle Estates have been extraordinarily generous in granting permissions. I am fortunate in the friendships of Denise Scott Fears, Elaine Sproat, Ian von Franckenstein, and Tappan Wilder.

Quotations from the works of Lola Ridge are by the kind permission of the Lola Ridge Estate; quotations from Evelyn Scott's writings are by the kind permission of the Paula Scott Estate; quotations from Kay Boyle's works are copyright Kay Boyle, reprinted by permission of the Estate of Kay Boyle. The unpublished letters, writings, and poems of Charlotte Elizabeth Wilder are published with the consent of the Wilder Family LLC c/o the Barbara Hogenson Agency and courtesy of the Yale Collection of American Literature, Beinecke Rare Book and Manuscript Library, Yale University. The unpublished letters of Isabella T. N. Wilder are published with the consent of the Wilder Family LLC c/o the Barbara Hogenson Agency and courtesy of the Yale Collection of American Literature, Beinecke Rare Book and Manuscript Library. The unpublished letters of Amos Niven Wilder are published with the consent of the Wilder Family LLC c/o the Barbara Hogenson Agency and courtesy of the Yale Collection of American Literature, Beinecke Rare Book and Manuscript Library. Quotations from *The Collected Poems of Evelyn Scott* are copyright 2005 National Poetry Foundation, reprinted with permission. Passages of letters by Lola Ridge, Evelyn Scott, and Kay Boyle that are housed at the Harry Ransom Humanities Research Center are reprinted with permission. Generous permission to publish materials by Ridge, Scott, and Boyle in the Lola Ridge Papers was granted by the Sophia Smith Collection, Smith College, Northampton, Massachusetts.

An earlier version of chapter 2 appeared as "The Loneliness That Sings: Evelyn Scott's *Precipitations*" in *Evelyn Scott: Recovering a Lost Modernist*, edited by Dorothy M. Scura and Paul C. Jones (Knoxville: University of Tennessee Press, 2001) and the revised version is printed here with the permission of the University of Tennessee Press.

Jim Denton and Linda Fogle of University of South Carolina Press have been outstanding to work with. I could not have invented better editors.

At a key time in my research, I received financial assistance from an Open Grant from the Humanities Center at Wayne State University. I thank the director, Walter Edwards, and I am also grateful for a year-long research fellowship in that oasis for scholarship.

I have had the pleasure of working in two academic departments at Wayne State University, and each of them provided collegial support during different stages of this project. In the Department of English I am grateful for the support of my chairperson, Ellen Barton, and colleagues Bill Harris, Julie Klein,

Christopher T. Leland, M. L. Liebler, Lisa Maruca, Ross Pudaloff, Barrett Watten, and Anca Vlasopolos. In the Department of Interdisciplinary Studies, which closed in 2007, I was sustained by the friendship and support of my chairperson, Roslyn Schindler, and colleague James Michaels. My partner, Frank Koscielski, deserves a medal for his forbearance, good will, and excellent readership.

Two important women in my life are present in spirit through these pages. I am in debt to my professor and friend Dorothy M. Scura for suggesting this project to me. Her death in 2009 was a severe loss to the many students and colleagues influenced by her generosity, wit, and keen insight. My mother, Laurette Maun, had the opportunity to read and enjoy this book before her death in December 2010. It staggers the mind to recognize all the small and large ways in which loved ones support the writing of books. Her notes of encouragement to me about each chapter she read remain on my desk.

Introduction

This book investigates the literary writings and friendships of a group of American women modernists during a period when their interactions and productivity were highest. For many readers Lola Ridge, Evelyn Scott, Charlotte Wilder, and Kay Boyle remain obscure. All of them were fearless in their artistic vocations.

These writers' lives and work intersected at various times in New York's Greenwich Village during the 1920s, 1930s, and early 1940s, and their contact was extended through letters and visits. This book is a study of the life span of a social network embedded in broader networks that may be more familiar in narratives of modernism. In examining the writing lives, poetry, and friendships of Lola Ridge, Evelyn Scott, Charlotte Wilder, and Kay Boyle, each of whom participated in the major currents of modern American literature early in their careers, one finds they cohere as members of a network of women authors who primarily thought of themselves as professional writers, who sought to grapple with major social issues in their poetry, and who had direct, personal connections with each other that advanced their careers as writers.

Aesthetically they are linked in their use of personal voice, in their use of poetry, fiction, and nonfiction as platforms to address social justice, and in their tendencies to employ modern, experimental artistic forms in their work. Ridge, Scott, Wilder, and Boyle negotiated paths from Imagism in the early periods of their careers toward alternative aesthetics as they matured, with Ridge Scott, and Wilder moving from free verse toward more formal poetry. While each had an individual trajectory through modernism, with considerable variety in their relationships and in their politics, this study shows how they grew individually and together within the framework of the professional publishing arena and grappled with modernist issues such as machine-age industry, individualism, and depersonalization. They all faced economic hardship for choosing to be professional writers, encountered challenges to their careers unique to women artists, and sought ways to negotiate what was often rocky terrain. The toll of placing writing at the center of their lives could indeed be high in terms of economic, physical, and mental health. On occasion they contemplated other paths because the obstacles to a professional writing life were formidable. They often had nowhere to turn but to each other for the sort of emotional support needed to sustain their dreams.

Their friendships supported and intertwined with their writing lives—they supported each other in ways that included recognizing the worth of each other's work, providing direct feedback on manuscripts, and simply acknowledging each other's talent. Not all the connections described here are of equal intensity or productivity, and in fact the friendships waxed and waned as events and misunderstandings arose. These were not always smooth friendships, but they were tremendously productive. Each author created space and permission for the others' writing. In addition to their individual achievements, their belief in each other made it possible to gather the will and sometimes the material resources for future work. When this network dwindled through death and separation, the support for the special challenges of writing also dwindled.

Lola Ridge established herself as an associate editor of two important little magazines in the late 1910s and early 1920s, and she was able to assist Evelyn Scott at the beginning of her career by publishing her poetry and introducing her to the circle of writers who most deeply influenced her early writing. Their friendship was central to both of them for more than twenty years. Lola Ridge introduced Evelyn Scott and Kay Boyle, and Scott's literary example provided an important influence in Boyle's early work. Scott was an energetic mentor to other writers, and she provided comments and encouragement for Boyle through a mostly epistolary friendship. They were an important, if sometimes ambivalent, support to one another, and later, when they again both resided in New York after periods abroad, Kay Boyle was one of the few friends who had the patience to remain in touch with Scott when she was deeply affected by a paranoid personality disorder. In the early 1930s Evelyn Scott introduced Lola Ridge and Charlotte Wilder, who became good friends. Scott's friendship with Charlotte Wilder was life changing and lifelong.

The circle as a site for inquiry—as opposed to a more formal sort of organization, school of thought, or club—is historically a productive approach. The circle is a private sphere phenomenon rather than an organized group, which might have a name or designated time and place to meet or other sort of protocol. Both public-sphere clubs and private-sphere circles are usually the result of one or more charismatic individuals who act—as Malcolm Gladwell has noted—as connectors, bringing others together. Ridge filled that role for this group. Not all these writers were always in the same location, so letters were a major part of how their friendships persisted. In fact letters are now the scholar's main access to the dynamics of the group. Visits occurred whenever health, travel, and finances allowed. For extended periods, Evelyn Scott and Kay Boyle lived abroad, but each continued to think of New York (particularly Lola Ridge's New York) as a home base.

The boundaries drawn for this study could be more or less circumscribed; I have limited the scope to several important, vigorous friendships and have uncovered themes familiar to scholars of American women's literature. This study may be placed alongside others that investigate circles or groups in American modernism. For example both Lola Ridge and Kay Boyle were close to Marianne Moore; Ridge, Scott, and Boyle were influenced by and friends with William Carlos Williams; Charlotte Wilder had a productive friendship with poet Louise Bogan. These individuals are all elements of the mosaic of American modernist writing, and the particular group on which I have focused was in many ways on fire—to follow the main motif in Lola Ridge's lifetime poetic project. Fire as a metaphor describes the drive these writers shared to be fully realized writing professionals, and it also describes a spirit flowing between and among them that allowed them—in the worst of times—to continue on that path.

Any examination that takes up neglected writers must speculate about why they are not well known in our time. This study participates in a tradition of criticism to refresh frayed cultural memory. Many critics working over the last twenty-five years have wrestled with the question of why we continue to seek out writers who are not especially visible even now, after much work has been done to recover texts. Some of the authors and texts who have been recovered fit comfortably into predominant aesthetic schemas, established historically and emergent. Some provide social and aesthetic value outside normative narratives of modernism. So much of modernist commentary is still wrestling with the question of canons. How writers did or did not achieve visibility is not reducible to any single theory. Canonicity depends on a complex tangle of influences and decisions by stakeholders at various levels over long periods of time. As scholars, we can have some effect on the visibility of modernist authors who were excluded for various reasons from histories, criticism, curricula, and anthologies during the 1940s, 1950s, and 1960s. The consensus about canonicity becomes less precise as one travels from decade to decade, anthology to anthology, however, and much of current modernist criticism has worked to uncover these landscapes in an atmosphere of greater liberality and curiosity about the modernist narratives we have not yet discovered.

Projects that attempt to recover modernist texts, particularly those that reflect a social orientation rather than a primarily aesthetic one (or who focus on authors who attempt to do both) are the grandchildren of Cary Nelson's *Repression and Recovery: Modern American Poetry and the Politics of Cultural Memory, 1910–1945*,[1] published in 1989. Nelson emphasized that he would "raise a number of difficult questions about literary history—some very much a part of current debates, some less familiar—and provide suggestions about how to seek appropriate, necessary, and yet altogether provisional answers to questions that cannot actually be settled" (3). The debates Nelson referred to, current in the mid to late 1980s and early 1990s, are what are now known as the "canon wars." Allan Bloom's *Closing of the American Mind* (1988) and E. D. Hirsch's *Cultural Literacy* (1988) were central to the popular perceptions of these issues.[2] Bloom's and Hirsch's books presented a conservative reaction to the expanding of the literary canon in university curricula and as reflected in the subjects of academic studies and emerging disciplines—including gender studies, ethnic literatures, and postcolonialism. Bloom argued that higher-education and general-education curricula were unduly influenced by the democratic movements of the 1960s. The expansion of texts rose concomitantly with a rise in scholarship that self-consciously explored underrepresented and alternative points of view. Bloom stressed that education had become relativistic to the point that it no longer produced discerning citizens who were able to evaluate texts or who had a common cultural background. The "closing" of minds was, according to his argument, the result of the opening of the aesthetic and social fields by which texts are judged.

Scholars undertook to read works and authors that did not neatly complete a dominant discourse of literary history, a discourse that had been contested and fashioned by a small number of academics in the 1940s, 1950s, and early 1960s. Both Bloom and Hirsch advocated a return to a traditional, mostly Great Books–style canon. They found a culturally conservative audience among those primarily outside the academy, who seemed ready to accept the conclusion that exposure to more literary voices led to cultural relativism. These forces lost the cultural battle, but in one sense it is good to recall what the dialogue was. Curricula, the discipline of literary studies, and literary history have been immeasurably enriched by the expansion of the canon and the refinement of critical tools brought to the task of excavation and interpretation. Nelson's response to these arguments was in part to demonstrate the cultural value of underrepresented texts by doing archival excavation and reconstructing the cultural contexts in which these works first appeared. He was able to broaden the criteria by which we evaluate outrider texts and artists.

Nelson stressed the provisional nature of any answers to the questions of canonicity, in essence saying that the urge for a transcendental truth, or a received and solidified tradition, or a list on which all are agreed, is an intractable problem of literary history. As he put it, "The challenge in thinking through the interpenetration of present and past in literary history is not to master the problem, or even to identify all its components—for neither goal is achievable—but rather to decide how to proceed in the midst of problems that can be acknowledged and clarified but not fully resolved" (3). He drew attention in a clear and compelling way to a large-scale forgetting (especially with regard to literary texts that engaged, to one degree or another, social issues) that took place as the story about literary modernism was developed and retold. What had been left out is "an immense amount of writing of great interest, vitality, subtlety, and complexity—writing, indeed, if one feels the need to argue the case on these grounds, of demonstrably high quality" (5). While there have always been narratives challenging the theories that were developed about high modernism, there have always also been alternative narratives. The present study contributes to an alternative narrative.

Canonicity varies among the authors studied here. Recovery of the work of Lola Ridge and Evelyn Scott was vitalized in the 1970s–90s by work to recover women's writing. The variety of verse forms in Lola Ridge's poetry makes her difficult to classify. Scott did important work in poetry, fiction, and nonfiction, but—because of her mental illness—her output varied significantly in quality from earlier in her career to later. Literary critics have made no attempt to recover Charlotte Wilder's work; the circumstances of her mental illness and hospitalization were tremendous impediments to her becoming more widely known. Alone of these authors, Kay Boyle has remained in a field of literary awareness, and she alone was able to maintain a writing career that most observers would judge broadly successful. She was a beneficiary of mentoring from Lola Ridge and Evelyn Scott, who both helped her at the beginning of her efforts, but she then mapped her own success independent from them. In analyzing the canonicity of these authors we arrive at a variety of circumstances and outcomes, which agrees with the idea that multiple factors and agents contribute to any artist's canonical fate.

To varying degrees the writers in this study used poetry as a platform to comment on and investigate social events and issues. Each was also informed and responding to the aesthetic trends of modernism. They were not "high" modernists, whose main focus in writing was to further the aesthetic experimentation of their art. If high modernism tended to focus on art as an autonomous object with the presentation being ahistorical, then the poetry of these women is different. A rough grid of these tendencies in poetry may be useful in placing these authors within a larger sphere. On the imagined and provisional axes of social/aesthetic and modernist/sentimental orientations for art, Lola Ridge, Evelyn Scott, Charlotte Wilder, and Kay Boyle would inhabit the modernist-social area. Social poetry refers to events, people, and acts specific to historical times and makes arguments about them in order to document events, change minds, or foment action. Aesthetic poetry often lacks such historical references and instead makes arguments for its own beauty. Modernist poetry espouses in one form or another Ezra Pound's edict to "make it new" and tends toward objectification of its subjects; sentimental poetry relies on traditional tropes that depend for their effectiveness on the rousing of the readers' emotions. These are of course imperfectly exclusive categories with a great deal of overlap. Modernist-social poets tend to produce art that is more modernist than sentimental and more socially oriented than aesthetically oriented, though not exclusively so.[3] One tendency shared by all the writers discussed in this book is an antisentimental approach to writing, which is one basis of their connection artistically. Other poets who have both modernist and social tendencies in their work are Carl Sandburg, Hart Crane, Robinson Jeffers, Langston Hughes, Genevieve Taggard, Muriel Rukeyser, Kenneth Rexroth, and W. H. Auden. In contrast most of the poets we recognize as canonical high modernists—such as Pound, Eliot, Stevens, Williams, and Moore—may be classified as modernist-aesthetic in orientation. Modernist-social poets use poetry to heighten social consciousness, address injustice, and articulate the voice of the underrepresented, either through the lyric "I" or in poems dedicated to representing minority or feminist points of view. Often poets of this orientation refer to specific events or people in their work to encourage solidarity. Some poets with this orientation, although not all, write to promote a political ideology.

In addition to Cary Nelson's *Repression and Recovery,* an important precursor in the effort to recover neglected writers is William Drake's *The First Wave: Women Poets in America, 1915–1945* (1987), which places Lola Ridge and Kay Boyle in a context of innovative women writers.[4] Drake's women's literary history made occluded authors visible and recontextualized more familiar authors within a broader matrix of figures. He recognized that friendship was an organizing and generating force in the work of many women writers of the period, and he introduced these women writers to a wider readership. As he put it, "supportive relationships among women appear to have been indispensable in the phenomenal wave of female creativity" (240) during the 1920s and 1930s. In expanding the range of writers considered for inclusion in his literary history, his study anticipated Nelson's *Repression and Recovery.* Drake's work attempts to "revive memory" (xviii), a project the two scholars shared.

Shari Benstock's *Women of the Left Bank: Paris, 1900–1940* (1986) and Gillian Hanscombe and Virginia Smyers's *Writing for Their Lives: The Modernist Women, 1910–1940* (1987) are broad surveys of writers, editors, and publishers who, during the early decades of the twentieth century, found themselves writing part- or full-time in Paris and became involved in thriving writing networks centered there. These studies consider women writers in their networks, including writers who have traditionally been central to broad understandings of modernism and those who were peripheral or (before these studies) not visible at all. Hanscombe and Smyers's study moves from node to node on a network that spans Chicago, New York, London, and Paris. Biographically driven, their book emphasizes a sense of discovery, the unconventional lives that women writers often led, and the ways in which women promoted each other's work and acted as facilitators and patrons. The book focuses on the networks created through publishing, reviewing, travel, friendships, writing, and the promotion of writing. Taking as their field of research not only personal correspondence, the publishing record, and autobiography, Hanscombe and Smyers also looked to the work itself, recognizing that many of the women in their study used life experience and relationships as the raw material for poetry and fiction. They traced many different kinds of ties, from life partnerships to financial patronage among women writers including H.D. (Hilda Doolittle), Amy Lowell, Gertrude Stein, Harriet Monroe, and Marianne Moore. The study also explores the fact that many women authors in the early twentieth century chose to live unconventionally, in part because to write professionally requires a particular relationship to space and time that traditional women's roles, such as wife and mother, do not support well. Some of the authors raised families, but it is rare in modern American women's poetry to find a writer who was in a conventional marriage. As Hanscombe and Smyers pointed out, women writers did carve out the security they needed to write, but they often did so with other women who could share the pioneering of boundaries with them. While centering their study on a network of female writers, Hanscombe and Smyers did not neglect to integrate the important ties and support that men in writing and publishing provided to these women. Interestingly most of the authors their book examines were not prominently involved with the major social movements of their time, such as suffrage. As they put it: "Those who are 'political' *intend* to effect change, developing analysis and tactics (which may include art) to bring about desired social and cultural shifts. By contrast, those who consider themselves—or who are considered to be—'artistic,' don't set out intentionally to effect such changes; and may be as astonished as any of their readers if their work turns out to be influential in promoting social change."[5] Because of their focus on writers who consider themselves "artistic," Hanscombe and Smyers's study excludes writers who are "political" or "social." Writers with these emphases tend to network with other writers who have similar goals.

Other authors have noted a schism between writers who wrote with predominantly aesthetic orientation and those who wrote from an urgency to develop art as a way to shape the social world. These are not mutually exclusive agendas, but they can describe broad tendencies in poetry. What makes some readers less comfortable with texts that inhabit a socially inflected modernism? To readers then and now, the mixed social and aesthetic motives may seem to be a contradiction. In *Poetry and the Public: The Social Form of Modern U.S. Poetics* (2002), Joseph Harrington has taken up the question asked with force by Jane Tompkins in *Sensational Designs* (1986): "Is it any good?" As Harrington pointed out, the "overall tendency of poetry studies in the United States (more so than other fields of criticism) has remained evaluative and canonical": "And the twentieth-century canon has remained high modernist: even if they are treated historically, when it comes to books of criticism, especially, at the turn of the twentieth century, it's still Pound, Eliot, Williams, Stevens, and maybe Moore, H.D., or Frost. Not only does this picture continue to marginalize other interesting poets, it presents a reified, inaccurate picture of poetry, including 'modernist' poetry, of the period."[6]

The hegemonic story is not only skewed but dull. Efforts to recover micromodernisms remain positioned and embedded in relation to modernism's most recognizable names. Even a poet such as H.D., herself the beneficiary of a longstanding effort at literary recovery, owes at least part of her success to her congruity with the main principles of aesthetic modernism. Nelson, Tompkins, and Harrington—among others—have promoted a project of reexamining outlier authors and texts to reevaluate the aesthetic tools wielded to produce the familiar results of canonization.

The recovery of individual authors has not been enough, particularly in modernism, which has continued to be largely canonical. Harrington has noted that, "if new writers eke their way into the penumbra of the modern poetry canon, it is only when they can be considered modern*ist* writers. The study of non-modernist modern poetry is not visible, let alone taken as interesting or valuable."[7] This is not entirely true, especially since Suzanne Clark's *Sentimental Modernism: Women Writers and the Revolution of the Word* (1991) increased appreciation for Edna St. Vincent Millay, whose "repetition of conventions" and absence of irony contemporary readers found comforting, but that many subsequent readers, attuned to appreciate aesthetic modernism, found grating.[8] The larger point—that discussions of alternative modernisms often import the dominant discourse—is accurate. So, when encountering writers new to us in modernism, it is hard to avoid repeating the pitfalls of literary history.

In *Women Poets on the Left: Lola Ridge, Genevieve Taggard, and Margaret Walker* (2001), Nancy Berke blamed the social themes in her subjects' poetry as part of the reason for their critical neglect: "[they] emphasize social commitment and radical, political consciousness as a poem's primary, although never exclusive, goal. Much modern poetry criticism has written off socially directed verse as propaganda without looking at its deeper nuances or its social and historical position within its culture."[9] Berke argued that a different set of poetic values may emerge from examination of poets who have social motivations for writing poetry. Like Nelson and Drake, she is interested in restoring cultural memory. Her work and Drake's constitute the major examinations of Lola Ridge in contemporary criticism.

Literary historian and critic Elaine Showalter has argued in *A Jury of Her Peers: American Women Writers from Anne Bradstreet to Annie Proulx* (2009) that the reason why many worthy women authors are still not widely known has to do with the failure of feminist literary criticism to construct a defined literary tradition.[10] Although in practice her book is extremely inclusive, Showalter is committed to making distinctions based on her assessments of the quality of the work she analyzes. The canon has historically been a contested space where scholars made valuations aggressively; in contrast "many feminist critics are very much opposed to any kind of selection, ranking, even chronology."[11] Showalter's point is that competing visions of women's literary history on a scale she attempts are relatively scarce and that there has been a reluctance within the feminist community to rank authors. She demonstrates the historical and widespread trend during the first half of the twentieth century for male reviewers to denigrate women's writing. What is not addressed is the difference any contemporary canon will have based on changes in media and how readers encounter and absorb texts through new technologies. Now that digital-publishing formats are used and more venues for publishing scholarship and primary texts are available, it is likely that the range and volume of texts that readers will consume will be changed, and the imperatives to exclude texts and authors will alter—but not disappear—as a result. What were primarily constraints of space have now become restraints of time. The limits of audience, or how many authors can be absorbed by readers and in curricula, exert more force than was previously felt. To a large extent, criticism on canonicity still responds to the technology of the middle and late twentieth century rather than adjusting to current practices that will tend to expand the field considerably.

Lola Ridge, Evelyn Scott, Charlotte Wilder, and Kay Boyle created, through their friendships and professional work as editors and writers, an outpost in the literary field. It is not surprising that Ridge—given the literary life she lived in Greenwich Village, including working as an editor on modernist little magazines and hosting gatherings for the circles involved in those projects—was able to help up-and-coming writers. The record of what she was able to do for others exists in the memoirs of her contemporaries, in the tables of contents of the journals she worked on, and in correspondence. For instance one author she helped introduce to the public was African American novelist and poet Jean Toomer. In their correspondence she commented on specific manuscripts and helped guide him in submissions to *Broom.*[12] Characteristically she facilitated a network of emerging writers by recommending Evelyn Scott's 1921 novel *The Narrow House* to Toomer, which he read and admired, calling the novel a "superb piece of etching."[13] In first approaching Ridge to respond to his manuscripts, he remarked, "Very seldom have I met one with intuitive appreciation."[14] The relationship was not strictly one way from the older poet as mentor to the younger; Toomer also offered comments on poems that Ridge had published recently in *Poetry* magazine. Ridge was solicitous of writers and offered them editorial guidance, moral support, and—enabled by the positions she held—direct opportunities for publishing. She considered as part of her work the fostering of connections between writers.

As in any social network, all the bonds are not equally strong, and all that was exchanged back and forth was not identical or without ebb and flow. However, this network was significant because the friends Ridge encouraged enacted some of the aesthetic and feminist principles she outlined in her 1919 lecture "Woman and the Creative Will." She found in Evelyn Scott, Charlotte Wilder, and Kay Boyle artists who modeled the courage necessary for women writers to overcome some of the social and psychological barriers to forthright expression. They were literary innovators who proceeded in part because of the possibilities and world their friendships with Lola Ridge created. By helping her friends to believe in themselves, she assembled around her a group that benefited from mentoring and that created an intertextual matrix of support.

An interesting if somewhat skewed glimpse into the circle that included Lola Ridge and Evelyn Scott exists in Cyril Kay Scott's 1923 novel, *Sinbad.* Evelyn Scott's common-law husband, Cyril Kay Scott had begun his career as a novelist on their return from a six-year self-imposed exile in Brazil in 1918. His novel is narrated from the point of view of a person who is greatly disillusioned with the lure of Greenwich Village, and the focus is on the destructive relationship between characters Emily Tyler (based on Evelyn Scott) and Howard Story (based on William Carlos Williams). The friendship he depicts between Emily and her closest friend, Genevieve (based on Lola Ridge), is a tender one. For the most part *Sinbad* is a roman à clef with characters who correspond to Cyril, Evelyn, Lola Ridge and her partner, David Lawson (known as Davy), and William Carlos Williams. The fiction follows the emotional track of Evelyn Scott's affair with Williams, which disrupted her relationship with Cyril (Lester Drane). As part of the foreground, however, the novel describes what it was like for the newly arrived pair (as in life, not married and living under assumed names) as they tried to find a group of sympathetic, like-minded friends among the careerists and double-crossers:

> Lester and Emily in coming to New York had innocently looked forward to finding individuals who would comprehend and sympathize with their aspirations. Thinking of themselves as misunderstood, wounded, and disheartened in a callous provincial atmosphere, they had both unconsciously made the meeting of "fellow artists" a last symbol. They had been naively religious in this faith. To know people who can share and inspire instead of hinder and destroy! Lester smiled now as he thought of it. A few months among the jealousies, anemia and nerves of various hostile coteries had driven him and Emily to gather about them a small circle of their own. Not great, perhaps, but here at least is a little kindness, he thought. Tonight in the obscure restaurant, warmed and confident for the moment, all were talking at once, not brilliantly or profoundly, but harmlessly.[15]

The passage has an elegiac air because this protective circle will not endure. The desire for a cohort of mutually supportive artist-friends is key, however. In this small group Genevieve Strang (Ridge) is Emily Tyler's closest female friend and tries to give her guidance when Emily's compass begins to spin after meeting Howard Story (Williams). Scott did in fact turn to Ridge often during the course of their friendship for guidance, literary and emotional. Emily, younger, impulsive, and prone to creating chaos, is grounded and supported by her older friend, Genevieve, who encourages her to repair her relationship with her long-time partner, Les, after things with Howard Story go bad (a characterization that served Cyril Kay Scott, who wrote the book in a way that prioritizes his relationship with Evelyn). Genevieve is represented as a gentle, compassionate, but firmly normative influence in Emily's life. In fact Lola's role in Evelyn's life was supportive and nonjudgmental; wherever Evelyn's heart went, it seemed, she had a friend who reminded her when she doubted it that she was an artist first. Often being an artist coincided with living an emotionally chaotic life. What Cyril Kay Scott depicted in his novel is the relationship of guidance and groundedness that Lola represented for Evelyn, which transcends the particular agenda that the plot of his novel forwards.

Evelyn Scott's life is documented in two biographies and in the two memoirs that she published during her lifetime.[16] She was southern by birth, although her hybridized family background included a father from the Midwest. She lived with her family in Clarksville, Tennessee, where she was born, and then in Russellville, Kentucky; Evansville, Indiana; St. Louis, Missouri; and New Orleans, where her parents moved to live near her paternal grandparents, who had settled there. As Scott's biographer Mary Wheeling White remarks, this early pattern set a template for rootlessness that governed Scott's adult life.[17] Evelyn was an only child and raised to believe that she was part of a great southern family, an ideology that she accepted critically, since her immediate family was often plagued by financial troubles. The gap between the image they sought to project and their actual circumstances was apparent to her and was something she had to make sense of. Her childhood, as she revealed it in her memoir *Background in Tennessee* (1937), was precocious and marked by an artist's insights. She was also frequently out of step with the dominant values of her environment. She was sexually liberated, having as a teenager invited a childhood friend to rid her of her virginity.[18] She was moved to a great extent by the inequalities of wealth and race surrounding her and involved herself in feminist social causes such as the suffrage movement when she was a teenager in New Orleans. By temperament an anarchist, she flouted convention when she left the country with a married man in 1912, Cyril Kay Scott (then Frederick Wellman), twenty years her senior, who would later become her common-law husband and father of her only child. The two traveled to London and then Brazil, where they spent the next six years, some of which were the hard years that are documented in her autobiography *Escapade* (1923) and subsequently in Cyril Kay Scott's autobiography, *Life Is Too Short* (1943). These autobiographies, widely different in perspective, make interesting parallel reading.[19] Before returning to the United States, Evelyn Scott began to send poetry manuscripts to little magazines. The appearance of her poems created a buzz as the couple arrived in New York from Brazil.

Scott's first literary appearances in print were in 1918 in Boston's *Poetry Journal,* where she published several poems and reviews of Brazilian poets. She also sent some poems to the *Others* American office, where Lola Ridge first became acquainted with her work. *Others* published four of Scott's poems. "Women" and "Young Girls" appeared in February 1919, and "Penelope" and "Young Men" appeared in the April-May 1919 issue. "Women" evokes some of the language of Percy Bysshe Shelley's sonnet "Ozymandius," and she transformed those echoes into a study of the brittle difficulty of women's contingent gender position: "Like crystal columns, / When they bend, they crack; / Conforming, yet not conforming— / Mirrors."

Scott likened the visages of women to mirrors that both reflect and absorb their subjects, prefiguring the contemporary poem of William Butler Yeats, whose colossus in "The Second Coming" has a gaze "blank and pitiless as the sun." The women in Scott's poem lack their own substance and are instead reflected beings, all their effort spent in conforming to vague expectations of what they should be. In Scott's poems, Ridge would have found much to complement her own theories about the difficulties women faced as artists, as she articulated them in "Woman and the Creative Will." She and Scott were in agreement about the struggle women face to become authentic artists in their own right and not simply create an art that is in opposition to or defined by male norms. In Scott's poems the eyes of the women become mirrors "winking in the sunshine"—dehumanized, their affect flattened. Scott approached her subject directly and used a vers libre format to create lines that accentuate the kaleidoscopic interplay of male and female.

In addition to having accepted some of Scott's poems for publication in *Others,* Ridge indicated her esteem for Scott's work through some words of review and a portrait she drew of Scott for *Playboy* magazine (published from 1919 to 1924 and not related to the men's magazine founded in the 1950s). About Scott's first novel, Ridge wrote, "*The Narrow House* is like a fork of lightning. It probes into hiding-places and shows you life—ugly, terrible, impotent—flayed of its last covering. Through all drips a bleeding beauty crucified, twisting on its nails, yet smiling with a pale radiance. I believe Evelyn Scott will take a high place in her generation."[20] Ridge gave unstinting praise and was willing to expend her own critical capital on behalf of the younger writer. Ridge's relationship with Scott continued—with only slight interruptions for misunderstandings—until Ridge died in 1941. In 1948 Scott contacted Ridge's widower, Davy Lawson, to propose doing a biography of Ridge, a project she did not ultimately pursue.[21]

Another of Ridge's protégés was Kay Boyle, a young writer from Cincinnati who arrived in New York to pursue her career in the spring of 1922. She was born in 1902 and was restless about home life, adoring her mother but in conflict with her father and grandfather, relationships that are the background of her autobiographical first novel, *Process,*[22] written in 1924 but not published until 2001. Boyle, like Evelyn Scott, lived in middle-class but strained financial circumstances. She came to New York to take a writing class at Columbia University and to work professionally as a writer.[23] In a letter to her biographer Sandra Spanier, Boyle reflected, "I naively took some of my poems to the *Broom* office, found Lola Ridge alone there trying to handle all the work, and we loved each other instantly."[24] Boyle distinguished herself as an assistant to Ridge and, with Lola's encouragement launched her career as a poet and later a novelist. As part of supporting both Evelyn Scott and Kay Boyle, Ridge introduced the two writers to one another by letter, and they corresponded, sharing their work and the details of their tumultuous lives.

Lola Ridge met Charlotte Wilder through Evelyn Scott in 1934, and although their ties were not as strong as those Ridge had with Scott and Boyle, Ridge played an important role in Wilder's life as she developed professionally as a poet. Born in 1898, Wilder was the younger sister of playwright-novelist Thornton Wilder and one of five children. She began her career as a poet and journalist in the early 1920s and was educated at Mount Holyoke and Radcliffe. She supported herself as a professor of English—first at Wheaton

College and then at Smith College—until she resigned in the early 1930s to pursue writing full-time. She probably met Evelyn Scott in 1931 during a residency at Yaddo, the writers' retreat at Saratoga Springs, New York. Lola Ridge was an important literary contact for Wilder, and one of the gifts of her friendship with Scott was Scott's introduction of Wilder to Ridge. Wilder called on Ridge for help with applications for grants and visited Ridge and Davy Lawson frequently. For example Wilder asked Ridge to help her with an application letter for a fellowship sponsored by the Houghton Mifflin publishing company in 1935.[25] Ridge's work influenced Wilder, and Ridge's spirit and belief in Wilder as a poet was sustaining.

Scott and Wilder were close, sometimes sharing lodgings or living nearby enough in Greenwich Village for frequent visits. Their friendship took a strange turn when both became victims of political harassment. They reinforced and amplified one another's perceptions about a hostile environment. The Wilder family was alert to and cautious about Scott's developing paranoia about people she interacted with in a rooming house where she lived. Scott contacted the FBI about her suspicions, which no doubt contributed to Wilder's emotional unrest and overall stress level. In 1941 Scott lost both Lola Ridge, who finally succumbed to a long-standing tuberculosis infection, and Charlotte Wilder, who entered a mental hospital and remained there, with a brief period of freedom in the early 1950s, until her death in 1980. These events coincided with a general decline in Evelyn Scott's mental health and the effective ending of her once-promising career as a literary artist. The last book she published was *The Shadow of the Hawk* in 1941. She continued to work on two novels, both of which remain unpublished, and a book of poetry, that remained unpublished at her death in 1963 and was finally published in 2005 as a section in *The Collected Poems of Evelyn Scott*.[26] Like the lives of literary artists, the friendship networks they inhabit also age and fray.

In their book *Women Poets on Mentorship: Efforts and Affections* (2008), Arielle Greenberg and Rachel Zucker point out how exceedingly rare constructive mentoring relationships were among modern American women poets. They focus on Marianne Moore and Elizabeth Bishop, but in generalizing about other women modernists they argue that most "who *were* published and read were mostly mentored by men, if they were mentored at all. Often they were almost completely isolated."[27] The women in this study had male and female mentors. Through the letters and works of these authors, we are able to understand the dynamic of the female network surrounding Lola Ridge. This study brings together the work of these women, whose contribution to American literary modernism is their blending of two principal veins of poetry that are often examined and lauded separately: socially engaged poetry influenced by left-wing politics and more aesthetic forms, such as imagism and forms celebrated by New Criticism. When the social and aesthetic impulses are blended, one potential result is poetry that does not fit comfortably into one orientation or another. Such poems may be judged as deficient by both critical camps, thereby falling between the historical cracks. Add to the aesthetic positioning of their work their personal and professional challenges as women writers, and there emerges a context by which to assess their role outside established and emerging literary canons. Ridge, Scott, Wilder, and Boyle represent a group that reinforced each other's commitments to participate in both modes of literary expression in spite of the risks to their art.

One

Imagism, Socially Engaged Poetry, and Lola Ridge

Irish-born, Australian and New Zealander immigrant-poet Lola Ridge has been described as an "anarcho-feminist," a "well-known poet on the Left," and "the most impassioned and certainly the most authentic of the proletarian poets." She has often and forcefully been identified with a left tradition in modern American poetry,[1] although the trajectory of her poetic career has made some critics uncomfortable.[2] Kay Boyle, who worked as a typist for Ridge when she was the American editor of *Broom,* described her as "an Australian poet of savage talent and fervent dedication to the arts."[3] Her books are suffused with empathy for those who struggle, and the choices she made as an artist and activist captured the imaginations of her contemporaries. Alfred Kreymborg, American poet, critic, playwright, and editor, introduced her poetry in his 1934 literary history *Our Singing Strength,* emphasizing her physical frailty, financial poverty, and strength of her spirit: "She has spent many years inside the frailest body on earth, so it seems, only to fight off death time and again after her many loyal friends had resigned her to the grave. . . . [S]he is an ardent rebel—a rebel fighting life and the forces of society in behalf, not of herself, but of the brotherhood of underdogs. In the face of her own poverty, she has devoted her labor to people much better off in worldly goods and health. The trenchant spirit holding her body intact is mostly at ease in revolution, among the pitiful shapes of slums, factories and tenements, and near the head of some insurrection she endows with her communal marching."[4]

Perhaps he was referring to her well-known activism in the Sacco and Vanzetti case of 1927. Emma Goldman described Ridge as a "sweet and lovely spirit" and "our gifted rebel poet," and Margaret Sanger said that Ridge was "an intense rebel from Australia."[5] Perhaps the highest praise of her came from her friend and fellow writer Emanuel Carnevali, who in his autobiography wrote "Emily Dickinson meant poetical solitude. . . . Amy Lowell meant voluminous and disorderly culture, wordiness, exaggeration.... But as for Lola Ridge, to fit her case no diminutive adjective would serve. It is not a case of sweetness nor any of those qualities, up to date, that have belonged to women writers. She is a poet, that's all."[6] He continued:

> Talk of propaganda here, was what I wrote of her poems. I wish every poet had something as strong and virile to uphold! It is not a matter of politics, it's a matter of such damning hatred and love as would turn a modern city to ashes. Virile?—it may be an insult to use that adjective since Lola Ridge has begun an era in which for a woman to be virile, i.e., masculine, might mean to be weaker. I think she is one of the most beautiful signs we have of woman's emancipation and independence. Let her be a socialist; this rebellion of hers is pure beauty, it is sanctified, it is nothing less than burning human blood. It is no longer that particular fact of the revolt against actual social conditions, which is, unfortunately, what affects today's socialists and anarchists. It is an eternal thing, the thing that caused Prometheus to be bound. It is the fire of heaven burning in this wonderful woman's blood.[7]

Carnevali situated Ridge as transcending the traditional categories of gender and their aesthetic valuations, going so far as to grant her a kind of mythological power. As these quotations highlight, several persistent tropes followed Ridge from the beginnings of her American career: she was a rebel; she was a mystic; she was poor at least partly by her ascetic choices; she had risked much for her art; she was physically infirm; and she was extraordinarily willful and passionate in her pursuit of art and the championing of artists she supported. She was also, because of her passion and commitment, controversial.

Not all her contemporaries found her as mystically inspiring as Goldman, Kreymborg, Carnevali, and Boyle. Of the gatherings at her home in Greenwich Village, William Carlos Williams wrote somewhat derisively, "she made a religion of it"—that is bringing writers together and seeming to take a vow of poverty in commitment to the artist's life.[8] Williams's friend was poet, fiction writer, and publisher Robert McAlmon, whom Williams met at one of Lola Ridge's gatherings. McAlmon created a character based on Ridge in his novel *Post-Adolescence*, first published in 1923. Named Dora (recalling Sigmund Freud's famous patient), she hosts frequent parties of artists and writers in Greenwich Village, just as Ridge did. It is not a sympathetic portrait—the main character, Peter (who is based on McAlmon), reflects: "poor old thing, pretending to be a revolutionary and flaming with passion when a few good meals would change all of that perhaps, except that she'd still be pathetic" (36). The Williams character, Jimmy, says, "I used to think she had a sense of what not to do once.... I used to like Dora, and thought I liked some of her things. What's there to say anyway?"[9] These fictional male poets behave in ways that mirror some of the gatekeeping that went on in the field of poetry with regard to women's contributions in general. Some male editors and publishers acted as governors and judges not only about the work of poets but about their social behavior. When one reviews those who championed Ridge and those who derided her, she uniformly evoked a strong response, negative or positive. Ridge received treatment similar to Williams's and McAlmon's from her colleagues on the little magazine *Broom,* Harold Loeb and Matthew Josephson, who had both aesthetic and temperamental differences with her. In concentric rings around her, Ridge had a rippling impact among artists and writers, especially those who inhabited the left-leaning, socially attuned camps of modernist literature. Closest to her was a network of women writers who were associated through friendship but also through sharing of aesthetic and political values.

There are two anecdotes about Ridge—one related by a fellow author and one a portrait from her unpublished journal—that suggest in brief how complex a figure she was. It becomes a question of how to reconcile these two portraits. In her 1940 diary, as she reflected on her life as an artist, focusing on iconic memories, the clarity with which she recalled a cradle memory after more than fifty years attests to the sharpness of her recall or the depth of her imagination—or both. As a toddler, she lay

> beside a table or chiffonier, my mother seated gazing into the mirror before her. She was doing something with her hair. Watching her, I suddenly became aware of her beauty (she was very lovely in her youth).
>
> Now, this luminous moment yet lives in me, her face in profile then turned toward me, the delicate, finely structured face and head, the sweet proud mouth, the large turquoise-blue eyes. The image hangs, the mingled sweetness and pride that was almost hauteur on her face—but there the unnameable haunting thing that is beauty. The light streaming on her and on my cradle—I suppose sunlight through a window.
>
> Of course I could not name this feeling for myself—I had no symbols, for I was at the pre-symbol age—I could not speak. But the sense of beauty was there and I distinctly remember a feeling of pleasure—a contentment in knowing that the beautiful object was in some way attached to me, was *mine.* The experience was so intense it automatically recorded itself on consciousness—the lighted moment, a perpetual oval, to be recalled at will, sometimes to reappear spontaneously, a soft serene shining.
>
> It must have been at that precise moment I first became conscious of my own identity, I lying watching from my cradle the mirror, glimpsed obliquely, my mother's face, aglow in the instreaming light.[10]

Near the end of her life, Ridge described in this image her "first world," as Gaston Bachelard might call it in *The Poetics of Space* (1994), which explores the psychological relationship between inhabited spaces and the development of the imagination. Our first house is in essence our cradle, and the house and the mother provide shelter in which the imagination can develop. This sense of shelter that the cradle, the mirror, the image of her mother, the sunlight, and accompanying comfort and pleasure represent was a moment of what Bachelard might call "Motionless Childhood," a heightened fusion of memory and imagination that stands outside time, where "we comfort ourselves by reliving memories of protection."[11] The moment is luminous because it was a defining time in which Ridge was mothered completely, and she relived it again and again through the years in order to mother herself. The infant is in immediate communion with her mother and with her environment. This sense of safety and shelter was pivotal to Ridge's development as a poet, and her mother became her first audience.

Rose Emily Ridge was born on December 12, 1873,[12] at 1 St. James Terrace, Dolphin's Barn, Dublin, Ireland. Her father, Joseph Henry Ridge, was a medical student, and her mother, Emma O'Reilly Ridge, was widowed a few years after Rose Emily's birth. Traveling with her young daughter, Emma resided first in Sydney, where they had family already settled, and then moved to Hokitika, New Zealand, a small gold- and gemstone-mining town on the west coast. In spite of the gold rush, prosperity eluded them. Ridge later wrote about the family's hardscrabble existence in her unpublished 1940 diary, painting a grim picture of their family life and setting the stage for an adult consciousness that was especially cognizant of poverty as an actionable social issue. Ridge's mother, Emma, married Donald McFarlane, a Scottish immigrant and miner, in September 1880. Theirs was a troubled marriage; Donald eventually entered a mental institution in 1896 and died there in 1906. In *The First Wave* William Drake presents a tableau of their lives in this period, which complements Ridge's early memory of being in the cradle. Her alcoholic stepfather regularly indulged in "raging drunken sprees when he would smash every stick of furniture in the three-roomed shack."[13] It was in such a turbulent atmosphere that the young girl first apprehended her calling to be a poet.

Despite the extreme poverty and emotional pain of that household, there was also abundant natural beauty surrounding them in Hokitika, a fact reflected in much of Ridge's poetry from her Australasian years. The figure of her mother—who is represented as caring and beautiful—also engaged and instructed her daughter's aesthetic sensibility. Her stepfather was emotionally troubled and defensive, but she recounted how on one evening, when the trio was sitting in relative peace as she attended to her homework, the sound of the nearby creek was elevated in her perception from the background to the foreground: the creek "so long docile, unnoticed ... endlessly vociferating, separating itself from all the other noises of the night—Suddenly talking in sweet clamor to my ears alone." It is interesting that for Ridge a significant part of the poetic act was observing and noticing—the shaping influence of perception and the way that a natural phenomenon, such as the sound of the creek, offered itself to her for consideration. What follows in the diary is also a moment of "Motionless Childhood": "An ache fell upon me and I looked at my mother . . . the pure pale cameo of her face—unmoved, disdainfully still sadness. . . . She did not hear my waters trebling." The silent and morose stepfather staring into the fire did not have ears to hear, but he shared in a moment of rare emotional vulnerability with his stepdaughter that he was thinking of his dead sister. Something about this tableau opened up the possibility of poetry for her, perhaps because she was singular in her ability to hear the music of the water and was called to write something of it, to share it with others in a way that captures its emotional significance. The young Ridge then wrote and showed to her mother what she believed was her first poem, written at age thirteen. Her mother's response was especially insightful: "My mother turned to me—an attention in her face—the Easter-lily face I was to see slowly wither—'There is something that it does—a poetic image.'" It was at this point that Lola says she knew that she was a poet, "one of them."[14]

Lola often referred to her mother in terms that highlight her physical and spiritual beauty and connected her early memories of her mother with her growing aesthetic sensibility and creative passion. Ridge often returned to these cameo-like images of her mother to calm the periodic rages she experienced as a child. Restlessness and subsequent peace formed a cyclic engine for her artistic production. In these images we see a young artist finding and cherishing safe spaces in the midst of a world that is conflict ridden and poverty stricken. She sought these spaces to develop the imagination and voice to write. We can understand that the passion Ridge brought to the poetic task was partly related to this desire to create and keep safe maternal spaces in which poetry could exist.

Contrast to these urges for enclosure and safety the description of Lola Ridge as protester of the executions of Nicola Sacco and Bartolomeo Vanzetti in Boston in 1927. By this point in her career, she had published *The Ghetto and Other Poems* in 1918, *Sun-Up and Other Poems* in 1920, and *Red Flag* in 1927. What she witnessed at these protests catalyzed her 1929 epic poem *Firehead,* which is a retelling of the Christ story inspired by the trial and execution of Sacco and Vanzetti. This extraordinary work was written and published in the two years following the protests. Her fifth book, *Dance of Fire* (1935) was also deeply inspired by these political and social events.

Ridge's early history of activism included close friendships with Alexander Berkman and Emma Goldman, as she was a founding member of the progressive Ferrer Modern School in New York, active in the Ferrer Center (where radical artists gathered in the early 1910s in Greenwich Village), and a founding editor of the magazine associated with the Ferrer Modern School. A self-described anarchist, Ridge was deeply concerned with the plight of individual freedom. The few modern critics who have written on Lola Ridge have all have cited the following description of Ridge given by Katherine Anne Porter in her autobiography *The Never-Ending Wrong* (1977).[15] Porter also attended the Sacco-Vanzetti protests and was an eyewitness to what transpired. At this time of international protest and scrutiny, Boston was an armed camp and crowd control was a serious issue. Outside Charleston Prison in Boston on August 22, 1927, when Sacco and Vanzetti were scheduled to die along with another inmate, many protesters had assembled and were confronted by mounted police:

> They galloped about, bearing down upon anybody who ventured out beyond the edge of the crowd.... Most of the people moved back passively before the police, almost as if they ignored their presence; yet there were faces fixed in agonized disbelief, their eyes followed the rushing horses as if this was not a sight they had expected to see in their lives. One tall, thin figure of a woman stepped out alone, a good distance into the empty square, and when the police came down at her and the horses' hoofs beat over her head, she did not move, but stood with her shoulders slightly bowed, entirely still. The charge was repeated again and again, but she was not to be driven away. A man near me said in horror, suddenly recognizing her, "That's Lola Ridge!"[16]

What would bring Lola Ridge, a poet who created and fiercely defended safe spaces and in fact found safe psychological spaces essential to her writing, to place her body before these horses? Surely she knew she was risking her life. She felt kinship to the accused because of their shared anarchist backgrounds, and no doubt she felt that what was at stake in the matter was of the gravest importance. For Ridge, under certain circumstances, perhaps the safest place to be was at the apex of danger when the cause was grave enough.

A picture included in Peter Quartermain's *Dictionary of Literary Biography* entry on Ridge shows her after this episode looking resigned yet matter-of-fact and being led away under arrest with Edna St. Vincent Millay, the two women on either side of a plainclothes police officer. Ridge went on to write at least three works directly inspired by her involvement in the Sacco and Vanzetti protest: "Two in the Death House," "Three Men Die," and *Firehead,* so her participation was a defining moment in her poetic career as well as in her revolutionary life. "Three Men Die," a poem acclaimed for its direct treatment of the trial, executions, and their effects, was published in *Dance of Fire* (1935). The poem presents Massachusetts governor Alvin T. Fuller as a Pilate figure whose impatiently tapping feet, insistent pulse, and jaded heart admitted no loophole and heard no plea in the time leading up to the executions. He considered the men "a menace to the state." Ridge effectively created a poetic portrait of a bureaucrat who must manage an international mess and a threat to the "many-storied fabric of our dream," the American dream, which many believed to be under direct assault by anarchists, who had a successful record of reaching government targets. Their activities culminated in the backlash known as the First Red Scare (1917–20), resulting in the deportation of many anarchists, including Ridge's friend Emma Goldman in 1919.

In "Three Men Die," Ridge is a participant-observer among the crowds assembled outside the prison, describing others who stood with her on that day and night. The sunset inevitably arrives, but the three in the death house are suffused with a "conscript light" as those outside the prison keep vigil. The light is part of the electrocution machinery, part of the system of death, items in the same series and conduit. The third man condemned to die that night, a thief, goes first. Sacco and Vanzetti are described:

> Two common men, they were not bred
> Through generations for the part
> Of brief authority. Each had
> That ancient singleness of heart
> That Bruno knew and Galileo
> And all the old discoverers
> Who held to their course amid veering winds
> And kicked death off like a shoe,
> The single aim, the pure intent,
> The virgin purpose, sharp as love,
> That neither love nor hate can move
> Or swerve to any meaner bent.

While Galileo did ultimately recant, it was after enormous pressure, being taken to the brink of execution, and Giordano Bruno, an Italian philosopher and mathematician, was burned at the stake for his heliocentrism. It was clear that no matter what the public controversy surrounding the particular guilt or innocence regarding specific crimes, Ridge, along with many others, saw the issues at the Sacco and Vanzetti executions as being as far-reaching. They were executed because of their political beliefs and because they were as immigrant-outsiders. Their deaths implicated a broad swath of the population of the

United States—people with alternative political views and those who had experienced ethnic prejudice.

The perspective of Ridge's poem lingers on the square outside of the prison, with fellow protesters surrounding her. Hearing "Drumbeats of the hooves" as the horses approach, she adopts a longer, Whitmanesque line and skillfully uses repetition to amplify the explosive percussions of the hoof beats. She makes a study of the animals themselves, imaginatively recalling the prehistoric taming of horses and the cultural transformation and transfer of power that occurred when that happened:

> Man, the soft-shelled thing, grew hard,
> He clinging to the meeked power, and valiant; breasted the rivers;
> outdistanced
> Tooth and claw, swept over prairies, heard the shrill battle-neigh
> Rising with his own and saw visible fire
> Flash from out the nostrils, foam on the curled-back lips, the hooves
> Clash like swords....

The power of human beings, Ridge argues, grew exponentially with the taming of horses.[17] She points out that they have been put to various uses in agriculture, warfare, and as domesticated show animals.[18] The advent of airplanes and other transportation has reduced human dependence on them drastically; yet they were a major component of effective crowd control, and film and photographic records of the August 1927 episode show the prevalence of horses deployed to manage the people gathered there. As she describes it:

> Drumbeats of the hooves ... so close, so close ... that one who had been
> there (and for some quite
> Unbalanced reason did not run ... but stood there in the hooves' path)
> had noted
> (Knowing horses) the lean head, straight nose, clean flank, the blooded
> Line of the onrushing shoulder, brought to this ... and feeling the wet
> foam of his mouth, glimpsed spread nostrils and the white
> Fire of the eye, rolling as in agony; one might have seen
> (All in the one beetling moment, there, awaiting the falling
> Cataract of hooves) the great body rear—swerve and plunge sideways
> And the lightning strike from the stone....

Ridge cannot explain the reasons for her rebellious stand, except to say that "for some quite / Unbalanced reason [she] did not run." One notes the solitude and isolation of her position, her reliance on intuition, and the fount of poetry that poured from this moment. One sees that she has created a safe space around herself where, at the last possible moment, the horse swerves and spares her. She imaginatively explores the conflicting roles of the beautiful horse as individual creature and as an animal put to a specific purpose by his masters. That the animal—which appears to be in agony—will not kill her is an act of mystical mercy. If Lola Ridge, with three volumes of poetry to her credit and pursuing a strong career in American literature, had died that day as a victim of police brutality, it would have radically underscored the aspects of the trials and executions that were prejudiced, predetermined, and unfair. She was prepared to martyr herself at a decisive moment in American history, where the future of a political movement she had been involved with for two decades hung in the balance, demonstrating that for her art and activism were one. The space of poetry, associated for her with safety, and the space of political radicalism, clearly a realm of personal risk, were not separate spheres for artist-activist Lola Ridge.

There is some uncertainty about the first decades of Lola Ridge's life. This complex woman lived abroad for more than thirty years before arriving in the United States, and the scholarly community will be assisted greatly when Elaine Sproat's biography of Ridge is completed. In the existing scholarship, the basic details about Ridge vary considerably from account to account. This protean critical history and biography are not made any simpler by the poet's having gone by several different versions of her name at various points in her life and her having published under different pen names. Add to this discrepancies in her date of birth, which she fostered, and the resulting confusion undermines her legacy with a basic instability at the origins of biographical information.[19] Her early writings—published in New Zealand and Australian periodicals—are difficult for readers outside these locales to obtain.

Not much is known about Ridge's early education, though she did report that she had a lonely, ten-mile round-trip walk through the woods to school each day.[20] Ridge led a disrupted life as a child and as a young adult. The documentary facts conceal much of the heartbreak that must lie behind them.

Rose Emily, by then known as Rosalie Ridge, married Peter Webster, a miner and mine manager three years her senior, on December 6, 1895, and they moved to nearby Kaniere from Hokitika. They had two sons. Paul Webster, born on December 9, 1896, died fewer than two weeks later of bronchitis. When Keith Webster was born on January 21, 1900, Rosalie Webster was twenty-six years old. She began publishing poems locally in New Zealand in 1892, slowly at first. Then she published a poem in the Sydney *Bulletin* on October 5, 1901, beginning a sustained record of poetry publication in Australia and New Zealand. The poem in the *Bulletin* was signed "Lola," and titled "A Deserted Diggings, Maoriland." It is a nationalistic ballad focused on the closing of New Zealand mines, revealing an early preoccupation with labor issues that informed Ridge's writing for the rest of her life. During the next few years, Ridge published poems that were enriched by the landscape and concerns of western New Zealand in newspapers in Dunedin and Auckland, New Zealand, and in Sydney, Australia. Something irrepressible had been stirred in her as she pursued her calling as a poet. Reflecting on this time near the end of her life, she wrote: "I felt surely, certainly, as I was sure that I was alive, there was some great thing to be done and that I was to do it, that I had been called, that I should be called again, that my life was for it."[21] Guided by her strong sense of intuition, she made major change after major change in order to secure the space in which to pursue this vocation. Her calling eventually took her from Sydney to San Francisco and then to New York.

On November 11, 1903, Ridge, her mother, and her young son emigrated from New Zealand to Sydney—without her husband, Peter. At some point after she had relocated to Sydney, she studied painting with Julian Ashton, a well-known Australian artist whose school continues to the present day. She began using the name Rosalie Webster with less frequency, asking journalist A. G. Stephens to not use it in publication. Instead she used her pen name, Lola Ridge, and at this time she began to report her birth year as later than 1873. This reinvented Lola Ridge persisted even until her death on May, 19, 1941, when her obituary notice in the *New York Times* erroneously reported that she had died at the age of fifty-seven instead of sixty-seven, her actual age.[22] It was also her habit to have editors withhold her birth year when her poems were reprinted in anthologies, even when those collections were often organized chronologically by the birth year of the poet.

During the early years of the twentieth century, Ridge made connections in the literary arts community, circulating a manuscript of her poems for potential publication. A. G. Stephens, an Australian literary critic, literary agent, writer, and editor for the Sydney *Bulletin,* retained a typescript carbon copy of "Verses by Lola Ridge," which is dated April 1905, indicating that she had sought his mentorship or his help as an agent.[23]

These early verses are of special interest to people who are familiar with Ridge's later works. Ridge was not yet as informed about currents in modern poetry as she became after entering the United States. In fact her ballads, which show skill and range within that idiom, seem more akin to Pre-Raphaelite or Victorian poetry, using sentimental tropes, iambic rhythms, and variations of traditional stanzas to explore themes that may be broadly classified as conventionally poetic. It is competent newspaper verse, and these early poems were a laboratory where Ridge learned meter, rhyme, and storytelling, aspects of the craft that continued to serve her well even after she had adopted the Imagist toolbox for much of her verse.

Still ahead was the infusion of the passionate sensibility present in these ballads with her later inflection of modern Imagism and its specificity and concreteness of language. The sentimentality of these early verses, however, is of interest to readers of her later poetry because this tendency informs her empathy and activism. Her early poetry does reveal continuity with tendencies Ridge exhibited later as she returned to poetic forms and even archaisms in language. In the early 1900s she had not yet found the motifs that unify her later books—light, fire, and spirit. She did, however, create protected spaces for poetry in her early works that reflect her iconic childhood memories.

A notable and transitional example of her early efforts is a blank-verse poem titled "Lake Kanieri," published in the *New Zealand Illustrated Magazine* in November 1902.[24]

Blue veined and dimpling, dappled in the sun
Lies Lake Kanieri, like a timid child
Wide eyed, close clinging to the spacious skirts
Of old Tuhua, the big, brawny nurse,
On whose broad lap I lie. No need to serve,
Or suffer, or regret: it seems life holds
No future and no past for me but this
Sun-lighted mountain and the brooding bush;
Nor art, nor history, nor written page
Could touch me now. It is enough to be,
And feel the slow and rhythmic pulse of Earth
Beat under me; and see the low, red sun
Lean on the massive shoulders of the range.
O lone, heroic, melancholy Hills!
You dim, gaunt peaks stand in the after-glow
Stern as Duty, implacable and cold;
Remote from the harsh clamour of the plains,
Whose pulse of life stirs dully at your feet.
O still, and calm, and pure, and wise, and strong!
My restless heart from your locked hearts shut out,
Leans on your strength, and craves the peace you hold—
Peace born of conflict. Ye old Stoic Hills,
Yield up your secrets! On your furrowed fronts
Are scars of fierce upheavals; in your grave,
Deep breasts what dreams are shut? Methinks you stand
Like pale, impassive monks whose chill looks hide
Forbidden memories of clinging lips,
Of passions conquered and of pains repressed
Within their breasts of snow. With outlines dim
The hooded slopes, like meek nuns grouped in prayer,

Kneel in the screenèd cloister of the bush
Dark robed and secret; and the laughing lake,
Smoothed by the slow, cool fingers of the dusk,
Has coiled herself to sleep. All light has gone,
Save on those heights where Day grown weak and old,
Close by the dying embers of the sun,
Sits, like an old man musing on his past.

Near Lake Kaniere is Mount Tuhua; the hills give the poet comfort and grounding; nature is a protective mother, creating a bower outside time for the poet to reflect. This blank-verse poem is carefully crafted to participate in the traditions of such poems by William Wordsworth, Robert Browning, and Alfred Tennyson. Some Victorian overlay occurs with the use of apostrophes, the manipulation of accented syllables to fit the iambic pattern, and the skillful stoppages in midline for emphasis. The poem is about a moment of peace, essential to artistic creation, one in which there is no need to contort to satisfy the social obligations that the world normally presses upon one. Outside literature, history, society, and time, the moment is simply for itself, but the consciousness of the persona quickly moves from the placidity of the scene of the long sunset, to the kinetic energy of the past, stored within the creases of the mountains that surround her, unspoken and ineffable, a record of ancient conflicts. The comforting and protecting hills become stoic hills that hold tragic and violent secrets. This is a transitional poem for Ridge. Her early efforts were much more reliant on the ballad tradition and tended to be portraits or narratives that resolved themselves within the confines and spaces of the poems. "Lake Kanieri" presents itself as the tip of a mountain of inferred information, which is suggested but not resolved by the poem and is thereby more modern in mood. Ridge drew from the transitional energy of Victorian literature in a move toward a modern sensibility, and the result shows some of the social consciousness that later took a more prominent role in her work as a writer.

Ridge's beloved mother, Emma McFarlane, died in Sydney at the age of seventy-four on August 2, 1907, of acute gastroenteritis and cardiac failure. Theirs was surely the most important relationship in Ridge's early genesis as a poet. The feeling of peace her mother provided remained the guiding light for the radical activist and social poet. Her admiration for her mother's perseverance and beauty informed Ridge's decidedly romantic early poetic tendencies. As "Lake Kanieri" shows, the role her mother played in the poet's early imaginative life was integrally associated with the landscape where she grew up in New Zealand. And, although she loved her mother greatly, her death no doubt freed Ridge to continue to pursue her dream of writing on a broader, more international stage. She left Sydney shortly afterward, accompanied by her young son, for San Francisco and then Greenwich Village.

Before settling in New York, Ridge published several poems in the *Overland Monthly* and *Gunter's Magazine* in San Francisco. She was using an assumed name, representing herself as ten years younger than her biological age. As a single mother, she had transplanted herself to a new environment having recently lost her mother and fled a broken marriage. These changes in name and how she reported her age indicate that she wished to shield her identity as she left Sydney, but she maintained that identity in the United States when her new life had begun. Her poems began to appear in New York periodicals in 1909.[25] While in Australia, she had published nearly forty poems and short stories. In the United States she did not mine the earlier Australian material extensively; only a few poems from her Australian period were republished, and only one of her early efforts was collected in an American volume of poetry.[26] Perhaps she did not do more in this regard because of the aesthetic shifts that she made or perhaps much of her early poetry was lost to her. She also quickly shed the backdrop of the Australian bush as setting for her reflections. Early work by Ridge appeared in Emma Goldman's *Mother Earth* in April 1909, indicating that Ridge found her way to the anarchist circle almost immediately upon her arrival in New York.

Ridge began a tradition of bringing writers together, a strong feature of her literary and editorial activity throughout the 1910s and early 1920s. In New York, as one of the founding organizers in 1910 of the Ferrer Modern School, under the leadership of Emma Goldman and Alexander Berkman, Ridge saw the power of the artistic and literary network as it formed around the Ferrer Center, which had a membership of approximately three hundred activists, artists, and educators. For many left activists, educational reform was essential to broadly construed social reform, and the Ferrer Modern School sought to educate the whole individual and to promote the creative arts as part of basic education for all students. Modern Schools, also called Ferrer Schools, were established in the early twentieth century mostly in the Northeast and Midwest. They were modeled after the Escuela Moderna of Francesco Ferrer y Guardia, a Spanish educator and anarchist who was executed without trial on October 13, 1909.[27] The curriculum of these schools championed individual rights and followed the curiosity of the students, children during day schools and adults in night classes. Many of these schools were fairly short lived; yet they provided powerful, life-changing experiences for students and instructors. In his history of the Modern School movement, Paul Avrich devoted generous portions of his study to the artists gathered around the political anarchists who organized the schools: "What drew these and other artistic and literary rebels to anarchism was their conviction that the freedom of the individual was indispensable for the flowering of culture. They believed that a libertarian society would be more favorable to the artist than any other, that art, indeed, depends on the full and free development of individual capacities."[28]

Gatherings at the Ferrer Center sometimes included the photographer Man Ray, novelist Upton Sinclair, playwright Eugene O'Neill, and novelist Theodore Dreiser. As first editor of the *Modern School* magazine (responsible for two issues before she and her partner, Davy Lawson, left New York for five years), Ridge gained valuable experience in editing that served her later when she was associate editor of *Others* and then American editor of *Broom*.

It was during her work at the Modern School that Ridge met Davy Lawson, a Scottish immigrant engineer with whom she lived for several years and then married in 1919. They were both committed to social causes, and Lawson was also dedicated to making Ridge's career as a writer a success. The letters they exchanged during extended periods when they were separated by Ridge's travels to the Middle East, to the American West, and Mexico to research her poetry show Lawson's tremendous solicitude and willingness to help her manage daily affairs and even to step in and help her other friends.

Asked by a reviewer for her thoughts on literature in 1935, Ridge responded: "There is a pernicious fallacy that the material of poetry and of the arts generally is necessarily limited to the subjects that are recognized as 'poetic'—i.e., that are without menace for the existing evils of social and industrial systems. For all life is the domain of poetry; not only the ancient rituals of love and birth and death, but all vast happenings, from wars, strikes, the endless crucifixions of labor to the being of the smallest flower."[29] For Ridge, and for the other writers in this study, art could be simultaneously about beauty and about action, about national events or about natural landscapes, about the political and the personal.

It has been in the interest of some modernist, aesthetic poets and critics to create and maintain a separation between poetry engaging social realities and that written primarily to delight. Yeats famously remarked: "We make out of the quarrel with others, rhetoric, but of the quarrel with ourselves, poetry."[30] In his poem commemorating Yeats, Auden said: "poetry makes nothing happen."[31] In *The Well Wrought Urn*, first published in 1947, Cleanth Brooks argued the tenets that became the New Criticism and subsequently dominated how poetry was read for decades: "The poem is an instance of the doctrine it asserts; it is both the assertion and the realization of the assertion."[32] In other words the poem is its own enclosed symbolic system, and one need not apply any outside reference points to its interpretation. A corollary is that the most successful, most artistic poetry is poetry that supports this sort of reading, especially poetry that makes no demands on the ethical dimension of responsibility or engagement. Ridge stood in stark opposition to this aesthetic-modernist viewpoint. For her the poem would always be about both beauty and the world.

Harold Loeb, editor of *Broom*, was acutely aware of and in opposition to Ridge's position on aesthetics. In his 1959 autobiography, *The Way It Was*, he revealed how he baited her regarding their differences,[33] and his criticisms are unjustifiably inflected by gender prejudice. The crux of their difference was that "Lola seemed to have a touchstone which instructed her what to choose and what to reject. Then she would defend her position passionately. A poem or article was good or bad because she knew it was good or bad. To her mind, its quality was staring one in the face. She would discuss it, to be sure, but anyone who failed to agree with her felt that she pitied his inability to see or feel the obvious."[34]

Ridge had a strongly developed and defended sense of aesthetic intuition. Loeb summarized their differences as aesthetic and political: "To her, capitalism was corrosive, its products corrupt; I felt that capitalism was impersonal, its products magnificent."[35] As others have noted, a good part of their rift had to do with Loeb's inability to accept a business partnership with a strong woman. As Peter Quartermain has rightly noted, their interpersonal disagreement should not obscure the profound differences of the theoretical positions that the two represented.[36] Ridge had suggested an all-American number of *Broom* from the beginning of her tenure as an editor (the January 1923 issue). This became the occasion of a wrestling match between the two editors. It is not surprising, given Ridge's commitment to American writers and her need to create a protected space for poetry to flourish, that she would request an issue exclusively devoted to American writers that she gathered and promoted. Loeb perceived that her request to have sole veto power over the issue usurped his authority. He would allow her veto power over any piece (in theory—in practice it did not work out that way), but he would not take "a few weeks' rest," as she suggested, for the duration of the editing of the issue (122). Loeb contended that there was not enough good American material to fill a single issue of the magazine and condescendingly stated, "Even with Kreymborg, I had clung tightly to veto power; I had no intention of giving it up to Miss Ridge" (122).

Ridge favored fostering an American idiom that was represented by writers such as William Carlos Williams, Sherwood Anderson, and Carl Sandburg and also by women authors such as Evelyn Scott and Kay Boyle. Loeb, perhaps as a result of his residing in Italy and Germany during the years of *Broom*'s publication, was more attuned to the American cultural contribution to European literature and art, admitting that his location abroad may have left him out of touch with what was going on in the United States—which was the purpose of having an American editor. In a letter to Loeb, Ridge described a literary history in which Ezra Pound would eventually be eclipsed by more native or populist poets. At heart Ridge had romanticized the idea of American literature. Clearly though, under the guidance of Loeb and Matthew Josephson, Loeb's associate editor in Europe, *Broom* had a different and emerging manifesto. As Loeb wrote to Ridge, "*Broom* is no longer a forum, as Waldo Frank put it, where anyone can hold forth who commands the English idiom. It is becoming an organ with a *strongly held* point of view."[37] The strongly held point of view evolved over many issues and editorials and was still in flux, but at the heart of it was an embrace of Dadaist aesthetics and the privileging of European over American contributions.

Loeb and Ridge's working relationship never recovered from several such aesthetic and political rifts. Ridge suggested a critical piece by Evelyn Scott for inclusion in *Broom*, and Loeb could barely conceal his nausea.[38] The permanent rift occurred over the publication of a short piece by Gertrude Stein in the January 1923 volume. Earlier Ridge had told Loeb, "Gertrude Stein has only an occasional gleam—it's mostly blah! blah! . . . In a few years her work will be on the rubbish heap with the rest of the literary tinsel that has fluttered its little day and grown too shabby even for the columns of a daily."[39] While this did not happen to Stein exactly, it is certainly a valid viewpoint. Loeb's point of view was ultimately also valid. He stated that he included Stein because she was pivotally influential to other important writers, regardless of one's opinion of her own efforts, and Josephson was in agreement with him. (Although one imagines that, if Loeb had been interested in pursuing things diplomatically, he would have held the contribution to another number, where Ridge was not at least tacitly to have controlling input on the contents, as she was for the January 1923 issue.) Ridge responded heatedly with the telegram, "RESIGN ON INCLUSION OF GERTRUDE STEIN IN AMERICAN NUMBER."[40] This turf war was cumulative and exacerbated by physical and aesthetic distance.

Although they did work together for a few more issues, Ridge's resignation was an expression of the intensity of the impasse and indicates the depth of their differences. About machine-age culture, Ridge was a skeptic but nevertheless one of the most powerful voices in American writing; regarding modernism, she championed writers who wrote with engagement in social issues, but she was able to support a wide range of writing styles. She did, however, stop short at Dadaism. She was, in spite of her range of opinion, misrepresented by her colleagues as retrograde.

In Josephson's account of the breach at *Broom* with Ridge, one finds a rigid chauvinism at work as well as an age gap. Josephson was quite condescending as he described their meeting in the early spring of 1923, when they had already had several failures of communication. Sent to New York to take over the American side of the publication after Ridge's argument with Loeb over Stein, Josephson met with Ridge in an effort to render her less "obstructive," and they attempted to talk about their differences and the fate of the magazine:

> There was one passage in our conversation which now seems amusing to recall. We had been discussing our different views of art and literature. With much emphasis Miss Ridge put the question: "Mr. Josephson, what is *your* definition of poetry?"
>
> "You know very well," I replied, "that up to this day the greatest of poets and men of letters have failed to provide us in the English language with a concise definition that is adequate. No more can I do so in a few words, although I can tell you what my preferences in poetry are."
>
> "I will tell you *my* definition," she went on very sweetly, narrowing her fine dark eyes and assuming a faraway expression. "My idea of the poem is a snowflake sparkling and melting in the sun."
>
> I said nothing, but bowed in acknowledgment of her metaphor. What could I have said to this excellent woman who had lived an arduous life up to middle age, suffered much poverty, and given expression to her experience in some poems that had the fire of a true idealist. There was a gulf between us. To my mind, the trouble with her and with a good many like her in America was that they still belonged to the "snowflake school" of poetry. We younger men, therefore, had a real job of modernization cut out for us.[41]

Josephson and Loeb seemed to need a foil against which to develop their aesthetic manifesto for the magazine, and they found a representative of the opposition—here depicted as a straw character—in Lola Ridge. If one compares Ridge's remark to Josephson to what she told the reviewer in 1935, one can see in the later comments a more developed point of view that more accurately reflected Ridge's views as poet and critic. Josephson and Loeb heard only what they wanted to hear, and for whatever reasons they needed a one-dimensional representative of a genteel tradition against which to rebel. That both authors made a point of putting the conflict with Ridge on the record is interesting. Both seem to have been determined to overwrite her presence and control the story. Both saw the conflict with her as a pivotal moment in the little magazine's history. Several factors converged to sink the magazine, including financial difficulties, government censorship, and a destroyed shipment of the magazine from Europe; yet the creative differences between these editors are an important factor. For a magazine in search of a manifesto, *Broom* became—at least in part—about personalities.

It is surprising that there has not been more current commentary on Lola Ridge. The most sustained study of Ridge's work to date was completed in 1987 by William Drake, who focused on Lola Ridge as a centerpiece to his study *The First Wave.* Drake's emphasis was on the importance of family roles in the lives of women writers and on their psychology and social circumstances as women. Lola Ridge's mother played a central role in her daughter's understanding of herself as a poet. Drake drew from Ridge's poetry and journals to highlight this relationship, arguing that it helped to crystallize Ridge's consciousness as an artist. Ridge's later descriptions of her mother in her unpublished diary are mystical in inflection, and Drake argued that "Ridge's poetry is marked both by rage at injustice and by a fiercely maternal urgency, as if the disorder of the world arose out of a separation from the spiritual center the mother represents" (4). He continued, "Ridge knew that her anger, her restlessness, her blunt force burned with the same fire as her spiritual aspiration and were inseparable from it. She differed perhaps from other women in not being fearful of these tendencies or dutifully trying to repress them, but seeking instead an individuation that would encompass the totality of herself" (185). This characteristic—that she did not tend, as many other women, to suppress the full range of her emotions and their expression in writing—is a core feature of Ridge's subsequent work. We also see evidence of this in the way that she is described and dismissed by Loeb and Josephson. Drake's readings of poems from Ridge's first two collections illustrate Ridge's idealism, mysticism, and desire to seek change through her writing.

In addition to Drake's chapters on Ridge, a substantial study of her poems "The Ghetto," "Submerged," "Electrocution," "Lullaby," "Stone Face," "Frank Little at Calvary," and "Morning Ride" is included in Nancy Berke's *Women Poets on the Left.* Berke selected these poems for their contribution to her overall focus on poets who "emphasize social commitment and radical, political consciousness as a poem's primary, although never exclusive, goal" (6). Viewing Ridge as a figure who has been occluded from cultural memory primarily because of her anarchist politics, Berke sought to bring Ridge's work to the fore in order to recover some of her now unfamiliar subjects and tropes and the ways in which she produced modernist texts. Berke has located her own critical precursors in Cary Nelson and Betsy Erkkila. Like Nelson, Berke seeks to recover authors who became obscure during the profession building of the 1920s and forward in the emerging discipline of American literature. The biases of primarily male professional critics tended to construct a discipline that was male, white, and middle class, and their work reflects ideological priorities of aestheticism and nationalism. While she emphasized that the poetry of Lola Ridge and of two other authors, Genevieve Taggard and Margaret

Walker, does not represent the whole spectrum of political poetry, Berke argued that they illustrate a portion of the topology of the progressive poetic trends of the time. Berke took from Erkkila the premise that the stories about American women modernists have served to emphasize the similarities between women at the cost of presenting the complexity and differences in their experiences. Berke has moved on from that position to say that feminist reconstructive criticism has not taken into enough account the historical events that are background for political poetry. Many scholars, even in works that focus on women writers, have chosen to reproduce similar canons. Berke has proposed that, should a scholar consider female poets who put "class before gender," it would likely result in a countertradition.

In 2007 Daniel Tobin edited *Light in Hand: Selected Early Poems of Lola Ridge.*[42] Emphasizing her Irish origins, he focused his introduction to the volume on a reading of Ridge's long poem "The Ghetto" and also assessed her contribution to modernism, praising her ability to render social situations with authenticity while at the same time finding tiresome her tendencies to write archaisms in her later poetry. Tobin's collection, as he has acknowledged, does not satisfy the need for a scholarly edition of her collected works, one that would recover the publication history of each poem and help scholars to solidify the texts. As it now stands, Ridge's works not in the digital or public domain (*Firehead* and *Dance of Fire*) are available only through a small number of academic and public libraries.

In addition to several unpublished dissertations and theses and a few articles,[43] including notably Peter Quartermain's essay in *Dictionary of Literary Biography,*[44] Drake's, Berke's, and Tobin's are the most substantial treatments of Ridge. Drake's, which draws extensively on archival materials, is the most detailed biographical treatment. In spite of such spare contemporary attention to her work, it is nonetheless the case that Ridge was at the center of an important node of American modernism.

Her partnership with Kreymborg on *Others,* her contributions as American editor of *Broom,* her gatherings that brought together other literary figures such as William Carlos Williams, Robert McAlmon (who went on to collaborate with Williams on the little magazine *Contact*), Marianne Moore, and Scofield Thayer show that she played a significant role in shaping American literary history during the modernist period. Her work and aesthetic were unique and marked by her sense of vocation and courage.

Readings of individual poems have been undertaken by several contemporary critics. An examination of two long poems from her early American publications demonstrates her essential themes and gives a sense of her adaptations of the modern aesthetic. These long poems are informed by and benefit from the Imagist idiom and show her development from her early writings, with their more Victorian sensibility. While most classic Imagist poems are short object studies, Ridge combined seeing imagistically with other narrative techniques (employing a first-person persona, creating a sense of story through various characters, and including some elements of plot) to create Imagist-inflected longer poems. The long poem format allowed her to mine the ethical richness of her subject matter. She also wrote many shorter poems, but all her poems are grounded in the social world in a way that classic examples of Imagist verse tend to avoid in their singleness of focus. One criticism leveled at Ridge by her contemporaries at *Broom* was that she was not "modern" enough. What is sure is that Ridge brought her own style, politics, passion, sense of justice, and humanitarian voice to the modern idiom in poetry.

Ridge's long poem "The Ghetto" was published in the *New Republic* on April 13, 1918, the same year that it also appeared in *The Ghetto and Other Poems*, published by B. W. Huebsch. Although she had been publishing verse in Australia and New Zealand since 1892 and in the United States since 1908, this book was in some sense her debut—the debut of the poet who subsequently went on to produce *Firehead*, a remarkable epic-length allegorical poem about Christ's crucifixion, which she wrote in the wake of the Sacco-Vanzetti execution and which critics agreed was her legacy contribution to American letters.[45]

"The Ghetto" begins with a deceptively simple opening section titled "To the American People," in which Ridge expressed anger and accusation in an attempt to reach what she anticipated would be an audience reluctant see the truth:

Will you feast with me, American People?
But what have I that shall seem good to you!

On my board are bitter apples
And honey served on thorns,
And in my flagons fluid iron,
Hot from the crucibles.

How should such fare entice you!

Ridge made her vantage point as an immigrant plain from the beginning, and her poem effectively echoes Walt Whitman in the use of repetition. The harvest the poem describes is not a Thanksgiving, and these lines make clear that what follows may make readers uncomfortable—something that most middle-class Americans, shielded from the sight of the ghetto, usually avoid. The questions in the second and seventh lines are not punctuated as questions, thereby giving the impression that they are instead pointed statements about the limitations of the audience in general, and she thereby created an immigrant English syntax. Ridge identified herself as a poet of the modern era, familiar with the currents of contemporary poetry, and willing to engage with machine-age America, unlike the characterizations of her by Loeb and Josephson.

It is worthwhile to compare Ridge's opening lines that so succinctly encapsulate her own disillusionment as an immigrant, with the famous poem "The New Colossus" by Emma Lazarus, which is engraved on the Statue of Liberty:

> "Keep ancient lands, your storied pomp!" cries she
> With silent lips. "Give me your tired, your poor,
> Your huddled masses yearning to breathe free,
> The wretched refuse of your teeming shore.
> Send these, the homeless, tempest-tossed to me,
> I lift my lamp beside the golden door!"

In Lazarus's poem America is a limitless resource, and the bounty is to be shared with everyone. In Ridge's poem there is limitation, pain, and disgust at the unfair rationing of resources and the struggle that begins as soon as immigrants land.

"The Ghetto" is a powerful poem written in free verse. Ridge used the concrete image to create scenes of the poverty she witnessed, similar to the 1909 project of photographic pioneer Jacob Riis in *How the Other Half Lives*, a sociological work that examines the lived facts and consequences of poverty in New York. As he did, she attempted to tell the truth about poverty with the idea that if others can see what is hidden in plain sight, then hearts will be moved, and change can begin. The unit of organization for Ridge was the image, and her long poem has a loose, associatively organized narrative that follows a family with whom the first-person speaker is staying in a Lower East Side Jewish ghetto on Hester Street. As others have mentioned, one of the most remarkable impressions one has when reading "The Ghetto" is how free of prejudice the controlling voice is. Contemporaries of Ridge, especially some of the most prominent modernists of the day, such as T. S. Eliot and Ezra Pound, voiced anti-Semitism publicly in their poetry and privately in their letters to one another. Ridge is present in her poem as the unnamed persona, and it is clear that she is a respectful and observant visitor to the ghetto. She was also invested in painting a range of human experience and making it clear to readers outside this world that they have more in common with Jewish immigrants than they have differences with them.

One feature of Ridge's modernism is an antisentimentality regarding motherhood. She frequently mined the language and images of maternity to illustrate a fierce point. The poem opens on Hester Street, a crowded neighborhood suffering from summer heat. In describing the prostration people feel, she emphasized their gothic stasis:

Bodies dangle from the fire escapes
Or sprawl over the stoops . . .
Upturned faces glimmer pallidly—
Herring-yellow faces, spotted as with a mold,
And moist faces of girls
Like dank white lilies,
And infants' faces with open parched mouths
        that suck at the air as at empty teats.

The air and the neighborhood itself are described as failing to nurture, and the corpselike images of citizens strewn in motionless poses, trying to get at some fresh air, is sinister and oppressive. The image is soon relieved by the description of young girls going to meeting halls: "Surging indomitable." This poem is about what people who are trapped in such a place can do—what actions are possible and relevant to orchestrate relief.

Ridge captured the crowding, the restlessness, and the historical scope of the ancestral ties between the current ghetto dwellers and ancient peoples. In moving back and forth from modern to ancient perspectives, Ridge referred to time as a minor impediment to a larger vision. The narrator wonders if women who overcame Egyptian bondage could have seen into the future to a time when their descendants would be caught in a different sort of trap, inhabitants of a modern, urban ghetto in a city so far removed from the Middle East as New York. Having overcome so much historically, Jews in the ghetto, the poem shows, are not yet fully free.

The family with whom the persona stays is named the Sodos. The son has moved away and married outside the faith; the narrator is staying in his vacant room, which is rented as a source of family income. The daughter, Sadie, becomes a focus of the poem. Her father was a saddle maker and is suffering from memory loss in old age. He is embittered and maintains a strong orthodoxy, which he has seen eroded in his family's religious practice. If he had his way, the candles would burn more often, but his wife hides them and his daughter blows them out either from indifference or out of thrift to save them for another occasion. The father's disillusionment and isolation as he prays futile prayers to "the Lord's shut gate" highlights the family's dead-end situation. They are constrained by space, money, and ethnicity to a narrow yet rich world.

Sadie works in a sewing factory, where the noisy and dusty conditions are not safe. Surely Ridge recalled in Sadie's situation the dreadful Triangle Shirtwaist fire that occurred in 1911 in nearby Greenwich Village. In that fire female employees on the upper floors of the building were trapped because of inadequate fire escapes and doors locked to keep people from going on breaks.

The management was able to escape, but many others were not so fortunate. One hundred forty-six people died, many jumping to their deaths. The tragedy was a catalyst for an upsurge in the influence of the International Ladies' Garment Workers' Union. The events of this tragic fire were no doubt vivid in public memory as they read about this young woman doing factory work. Sadie is doing piece work and admonishes the other girls to "slow down" to prevent their wages from being cut. (The more productive workers in this system were, the lower the price set per piece by the employer.) The description of her work suggests that she finds a flow and becomes one with the machine, although she has in the past been injured by the needle. She is described as "a fiery static atom, / Held in place by the fierce pressure all about—." The pressure is economic, social, and interpersonal. There is nowhere else to work; the conditions are horrific; and individuals have little autonomy to change the circumstances of their lives.

In the precious time that she is not working, Sadie reads modern literature ("those books that have most unset thought, / New-poured and malleable"), speaks at rallies, attends protest meetings, and goes to dances. Her work as a labor organizer sustains her, as does her "Gentile lover," a cause of worry for her mother, who chaperones them as best she can. Her daughter is an adult and a modern woman and will do what she wants. That both Mrs. Sodos's children have found love outside the faith illustrates another social pressure that Americanization exerts on immigrant cultures.

The poem provides portraits of other personalities in the neighborhood, describing recent immigrants' struggles to learn English, a small immigrant child's bewilderment at the light and noise of a neighborhood parade (which reminds her of pogroms she has witnessed in Europe), and a local merchant focused on his trade with one eye to the west, toward Wall Street. The poem turns to an "old grey scholar," a figure who knows the history of his people and can place his current situation in a broader perspective. Now working as a tailor, he represents a generational divide in the ghetto. He is imperturbable, even if "a rigid arm and stuffed blue shape, / Backed by a nickel star / Does prod him on." This ironic description of a police officer as a sort of "hollow man" (Eliot's well-known poem came much later, in 1925) will not touch the tailor either: "All gutters are as one / To that old race that has been thrust / From off the curbstones of the world." Ridge fortified this scholar with a quiet and iron dignity that cannot be eroded by the taunts of the young or police intimidation.

Echoing in the neighborhood is the voice of a parrot—the pet of a nameless woman in a tenement across the way from the Sodos—crying "*Vorwärts!*" over and over again. *Vorwärts* (Forward) was a newspaper of the Social Democratic Party of Germany, published in Berlin from 1891 to 1933. In this poem, however, it is an irritating scream of a caged bird. The parrot is as incapable as anyone trapped in poverty to find a way forward. The candles in the woman's flat burn for Shabbat:

On Friday nights
Her candles signal
Infinite fine rays
To other windows,
Coupling other lights,
Linking the tenements
Like an endless prayer.

This image of repose, community, and tranquility is in contrast to the bird's futile and dissociated squawking and the woman's social isolation. Although she is old and alone, the poem gives details about her that reveal her dignity: "Her thews are slack / And curved the ruined back / And flesh empurpled like old meat, / Yet each conspires / To feed those guttering fires / With which her eyes are quick." The candlelight communicates her presence to the neighborhood and to her God, and that light is also reflected in the intelligence in her eyes.

What sort of vision does Ridge's poem offer? The poem includes portraits of those who organize for change, but notably activism is not romanticized. In fact all the pitfalls and foibles of being human are part of the process of organizing a way forward:

Words, words, words,
Pattering like hail,
Like hail falling without aim . . .
Egos rampant,
Screaming each other down.

Those at a meeting are depicted in the language of the parrot: they are "Egos cawing" and "naked, unformed, unwinged," just hatched in the nest and full of primary, enormous need. One organizer is "Garbles Max Stirner," a nineteenth-century philosopher and anarchist: "His words knock each other like little wooden blocks. / No one heeds him." Yet the group tries to grapple with issues of leadership, imbalance, fanaticism, and need.

Egos yearning with the world-old want in their eyes—
Hurt hot eyes that do not sleep enough . . .
Striving with infinite effort,
Frustrate yet ever pursuing
The great white Liberty,

Trailing her dissolving glory over each hard-won barricade—
Only to fade anew....

Unlike Lazarus's depiction of Liberty as a maternal, nurturing figure, where the main part of the question and struggle is simply to land and be accepted, Ridge's Liberty is distinctly white; her torch and the dream it signifies tantalize but do not last. Rather than lighting a clear path with a sure lamp, the light illuminates formidable obstacles to freedom. Immigrants are not welcomed, and their lives are transformed; Ridge created a world in her poem where, while everything is not bad, people are indeed trapped. Instead of being drawn to a great torch, visible from a far distance, the group of activists huddle together in a local pool of lamplight:

A gas jet throws a stunted flame,
Vaguely illumining the groping faces.
And through the uncurtained window
Falls the waste light of stars,
As cold as wise men's eyes ...
Indifferent great stars,
Fortuitously glancing
At the secret meeting in this shut-in room,
Bare as a manger.

Despite the challenge of organizing for change and the indifference of the outside world, the message with which Ridge ended the poem is one of life. All the strivings in the ghetto against the social barricades and the imperfections of activism, the struggles with ego—all these signify the abiding force that is larger than any one person or movement. Ultimately the parrot screaming "*Vorwärts!*" is a triumphant figure:

Life!
Startling, vigorous life,
That squirms under my touch,
And baffles me when I try to examine it,
Or hurls me back without apology.
Leaving my ego ruffled and preening itself.
Life,
Articulate, shrill,
Screaming in provocative assertion....

Ridge's poem ends in affirmation that the life force she witnessed in the ghetto was freighted with challenge and pent-up frustration, but ultimately indestructible. On the one hand the ghetto is a trap that stifles its inhabitants, as symbolized by their prone figures gasping for air at the beginning of the poem; on the other hand it is a space of shelter where immigrant traditions have some hope of being preserved, even as they are eroded and encroached upon by the larger culture.

"The Ghetto" is Lola Ridge's mature fusion of modernist poetics with a social agenda. She was commended by critics for her "exactness of observation," her vivid and arresting art," and her "acrid dynamic description." Louis Untermeyer in the *New York Evening Post* wrote, "In 'The Ghetto' Miss Ridge achieves the sharp line, the arrest and fixation of motion, the condensed clarity advertised by the imagists—and so seldom attained by them. And to this technical surety she brings a far more human passion than any of them have ever betrayed." In the *New Republic,* where the poem first appeared, the critic declared, "'The Ghetto' is beyond doubt the most vivid and sensitive and lovely embodiment that exists in American literature of that many sided transplantation of Jewish city-dwellers which vulgarity dismisses with a laugh or a jeer."[46] Conrad Aiken's review in the *Dial* was a substantial critique of Ridge's method, but even from a fault-finding standpoint he commended "The Ghetto," where "the vigorous and the tender are admirably fused." *The Ghetto and Other Poems* was the first opportunity for Ridge—in a writing career that spanned more than twenty-five years at that point—to engage with the critical community and experience the full reception of her work. In that book she chose to find the intersections of personal and political poetic spaces.

"Sun-Up" was published by B. W. Huebsch in 1920 in the volume *Sun-Up and Other Poems.* In this collection Ridge returned to her roots and explored themes and images from her childhood, as well as writing labor poetry in tributes to Alexander Berkman, Emma Goldman, Rosa Luxemburg, and James Larkin. The dedication, to her mother, is an incantation that likens the mother to a dead queen Ridge was trying to resuscitate through her poetry. Throughout the volume, she credited her mother with providing her with an impetus to poetry, as unsentimental as it sometimes is.

Let me cradle myself back
Into the darkness
Of the half shapes . . .
Of the cauled beginnings . . .
Let me stir the attar of unused air,
Elusive . . . ironically fragrant
As a dead queen's kerchief . . .

Let me blow the dust from off of you . . .
Resurrect your breath
Lying limp as a fan
In a dead queen's hand.

The air is "ironically fragrant" because the subject is long dead, desiccated, and turned to dust; yet her perfume lingers in a way similar to the way her mother's memory lingers in the poet's mind. The mention of the cradle is significant, as are the "cauled beginnings." Several of the main images in the volume are introduced here. *Sun-Up and Other Poems* is primarily about the past and concentrates a good deal on the influence Ridge's mother had on her daughter's imagination. This dedicatory poem effectively uses repetition to ask for permission to disturb those materials, to disrupt her mother, who may have attained something like an attenuated peace, not having been disturbed in such a long while. "Cauled," as an adjective suggests the piece of fetal membrane that occasionally covers an infant's head at birth, marking the baby, according to tradition, as lucky or possessed of special powers. Ridge's use of the image associates her mother with her daughter's creative genesis, suggesting that she was marked from birth to pursue her vocation. Childhood, for Ridge, is where poetry began, and the mysticism of the calling is something she excavates in this volume.

"Sun-Up," the title poem, is a long meditation on early childhood. The speaker is a four- to five-year-old who lives first with her mother in, presumably, Dublin (unnamed in the poem) and then is relocated when she and her mother move. A primary theme is isolation. The father is a not fully remembered outline; some lines of the poem recall nurses who tended to the child in the mother's necessary absences for work, and the depictions of playmates—male and female—are not especially comforting. The persona is an only child and singled out as such, with playmates who may or may not be completely imaginary and with a complicated relationship to a doll named Janie. The child can find comfort with the hired caretakers, although at the beginning of the poem Ridge effectively conveys the child's sense that these nurses cannot really protect her from her environment: "When God throws hailstones / you cuddle in Celia's shawl / and press your feet on her belly / high up like a stool. / When Celia makes umbrella of her hand. / Rain falls through / big pink spokes of her fingers." Celia is also unable to prevent the child from playing in the fire and by being burned by glowing "cherries" picked up from the hearth. Celia tells the child her absent, dead father will bring her a "golden bowl." The message the nurse delivers from Ecclesiastes is not an especially comforting one to convey to a small child who has lost her father because it has much to do with skepticism about an afterlife. The image of the golden bowl, broken and unable to hold whatever riches or potentialities a life promises, is hauntingly superimposed on the child's understanding. Ridge effectively created a child's apprehension of the situation:

When I think of my father
I cannot see him
for the big yellow bowl
like the moon with two handles
he carries in front of him.

In a play of symbols, the golden bowl becomes literally a yellow bowl, the moon, in an associative chain. The golden bowl becomes a shield, occluding the direct perception of her father, and he takes his place in her imaginative constellations.

The child's understanding of death is also conveyed through remarks about her grandfather, who has "gone away and left his great coat." The child does not believe the sanitized explanation of his absence. The persona of the poem begins to use the pronoun "you"—a direct address from the adult, interpreting poetic consciousness and the "I" of the child's consciousness. The poem shifts back and forth between this child's understanding and an adult interpretation. Visible in the poem is Ridge's effort to counsel and nurture her younger self.

There are dark hints of abusive relationships between adults and children in the poem, which describes kaleidoscopically what may have been a fire at St. Joseph's Church in Dublin. The persona and another young girl are running from the area, which "isn't a dream":

It comes again and again....
You hear ivy crying on steeples
the flames haven't caught yet
and images screaming
when they see red light on the lilies
on the stained glass window of St. Joseph.

The young girl spins "like a penny thrown out into the street," and a mysterious man grabs hold of her friend's hair:

He always clutches her by the hair....
His eyes stick out like spears.
You see her pulled-back face
and her black, black eyes

lit up by the glare. . . .
Then everything goes out.

The combination of apocalyptic imagery, the sacred and the profane, a church fire, and the suggested sexual aggression adds up to a troubling portrait of a four-year-old consciousness. The situation underscores the absence of safe spaces. The church on fire is not a spiritual or physical shelter, and the man, potentially a priest, is a predator. Later in the poem the persona is also described as sexually precocious while engaging in play with a young male friend. She exchanges kisses with her friend Jimmie, whom she did not believe at first was "different" until "he / showed you." The persona refers repeatedly in this passage to freshly laundered sheets being hung by another nurse, named Mabel, who is eerily singing "Three Blind Mice" to the child, who slips away to play with her male playmate. In a sort of disjointed logic suggestive of shock, the persona then describes time standing still "as when a clock stops" and the "sun glaring bright as God" on them. They are discovered, and in a panic Mabel puts an end to their game. The voice who says "you" is the adult self speaking back to the child's understanding: "Mabel pulls you in the gate and shakes you / and tells you not to tell your mama. . . . / And you wonder / if God has spoiled Jimmie."

The child's simplicity introduces Ridge's observation of the inequality of gender roles. The sexual experimentation will be measured differently according to gender—while she is spoiled, presumably Jimmie gets to go home without the stigma of defilement. The poem refers to the sheets drying on the line several times in these passages, and the sheets serve as a suggestion of the entire world of adult sexuality, to which the child is not yet privy but will be soon. In a disciplinary way, the young girl is pulled forcibly back into the gate and the protected space shared by the guardian. The sheets foreshadow a public and private negotiation of sexuality. For her, yet a child, they remain a blank but meaning-filled signifier.

The world the young child inhabits in "Sun-Up" is marked by poverty, relocation, isolation, and a growing awareness of the limitations of her powers in terms of sexuality and class. The mother is single and working, thoughtful and compassionate but also deeply preoccupied with the tasks before her. She has a child who is imaginative and has found an edge—a cruelty—that becomes compensation for the powerlessness she otherwise feels. As William Drake observed, the young girl in the poem is "not a 'nice' girl"; she tests the limits of her powers by pulling wings off flies and abusing her doll, which she finds lacking because it depicts an unrealistic and shallow representation of girlhood.[47] The behavior described suggests antisocial patterns that may come from witnessing or experiencing abuse. The descriptions of the doll are unsentimental. Made of rubber with her clothes painted on, she has a hole in her head where a whistle was once fastened and through which the persona tries to feed her.

> My doll Janie has no waist
> and her body is like a tub with feet on it.
> Sometimes I beat her
> but I always kiss her afterwards.
> When I have kissed all the paint off her body
> I shall tie a ribbon about it.

The persona says "I beat Janie / and beat her . . . / but still she smiled"; the child continues the abuse to the point where she imagines the doll "doesn't love me anymore." The relationship between the girl and her doll is portrayed as pronouncedly nonnurturing, and the child eventually throws her toy in a ditch. The testing of social limits with the inert doll suggests a childhood that on some level was shaped by emotional abuse. Although Ridge's stepfather is not represented in the poem, the violence of the girl's play seems to suggest the shadow of his influence on her.

In contrast, although the mother in the poem is preoccupied with her responsibilities, she is consistently portrayed as caring and is associated with natural beauty in the form of the moon and stars—sources of inspiration for the emerging poet. The poem successfully mines Ridge's early imagination to draw up a complex welter of feelings establishing early inspiration. These associations balance with the later linkage of her mother with art and nature.

In one section of the poem, Ridge drew on Plato's myth of the cave, rewriting it for the young girl's sensibility. The persona remarks on the active presence of silence—a silence so present that it can make one scream. Elsewhere in the poem Ridge developed the idea that some shadows tied to things are safe, but other shadows are separate from things or symbolic—or seem to have a life of their own. They are terrifying: "There is a shadow / that is not the shadow of a thing . . . / it is a thing itself. / When you meet this shadow / you must not look at it too long." In Ridge's cave

> Little girls sit there
> dressed in white
> and the dolls in their arms
> all have white handkerchiefs
> over their faces.
> Their shadows cannot play with them . . .
> their shadows lie down at their feet . . .
> for the little girls sit stiff as stones

with their backs to the mouth of the cave
where a little light falls off
the wings of the silence
when it comes down out of the sun.

The inhabitants of Ridge's cave are all anonymous little girls who appear manufactured, like their dolls. The girls do not appear to be chained to their seats like the inhabitants of Plato's cave. Instead they are dressed in white, are diminutive, and above all are sitting obediently. Their chains are not external but mental, a result of their socialization as little girls. Their world has shrunken to the dim, occluded sun, the still shadows, and their mechanistic poses—a result of the stultifying effect of their internalized gender roles. They are more or less tamed, sitting there with their dolls, which are striking, miniaturized symbols of their own attenuated life force.

The fifth section of "Sun-Up," titled "Jude," begins with a reflection on the future, a sense of poetic calling, and her mother:

When you tell mama
you are going to do something great
she looks at you
as though you were a window
she were trying to see through,
and says she hopes you will be good
instead of great.

Ridge was shaped by this sense of impending, potential work ahead of her, and she also anticipated the sadness and social isolation that can result: "When you do something great / people give you a stone face." One form her mother's protective love takes is that she hopes her daughter will not deviate too much from the norm—that there is safety and comfort in anonymity, especially for a girl. The implication is that there is no comfortable fame for a woman. The daughter becomes a window her mother tries to see through—an extension of her identity and a medium through which the future can be glimpsed. Windows are developed as a symbol throughout the poem. A complicated symbol, they are as often something that blocks sight rather than facilitates it. They join a multilayered system of related symbols: mirrors, windows, stars, and her mother, which are gathered up in the passage from Ridge's 1940 diary quoted earlier.

"The Ghetto" and "Sun-Up" contain the primary features and principles of Lola Ridge's aesthetic vision in the late 1910s and early 1920s. Her poetic project focused on an antisentimental rendition of experience in forms that took advantage of key Imagist techniques, especially the concentrated line governed by breath and sharpened by distinct images, and she achieved success in long poetic forms using associative and narrative methods of organization. In "The Ghetto," the first-person "I" is a participant-observer in the ghetto, who draws conclusions about her environment from close observation; in "Sun-Up" Ridge created a dual persona, a child consciousness and a reflecting, adult consciousness, as she unfolded an autobiographical narrative that fully exploits the sort of iconic memory she revealed in later diary passages where she described her younger self at a "pre-symbol" age experiencing a direct apprehension of beauty and pleasure. "The Ghetto" and "Sun-Up" demonstrate that Ridge could blend aesthetic and social motivations in her literary work—her early poetic career was a locus for both political activism and an activism grounded in personal and feminist insights.

Two

"Unwieldy with enormous births"

Lola Ridge and Evelyn Scott

Lola Ridge was a remarkable poet, writer, thinker, and human being. She influenced, mentored, and promoted many other modernist writers, who were mostly, but not exclusively, female. One such writer was Evelyn Scott, brilliant in her own right, who benefited from a close friendship and working relationship with Ridge.

While a member of Alfred Kreymborg's editorial staff at *Others* magazine, Ridge was one of several lecturers (also including Conrad Aiken and William Carlos Williams) who spoke as members of the touring Others Lecture Bureau in 1919. The topic she chose was "Woman and the Creative Will," which was later published as a number of the Michigan Occasional Papers series in 1981, edited with an introduction by Elaine Sproat. Noting that Ridge's lecture makes a point similar to that of *A Room of One's Own* ten years earlier than Virginia Woolf, Sproat also pointed out that, while the lecture was written during the final stages of the suffrage movement in the United States, Ridge chose to place her argument outside that particular struggle. At once inclusive of that movement but much broader, Ridge's vision is more radical. Believing that we live in a "dynasty of fire," Ridge asserted that for justice to occur, reform was simply not enough. She worked toward "the construction of a completely new social and economic fabric."[1] Calling the time she lived in a "Woman Renaissance," she reflected years later on the pain and destruction wrought by male leadership over two world wars, saying that these conflicts were "the primal male dance—from which woman is shut out, save as a chattel, a breeder of warriors, or the industrial handmaiden of warriors, to take her dead husband's place. [But] beware . . . there may [yet] be a woman dance."[2] Ridge worked intermittently on expanding the lecture into a book, but her publisher responded about one sample of it that he "could not bring out a book written in this way as not more than three hundred people in America would buy it."[3] Ridge never completed the longer version; yet the lecture alone provides an important statement of her aesthetic and feminist perspectives. "Woman and the Creative Will" constitutes an early manifesto for women's writing and contains principles that guided Ridge's judgments about other writers—judgments she made as an editor and also those regarding how she invested her time to promote and nurture other women writers. Ridge's manifesto foreshadowed not only the feminism of Virginia Woolf by ten years but also the radical French feminist writing of Helene Cixous by fifty years.

Ridge was speaking in an environment of tremendous change for women and in a burgeoning period of growth for women's writing. While in 1919 the amendment granting American women the right to vote was about to be ratified in the United States, individuals were still working out new women's roles in more liberated sexualities and in the workplace. Women were at the editorial helms of leading intellectual periodicals of the day: Harriet Monroe at *Poetry,* Margaret Anderson and Jane Heap at the *Little Review* and later Marianne Moore at the *Dial.* Ridge's own energy sustained *Others* when Kreymborg was ready to give it up.[4] In addition to women's suffrage, women were taking a greater role in industry as a consequence of the absence of men and the need to ramp up material production during the recently ended First World War. The writings of Elinor Wylie, Sara Teasdale, Marianne Moore, Djuna Barnes, Mina Loy, and Edna St. Vincent Millay were increasingly prominent in literary periodicals. The new woman of Greenwich Village became a nationally recognized stereotype. Nevertheless Ridge asked and answered some vexing questions about women and their literary achievements, which transcend the local concerns of that time.

Ridge was responding to criticism of women by writers such as playwright and novelist August Strindberg, psychologist Otto Weininger, and philosopher Friedrich Nietzsche, all inveterate misogynists. Perhaps in response to the gathering power of the "woman movement," these artists and thinkers attempted to make the case that women were by nature inferior, and their arguments sound strident to later readers. Ridge conceded that the historical record of creative achievement for women reflects disparity, but women have also been determined to be inferior by a history narrated by men, and that in itself has an impact on women's potential. Ridge described a "double-dealing with life—a kind of made-to-order wholesomeness" that women developed as a survival strategy[5] and that constitutes a filter through which life is experienced. Her argument mirrors in some ways W. E. B. Du Bois's famous formulation of double consciousness with regard to being black in America. This doubleness of mind is a result of the intense pressure dictating the many aspects of social control that have been applied to women. It is extremely difficult to escape; if women rebel against social pressure, then their work is still shaped in opposition to the artificial situation—it still derives its form and meaning from being oppressed. It has consequently no independently developed system of symbol or meaning. At that time women were underrepresented in poetry, philosophy, psychological novel writing, music, and religious life; they were sparsely involved or absent in every major field of human cultural and intellectual endeavor, according to Ridge. In fact, when a woman does achieve a high water mark in cultural production, Ridge pointed out, she is often accused of being "male" or of her creation being "masculine." Emanuel Carnevali, in his praise of Ridge, was careful to say Ridge represented a new feminism that transcends the categories of masculine or feminine—and thus paid her a higher compliment.

Central to Ridge's thesis is the idea that, in spite of the disappointing historical record and the tendency of success to be gendered male, women have a strong and equal "creative will," and they have a future in art in large part because of their strong intuitions, which are an essential ingredient in creative production. Ridge herself may have been guilty of gender essentialism with this claim, but her advocacy for women was strong. While the promise of female creativity in art had not yet been fully realized at the time she was writing, she argued that real changes to the social fabric will make the playing field more level in the future and that, once fairness is accomplished, there will be no natural or biological bar to women's successes.

Ridge pointed out three "great deficits" in women's creative work: "poverty of imagination, absence of form (... by form I mean not technique, but spiritual unity); above all, [lack of] sincerity."[6] In what ways do women fall short of these attributes? Ridge regarded women artists as crippled by social fear. The pervasiveness and comprehensiveness of male chauvinism has tamed women to the extent that their own artistic visions are limited in scope by this social fear. Spiritual unity or form is rare in women's work, according to Ridge, because women have not had the centuries of mental discipline in creating and organizing large social structures: "[Men] have handled large undertakings and seen things in masses and people in crowds. They have always been shaping things on a large scale and drawing parts into a whole, so perfecting their sense of unity and form."[7] Women lacked training to develop these aptitudes, and they have historically been limited to a domestic sphere.

On this point Ridge was in opposition to another great theorist of women's art, playwright Susan Glaspell. Her 1916 play *Trifles*, produced by the Provincetown Players, was a dramatization of the principle that domesticity is a valid sphere of knowing and being. Following the example of Emily Dickinson, who found a world within her home and near her doorstep, Glaspell had the characters in her play demonstrate male and female ways of seeing. The men, who are investigating a murder and are there in an official capacity, miss all of the available clues that their wives, lingering in the kitchen, discover.

Since the murderer is also a wife and woman, it is obvious to the audience and the wives that the story of her crime is part of the fabric of her domestic life. In contrast to Glaspell, Ridge saw women's experience on a larger map. Rather than rescuing the domestic sphere, she wanted women to enlarge themselves to a world stage. Domesticity is part and parcel of the "arrested development" Ridge sought to uncover and indict. Regarding the women's rights movement in particular, Ridge predicted success for it and saw it as part of a "human rights movement" that includes racial justice and labor justice. Women stand "squarely linked to stand or fall with the rise and fall of the proletariat of the world."[8]

Ridge's concluding remarks urge women as creative artists to move forward without fear, since fear is what sets up limitations and mental blocks to full expression. She encouraged women to inhabit confidently the spheres that are conventionally dominated by men, not the least reason being that they need to develop the mental discipline that organizing in the public sphere can give them. Already having intuition in large measure—which, according to Ridge, is a precondition of genius—they have yet to become "masters of dreams." To do this women must enlarge their minds and experiences to transcend the social fear of domination and to develop a mental discipline able to give unity and order to experience. Most of all, with the attributes of confidence and experience, she urged women to find meaning independent of old structures of gender domination.

Ridge's "Woman and the Creative Will" is startlingly prescient of some of the major insights of Helene Cixous's "The Laugh of the Medusa," which was published in *Signs* in 1976.[9] While it is not likely that Cixous was influenced by Ridge, it is noteworthy that one aspect of Ridge's reception was that she had insights for which her readers were as yet unprepared; she was ahead of her time. Cixous's main point—which is infused with postmodern psychoanalytic theory to which Ridge of course did not have access—is that women have been historically and culturally alienated from themselves, both their bodies and their writing voices, which are linked. Cixous, like Ridge, admitted that the legacy of this history of oppression is still evident in the works of women, especially in the ways they strain under the weight of social expectations. While Ridge did not explicitly mine the erotic alienation of women from their bodies, she is a poet whose work is intricately tied to mystical ecstasy, and thereby she explores similar ground. Through sermonic flourishes and powerful rhetoric, Cixous tried to blast women out of complacency with their limitations. Congruent with Ridge's insights about the deadening restrictions on little girls, Cixous argued: "[Women] have wandered around in circles, confined to the narrow room in which they've been given a deadly brainwashing" (877). Writing in what could be a gloss to Ridge's representation of Plato's allegory of the cave in "Sun-Up," where young girls sit immobile with their dolls, Cixous commented: "The little girls and their 'ill-mannered' bodies immured, well-preserved, intact unto themselves, in the mirror. Frigidified. But are they ever seething underneath! What an effort it takes—there's no end to it—for the sex cops to bar their threatening return" (877). Reading backward through Cixous, one can see one of the major insights of Ridge's "Sun-Up" is the way in which the dolls represent the cultural ideal of women's sexuality: clothes painted on, bodies inert, they are receptacles of abuse. Ridge's insight about the incarceration of women's sexuality is essentially the same as Cixous's.

One of Ridge's main goals in "Woman and the Creative Will" was to shed light on the difficulty for women writers to evolve beyond the influence of their roles as women. Cixous was more radical, arguing that there is a women's writing that will engender new organizations, new inflections, and new meanings. Cixous has contended that there "is such a thing as *marked* writing. . . . [W]riting has been run by a libidinal and cultural—hence political, typically masculine—economy; that this is a locus where the repression of women has been perpetuated, over and over, more or less consciously" (879).

A truly liberated woman, Cixous argued, would be impossible and untenable in a real social framework. "Her appearance would necessarily bring on, if not revolution . . . at least harrowing explosions" (879). Ridge did not argue specifically for a separate, marked, women's writing, although her later remark about a coming "woman dance"—an alternative history that is written by the minds and actions of women according to their emphases and priorities—makes a similar point.

If one considers the ways in which she disrupted the expectations and limitations placed on her because of gender chauvinism from fellow editors and some male fellow writers, one could indeed describe Lola Ridge as a woman of "harrowing explosions." She sought most of all to break women's silences, a goal shared with Cixous later in the century. Both thinkers saw the emancipation of women, not only from direct political and social oppression but from spiritual oppression, as a radical, political act. Both writers were attempting to unshackle repressive structures that bar women's thinking and creative endeavors. It became an important aspect of Ridge's personal as well as professional life to promote the attributes of creativity, independence, honesty, and courage in other women writers. These goals are congruent with the position on women's aesthetics she outlined in "Woman and the Creative Will."

Between the work Ridge produced as a mature modern writer and the remarks she delivered in "Woman and the Creative Will," readers find a coherent aesthetic position regarding women's literature and modern art. Ridge used some of this overflow of energy, care, concern, and thought about women's writing to guide other writers, including the women considered in this study, in their own attempts at liberation.

One of the most important professional and personal friendships in Ridge's life was with Evelyn Scott. Scott's work has been neglected. Her productive life as a writer spanned more than twenty years, including published novels, volumes of poetry, autobiographies, and a play produced by the Provincetown Players in Greenwich Village in 1921. One of the first American editors to receive, evaluate, and publish Scott's early poems, Ridge was struck by their subjectivity, the immediacy of the world they inferred, and the ways in which they express the self. She regarded their fine courage highly. Seeing an innovator, Ridge later said, "These poems show an astonishing and essentially modern awareness. . . . [I]t is a consciousness that, while close to and keenly aware of instinct, has yet obtained its release; so that it watches, intent but calmly elect."[10]

When Evelyn Scott returned to the United States in 1919 from a voluntary personal exile in Brazil, she found herself—thanks to Lola Ridge—at the center of the Greenwich Village nexus of the modern literary world. From that platform Scott began what seemed for the first fifteen years a brilliant, celebrated, and promising career. Scott's greatest literary accomplishments include her first volume of poems, *Precipitations* (1920), noteworthy for its Imagist innovations; the novel *The Narrow House* (1921), which combines naturalism and a powerful critique of domesticity; her autobiography *Escapade* (1923), which documents in detached subjectivism her elopement and exile in Brazil; and the novel *The Wave* (1929), which tells the story of the American Civil War in a cinematic panorama of more than a hundred characters and episodes. Scott produced other noteworthy works as well, including her autobiography *Background in Tennessee* (1937), which documents her early debt to her southern upbringing. Although she continued to write novels that garnered critical success into the 1940s, she was often left out of literary histories of the 1950s, and her work was not revived again until briefly in the 1970s and in a somewhat more sustained way in the 1990s. Lola Ridge's literary reputation suffered a similar fate, although her more direct treatment of social issues brought her recognition by leftist and social critics who sought to reformulate the academic literary canon. Scott's critical neglect is a puzzle of American literary history worthy of its own full-length study.[11]

It is not known what sort of gift initiated their friendship, but Scott sent some anonymous token of respect and affection to Lola Ridge in 1919, presumably after Scott's poems first appeared in *Others*. She had sent her poems

"Women" and "Young Girls" from Brazil. Ridge made reference to the gift in the first letter Scott received from her and also set up some of the major themes of their correspondence. It is noteworthy that the correspondence between the two friends is not equally represented by the existing manuscripts. Ridge assiduously saved her correspondence with Evelyn Scott, and the manuscripts have survived and are preserved in the Sophia Smith Collection of Smith College (with photocopies of that collection available in the Evelyn Scott Collection at the University of Tennessee). There are hundreds of letters from Scott to Ridge spanning the years 1919 to 1941, and related correspondence going even beyond Lola Ridge's death as Evelyn Scott wrote to Ridge's widower, Davy Lawson, into the 1950s. In contrast, and for reasons that are unknown at this time, there are only a few extant letters from Lola Ridge to Evelyn Scott.[12] Most of Ridge's letters to Scott were not preserved after Scott's death in 1963, perhaps destroyed by her widower, John "Jack" Metcalfe. The gift Ridge mentions in the earliest letter to Scott may have been a note of encouragement or perhaps something more material. Ridge wrote to Scott, not yet knowing her name:

> Dear Unknown Friend:
>
> This is a beautiful thing you have done for me. It is a poem too. Not all the poems are written or painted.
>
> How shall I convey to you my gratitude—make you understand how deeply touched I am by your action and the loving kindness that suggested it.
>
> Thank you for believing in me. I shall try not to disappoint you. I feel happier in the work I am now doing. I see more clearly. There are seven veils before the eyes of the creator—but you too must know this. This last year one of mine has parted. You have helped in this. Your aid gave me a great stimulus. I am now writing a long poem—night and day for the last month except when actual illness intervened. If you have not written and disclosed yourself to me by the time it is finished, I shall send you a copy through [illegible].
>
> One thing I ask: do not I beg of you deplete yourself for me. If you have already done so by giving to me a part of what you needed or could well have used, then please give me the opportunity of making good the actual and material outlay. This beautiful thought that suggested your action is the greater gift, that I would not return if I could but shall keep always like a flower.
>
> Do you smile at me and take my hand?
>
> Do I know you well?
>
> This can hardly be as I have asked many.

My thought reaches out to you. When it returns without touching you, I am as surprised as though a light had gone out. But thoughts run brightly only a little way. Then they weaken and go dark.

Many times I thank you in my heart—suddenly and without premeditation as one notes the beauty of a morning or a soft wind.

May I not know your name?

Lola Ridge[13]

Ridge's description of sharing thoughts and encouragement through the metaphor of light is interesting. The energy and insight for thought must be refreshed with the help of one's artistic community. The light that emanates from the work is generated collectively.

The letter highlights the start of a friendship between two poets, and an essential aspect of such a friendship was the encouragement of their work. Ridge wrote poetry for her entire career, and in these early years, Scott was building on poetry, specifically Imagist-style verse. Scott soon secured a contract with Nicholas Brown for *Precipitations,* and poems from this collection were appearing (and would yet appear) in *Poetry Journal, Others,* the *Dial* and *Poetry.* There are no subsequent references in later letters that define what the gift was, but it is clear that it was deeply touching, and the letter is romantic in tone, an element of their correspondence that did not vanish once Scott's identity was revealed. Scott shared who she was with Ridge a short time later, and expressions of devotion and in endearments such as "Sweetest Dear," "Lola darling," and "darling girl" continued to appear in their letters.

What flowed between these two authors through the connection of their letters? Even from the first communication we see their belief in one another as artists. There is an exchange of energy that helped to enable present work and allowed each woman to imagine a future as an artist. Each author helped the other to see her work. Ridge stated that "there are seven veils before the eyes of the creator" (small *c*), metaphorically stressing how difficult it is to have perspective on one's work. Criticism of one another's writing—constructive, supportive, and loving feedback—became a kind of dance between them. The long poem Ridge referred to in this letter is her "Sun-Up," a poem Scott loved and shared with her closest friends. The two writers also shared a consciousness of the price of creative work—that it takes one's best energy, and each encouraged the other to save her best vitality for the creative efforts she knew would be her contribution to literary history.

Ridge turned to editing in order to have money to live. Editing allowed her to have an important role in the literary field, but it did take great chunks of time and consumed energy in promotion, advertising, and processing subscriptions. Later she found support through writing awards, and she also had the combined household with her husband, Davy, who helped them to subsist in their spare lifestyle.

Evelyn Scott, except for a brief exception when she taught at Skidmore College in 1939, lived by her pen and also combined households in creative ways with her common-law husband and various other partners in complicated domestic configurations. Ridge and Scott were acutely aware of the psychic and financial tolls that the life of an artist could take. As Ridge mentioned in this letter, "my thought reaches out to you." More than anything that passed between Ridge and Scott via their correspondence was the reaching out of thought, the connection made corporeal in words on paper, which constituted their support for one another as gifted and successful individuals. In many ways their simply asking to see one another's work in progress helped to move that work along. For years, in practically each letter, Scott inquired after Ridge's health and her progress on manuscripts, offering her moral (and when she could afford to) material support.

The friendship was mostly conducted by letter, but there were also periods when Scott resided in New York and they were able to visit in person and by phone. The partners of both women (Davy Lawson with Ridge and various men, including Cyril Scott, Owen Merton, and later Jack Metcalfe, with Scott) were also close. It is an interesting issue that so much of Scott's and Ridge's connection was long distance and on paper. They did have some misunderstandings, especially in the late 1920s, when Scott organized a fund among other authors to help support Ridge's creative work financially without consulting her before doing so, and near the end of Ridge's life in 1940 and 1941, when Ridge was extremely ill with tuberculosis and Scott was in mental and emotional turmoil. Indeed most of Scott's supportive, long-term friendships with women were epistolary—including those with Emma Goldman, Jean Rhys, Jean Stafford, Louise Theis, Charlotte Wilder, and Kay Boyle. In contrast there are few female friendships that occurred proximally and over a long period of time between Scott and other women. She was close to and proximal with Charlotte Wilder for a time, but that relationship had complications. Also there are no strong examples of successful female friendships in Scott's fiction. For the most part, the innate (at least in her interpretation) rivalry among women is a perennial theme, beginning with the rivalry and antagonisms Scott had with her mother. It is clear from Scott's correspondence with Lola Ridge that Scott treasured and worked to preserve her crucial connection with her mentor, long distance though it was most of the time.

Evelyn Scott met a need for Lola Ridge, just as Lola Ridge met a need for Evelyn Scott. The early Scott poems that appeared in *Others* magazine, "Women" and "Young Girls," speak directly to issues that Ridge had identified as areas lacking in women's literature historically. "Women" is a vers libre meditation on the compromised and muted presence of women who take their shape and draw their energy from masculine worlds. "Young Girls" is an Imagist poem that describes a world that is "not for" the females who perceive its beauty; their souls are "bathed in kisses and blood." The speaker maintains, "All you know / Is to burn, tremble, and yearn." Both poems are unsentimental in viewpoint, carry focused insights, and employ modernist form. They express a clear and determined vision to say something true and unconventional about their subjects. Representative of Scott's early work as a poet, they summarize some of the contributions that her first volume of poetry, *Precipitations,* made when it appeared in 1920.

The poems of *Precipitations* defined Scott as an Imagist whose primary topics were subjectivity, sexuality, and exotic Brazilian landscapes, which catalyzed her writing from 1913 until 1919. Her imagism, however, developed independently and in isolation from that of Ezra Pound, H.D., and Amy Lowell (although in 1921 Scott circulated for publication a poem titled "Nike," which was a tribute to H.D. and which eventually appeared in her second book of poetry, *The Winter Alone,* in 1930). The poems of *Precipitations* broadened Scott's scope from early appearances in little magazines with the inclusion of poems about the city, race, sexual politics, and nature. Scott's particular contribution to Imagism is that, while she depended on the evocative power of intensely realized imagery, she also used the imagery to provoke the emotional responses of her readers in ways that refer beyond the poems themselves. She developed a harshness of vision in common with Ridge and later Kay Boyle. Open forms, influenced by the work of D. H. Lawrence and William Carlos Williams, provided her with the freedom to experiment. When rhyme and rhythm appear in this early poetry, it is toward specific effects of juxtaposition rather than establishing form for form's sake. That Scott did not entirely eschew the tools of rhythm and rhyme is another trait she shared with Ridge; both poets relied on traditional forms with more and more frequency as they matured poetically.

Early reviewers of *Precipitations* situated Scott as a modern poet. Padraic Colum in the *New Republic* stated that Scott "takes us to a place where there are no shared possessions and where there are no springs of action." He associated the isolation and experimentation in the poetry directly with "territory that the moderns have opened up" in new subjectivities, although he also thought this territory more fruitful for novelists.[14] For example a riot is described with detachment, graphic detail, and concentrated accuracy but without any sense of action or emotional processing. This treatment establishes detachment as a primary feature of her voice. Rather than expressing outrage, the persona has a distance that allows a more objective voice, one influenced by Scott's reading of philosopher Henri Bergson.

Mark Van Doren reviewed *Precipitations* for the *Nation,* describing Scott's poetry as radical impressionism and finding Scott apprehending new subjects in new ways: "At no time do the walls of tradition serve her, either as mirrors or as sounding boards."[15] His remarks underscore that in a field of artists doing what was "new," Scott brought originality to the task.

Reviewing *Precipitations* for *Poetry,* Ridge characterized Scott's poetic voice as "like an electric ray, that seems to focus—almost lovingly—upon decay and death, a child's simplicity and eager response to every mood of earth." She also placed Scott as a modernist: "These poems show an astonishing and essentially modern awareness. . . . It is . . . a consciousness that, while close to and keenly aware of instinct, has yet obtained its release; so that it watches, intent but calmly elect."[16] In these poems Ridge was able to find imagination, form, and above all a type of ruthless sincerity that would fulfill what she identified as accomplishment and independence in women's writing.

As the title of Scott's first volume of poetry suggests, her early poetry functioned for her as a precipitate, or condensation, of thought and feeling. The poems are short, free verse; some are rhythmical; some are rhymed. They are frequently synesthetic. The volume is arranged in six main sections: "Manhattan," "Vanities," "Bruised Sunlight," "Contemporaries," "Brazil through a Mist," and "The Coming of Christ." Each of these sections has two or three poem cycles, each with separate titles, and each cycle comprises between four to sixteen short poems, also titled separately. This hierarchy of structure promotes an interweaving of themes throughout the volume while also emphasizing continuity within the parts. The poetry cycle was a method of organization that Scott frequently used in the earliest of her published poetry. It seems to provide a combination of focused investigations through individual lyrics as well as opportunities for sustained development across poems.

The poems in *Precipitations* have a broad surface scope, and they have subterranean commonalities as well. They deal broadly with Scott's experience of Brazil, her transition to living in New York, the female body, physical pain, maternity, character studies and portraits of contemporaries, and evocations of mood. Scott wrote vividly in concentrated lyrics on subjects deeply informed by her experiences as a woman. She dwelled on color, light, and shape with precise detail while allowing a blending of perceptions to inform the representations in the poems. Poems often blur the distinctions between subject and object. In these poems Scott also identified several forces that work against rational thought, such as maternal instinct, mob violence, and narcissism, which she depicted as monstrous and threatening. In fact her primary critique of modern culture rests with her examination of forces and urges that thwart rational thought. Scott's entire artistic project and most of her personal preoccupations stemmed from this tendency to question totalizing social influences on individuals. With increasing stridency as she aged, she obsessively opposed any forces that encouraged automatic thought, response, or behavior—whether they were political movements, the actions of governments, or personal lapses of mindfulness.

Scott's project in *Precipitations* is not only to capture sensual images but to reproduce specific experiences of perceiving the images and to construct associations that unseat the reader. This urge to discomfort the reader is what provides the volume of lyrics with its unity of form. The anxiety these techniques produce in readers seems to have been one of Scott's main goals in writing. The tension she created may serve to highlight certain philosophical or social dilemmas or contradictions that she chose to focus on in a particular poem. In order to achieve these effects, the voice in her poems is frequently narcissistic to the point that the boundaries of self are called into question. Added to this experimental voice in her poetry, Scott also persistently interwove references to female eroticism that were daring for her time. She also focused in many poems on what one might identify as the hideous. Scott was one of the earliest writers to recognize and exploit the socially constructed association between the female body and irrational thought that found especial championing in the writings of Freud. By reinscribing the cultural links of the female body to irrationality and generating anxiety about them, Scott intended to force her readers into new ways of thinking about women that question the nature of these patriarchal links.

The natural world, also associated with the female body, is portrayed as indifferent to the joy and the suffering of the persona although it evokes both emotional responses. In contrast the city (specifically New York) becomes an adjunct of nature, both terrible for the mobs it contains and beautiful in its stony composure and implacability. Neither it nor nature, it seems, will be altered by the boundless and frantic persona, who looks at both beauty and ugliness with an equal share of fascination and wonder. In reading Scott's poetry, the reader is absorbed by the perspective of this persona and engulfed in the natural forces that seem to buffet her.

A unifying theme in *Precipitations* is the isolation of the individual. The first section, "Manhattan," containing two poem cycles, "The Unpeopled City" and "Crowds," explores the paradoxes of isolation within a most populated place, New York City. In "The Unpeopled City" the poem "Midnight Worship: Brooklyn Bridge," the first poem of the volume, describes street lamps along the bridge as subjectively perceived saints whose nimbuses hover above as a trick of the light. In contrast to the paralysis of the speaker, the lamps have will and agency. In "From Brooklyn," a later poem in "The Unpeopled City," the persona describes the perceived floating of Manhattan across the river: "Dim gardens of fire— / And rushing invisible toward me through the fog, /

A hurricane of faces." Other people, crowds in fact, pose a direct threat to her viability as an individual. Robert Welker appropriately described "From Brooklyn" as an example of purely Imagist verse, emphasizing the way in which the description exists for its own sake and does not seem to reach out toward a larger web of meaning beyond itself.[17] The persona perceives Manhattan as a unity floating across the river, but at the same time she is overwhelmed by the crowds that she knows the city contains. Faces, the vehicles of individuality, merge in a storm that overwhelms her.

"Crowds," the second poem cycle of "Manhattan," further examines the isolation of individuals and their control by natural urges within the framework of civilization. In "New York," a brief poem, Scott subjectivized the landscape of New York to include natural images of destruction: "With huge diaphanous feet, / March the leaden velvet elephants, / Pressing the bodies back into the earth." The city's buildings are described as a herd of animals large enough to dwarf the individual human lives contained within. Scott's use of the descriptive terms "diaphanous" and "velvet" depict sensual contradictions, a favorite device. The buildings are diaphanous because, while seeming solid from a distance, they are in fact hollow; perhaps the lives that are led in such buildings, lives of business and commerce, exert the velvet yet inexorable forces that press humanity back into the earth. The buildings take on the attributes of the human activities performed within them. Commerce and commercialism, the persona suggests, are crushing forces. Human beings are described as merely bodies, dwarfed and inconsequential; they may as well be ants, for all the individual significance they exert.

The indifference of the city is further elaborated in this cycle in "Sunset: Battery Park," where the sunset, reflected from the windows of houses, turns the windows to eyes that gaze back at the persona in sightless, expressionless judgment. The sight lines "obliterate all they see," and the poem concludes with a description of the crowds below the buildings as contiguous, one being, melting "seaward and deathward" to the ocean like those not fully alive. They cannot recognize the landscape around them or the cost to themselves of following their blind urges. The persona is a lone voice of protest among many who seem themselves to refrain from thinking and judgment.

"Riots," also in the "Crowds" cycle, likens the action of riots to that of birds flying in a flock: every individual is a part of something larger than him or herself and subject to that new, larger thing's demands. The riot, once it begins, becomes something that can be referred to as an "it"—something unitary, singular, and willful. The poem describes this communal identity as monstrous. "Faces float off in a red dream" of spilled blood, which suggests that under our surface features we consist of the same matter, the same red flow. The detachment with which this scene is described further deemphasizes the personal nature of loss of life. The monster seems to feed on and is sustained by the blood. The poem concludes with a detached statement: "Blood / I think it oozes from my finger tips. / —Or maybe it drips from the brow of Jesus."

The first possibility, offered as it is, suggests rather uncertainly that the blood spilled is on the persona's hands, but the second possibility, offered as an afterthought, indicates that the stain may be a divine one. Offering both possibilities juxtaposed in this way that suggests emotional shock and incomprehension gives an arbitrary quality to the assignment of responsibility. This thing that the riot is, is larger than any individual's responsibility, even of God's.

Life itself is described as a monster in "The City at Night," the last poem of the "Crowds" cycle. In a remarkable image, Scott described life:

Life wriggles in and out
Through the narrow ways
And circuitous passages:
Something monstrous and horrible,
A passion without any master,
Male sexual fluid trickling through the darkness
And setting fire to whatever it touches.

That is the master
Bestowing a casual caress on a slave. Quiver under it!

The unconscious, multiple will is a monstrous force made up of individuals and subjugates their will to its own. In "The City at Night" this is expressed in the image of life as wormlike, wriggling, and without mind. The individuals who travel in the night are described as subject to a will larger than their own. The monstrous quality seems to be caused by a lack of specific intelligence or realized personality. "A passion without any master," in whatever form it takes in Scott's poetry, is depicted as dangerous. Molten sexual fluid is responsible for new life, but it is also a scalding harbinger of the strife new life may bring. The city represents a human hivelike existence, which is contrasted to the terrible peace Scott knew in the isolation of the Brazilian ranch.

In several poems in *Precipitations,* Scott explored the sensual experience of the female body in ways that rivaled the experimental poems by Mina Loy that infamously opened the first issue of *Others.* Scott's poems are in company with Loy's "Pig Cupid his rosy snout / Rooting erotic garbage."[18] Scott's "Embarkation for Cythera" is a brief poem of stasis and stagnation. Cythera historically is a Greek island associated with the goddess Aphrodite. Sexual pleasure and death are distinctly linked in this poem:

Like jellied flowers
My inflated curves
Melt in the peaceful stagnance of the bath.
If I were to die
I would resist the final agony
With only a faint quiver
From my escaping thighs.

The libidinal knowledge of the persona's boundaries are blurred in the warm stagnancy of the bath. In the flow of water the distinctions between inside and outside grow confusing. The water that penetrates the persona makes the sense of her particular self seem less definite. The climax of the poem, it is suggested, is a synchronous experience of orgasm and death.

"Christian Luxuries," "The Maternal Breast," and "The Shadow That Walks Alone" join "Embarkation for Cythera" in exploring the sensual experience of the female body. "Christian Luxuries" indicates that the luxury Christians enjoy is their sense of sin. The feeling of sin is described as a delicious indulgence, a debauching of responsibility for one's actions. Once again we find the persona in a bath; yet this time it is described as a "red fountain of shame" that generates from her heart. The fountain is simultaneously the natural flow of blood in veins as well as an explosive display of excess suggestive of water stained by menstruation or a suicide attempt. In an exercise in sensual paradox, the persona claims that "the fire is cool. / It cannot burn me." Sensual paradox is one of Scott's anxiety-producing poetic devices. By saying sin is a cool fire, she indicated the central paradox of sin—it is felt both openly as pain and as a subterraneous pleasure—it is both a thing avoided and a compelling thing. In this poem she directed the reader's attention to long-held assumptions about sin and religious practice, with the intention of debunking them as self-serving and hypocritical. The female body is an appropriate trope for this admixture of feeling in its experience of a monthly cycle beyond its own control, and the social stigma historically placed upon the menstrual cycle.

In "The Maternal Breast," the persona experiences a deep desire for a maternal sanctuary—a theme that may help explain Scott's ready and durable attachment to Lola Ridge, who was a nurturing, maternal, and mentoring figure for her. The mother, it is suggested, can be a location of refuge, a place. This poem is additionally interesting when one is aware of the deeply conflicted relationship Scott had with her own mother, Maude Thomas Dunn. In *Escapade* Scott changed the identities of her parents to an aunt and uncle, which may have served, as she claimed, to protect them from the scandal of her "elopement," but it may also have provided a crucial psychological distancing from her mother, who became a key character in the narrative. In this poem the persona seeks an ideal mother, a figure of plenty, like the statue of Diana of the Ephesians, with her many breasts. The quest for the ideal mother, who is a function of giving beyond all reason with no sense of her own self, goes unfulfilled in the poem. "I was looking for a hill of mounds hairy with grass, / And a place to lie down." The closing of this poem suggests not only a return to the safety of a womb but also a final resting place, a graveyard. It coincides with an early remark Scott made to Ridge, explaining that from a young age she sought a female friend but had never—until meeting Ridge—found someone who could fill that role for her.

The title of "The Shadow That Walks Alone" presents yet another paradox. Shadows by necessity accompany their source objects, but here Scott sought to separate the shadow from its origin. In doing so she created a persona who inhabits a diaphanous and ghostly form. In addition the poem is a frank exploration of the maternal instinct, which Scott saw as running counter to rational thought. The silence is like a child who feeds on her milk; however, in the second half of the poem the perspective shifts, as though the role of the persona had been drawn through Scott herself, and mother feeding child becomes child incubating in the "womb of an idiot." The result of this role reversal is to depict a self in radical flux. The figure of maternal love is a flap-eared ass, whose inability to think is contrasted to its extreme capacity to feel. The persona is horrified by it, and yet her own body contains the capacity to be both child and mother, both roles that Scott saw as necessary but terrifyingly subversive of individual will.

Scott's poems of community and the family paint no less isolated a portrait of the individual self. "Love Song" suggests the tangle of the persona's familial relations. It is dedicated to Cyril Kay Scott (C. K. S.), and in the poem the complicated nature of their relationship becomes evident. "Little father, / Little mother, / Little sister, / Little brother, / Little lover"; Scott expresses the confusion of being apart from the one who defines her identity. The repetition of these roles suggests their coequality and interchangeability. It also reflects the autobiographical twists and turns of the on-again, off-again sexual side of their relationship. This poem captures the thought expressed early in *Escapade* that when Evelyn's companion, John, is absent, she finds herself psychologically adrift and undefined. The double sense of the word "bear"—to withstand or to bring forth—both apply later in the poem when the persona asks:

How can I get up in the morning
And go to bed at night,
And you not here?
How can I bear the sunrise and the sunset,

And the moonrise and the moonset,
And the flowers in the garden?

How can I bear them,
You,
My little father,
Little mother,
Little sister,
Little brother,
Little lover?

The persona finds it difficult either to bring forth meaning and appreciation of nature or to withstand the absence of her defining relationship when her companion is gone. The repetition of the diminutive "little" suggests a convolution of child and adult roles, in addition to the sheer proliferation of roles that each is to the other.

This proliferation of familial and sexual roles Evelyn Scott assumed was the dominant impression that Kay Boyle later retained from their brief meeting in 1927 in France. Boyle wrote, "One was aware at every instant of the nervous complexities of Evelyn's marital, and sexual, and professional lives, and in the smoke-filled, crowded hotel room I found it impossible even to hear what was being said. . . . I trembled for Evelyn's shattered depths. Was she wife, lover, mother, or none of these things, or all of them?"[19]

Not one to follow a traditional path either, Boyle nevertheless found Scott's domesticity exhausting. One way to understand the importance of Scott's attachment to Ridge was that Scott had found a relationship where the role she played was not layered by the same sexual imperatives as her relationships with the primary men in her life. Given that her mother's sexuality also complicated the attachment she had with Cyril, her relationship with Lola was an oasis.

In a poem titled "The Tunnel," Scott more directly acknowledged the eroticism of the mother-child relationship and conflated the roles of mother and lover. Her insights on this topic are one of the most original contributions of her early poetry. In contrast to other poems in the volume, where Scott's persona is a passive observer characterized by stillness and isolation, she takes on a malevolently active role as mother and creator of the child. Note the use of rhyme and cadenced language to contrast the content to form:

I have made you a child in the womb,
Holding you in sweet and final darkness.
All day as I walk out
I carry you about.

I guard you close in secret where
Cold eyed people cannot stare.
I am melted in the warm dear fire,
Lover and mother in the same desire.
Yet I am afraid of your eyes
And their possible surprise.
Would you be angry if I let you know
That I carried you so?

I could kiss you to death
Hoping that, your protest obliterated,
You would be
Utterly me.
Yet I know—how well!
Like a shell,
Hollow and echoing,
Death would be,
With a roar of the past
Like the roar of the sea.
And what is lifeless I cannot kill!
So you would make death work your will.

In most intimate touch we meet,
Lip to lip,
Breast to breast,
Sweet.
Suddenly we draw apart
And start.

Like strangers surprised at a road's turning
We see,
I the naked you;
You, the naked me.

Unable to reincorporate the child into her established identity, the persona fears the judgment of the child and the separation that will inevitably develop with the growth of his will. The mother is lover and shot through with guilt for feelings that have no social sanction and are potently taboo. The mother-poet gives range to incestuous impulses—for her the truth of the relationship is a Freudian cocktail of love and desire. She expresses the longing to engulf that which has separated from her—so much so that she speculates about whether killing the child would solve the contradictions she faces. But while that which she has made is other than herself, it is most of all a living part of her. The child's competing interests and complex, intertwined fate leave Scott's persona in a state of unfulfilled expectation.

The poems in *Precipitations* give an indication of Scott's relentless and earnest desire to speak the truth she experienced as a poet and as a woman, no matter how uncomfortable doing so would make her or others. She was extremely fortunate to find in Lola Ridge a more senior poet who was seeking these qualities in other artists.

Significantly *Precipitations* also includes a poem dedicated to "L.R.":

To rush over dark waters,
A swift bird with cruel talons;
To seize life—
Your life for hers—
To hold it,
Hold it struggling—
To kiss it.

This is the first of three poems Scott specifically dedicated to Lola Ridge. Poems for Ridge also appear in *The Winter Alone* ("To Lola Ridge") and *The Gravestones Wept* ("To Lola Ridge: Poet").[20] The first poem for Ridge is one of three vignettes in "Portraits of Poets." The other two vignettes are inspired by William Carlos Williams and Alfred Kreymborg, both members of her circle in Greenwich Village for a time. What Scott identified in Ridge is something that she also saw in herself: they both had a quality of vision that made them predatory in their effort to capture the essence of experience and life in concentrated, poetic language.

Contrast Scott's poem to the poem Ridge wrote for Scott, which appeared in *Sun-Up and Other Poems* (also published in 1920):

(To E.S.)
You inevitable,
Unwieldy with enormous births,
Lying on your back, eyes open, sucking down stars,
Or you kissing and picking over fresh deaths . . .
Filth . . . worms . . . flowers . . .
Green and succulent pods . . .
Tremulous gestation
Of dark water germinal with lilies . . .
All in you from the beginning . . .
Nothing buried or thrown away . . .

Only the moon like a white sheet
Spread over the dead you carry.

Ridge and Scott celebrated qualities in one another that they themselves possessed. Each valued the vision of the other poet and her courage and will not to turn away from psychological, social, or personal truths that might in general be terrifying, grotesque, or compromising. For Ridge, Scott was "inevitable," pregnant with creative possibility, immense with her observations, and picking through the detritus of life to craft her art. We recognize in her poem a celebration of Scott's complete sincerity as an artist. Through "To E.S." Ridge christened Scott as the incarnation of the next stage of women's writing. Both writers acknowledged that in order to be artists, they had to live vital and risky lives, but most of all they must not place governors on their capacities to feel.

Ridge was in a sense Scott's Diana. It is important to note that Scott had spent a trying number of years in various locations in Brazil with Cyril Kay Scott, her young son (born in Brazil in 1913), and her mother, Maude Dunn, who had traveled to join them after Evelyn and Cyril had eloped. Maude arrived on a one-way ticket, supplied by her husband and Evelyn's father, Seely Dunn. Dunn thus stranded his wife in Brazil, where she was a constant irritant to both Evelyn and Cyril, and then divorced her on grounds of desertion.[21] Evelyn, Cyril, and Maude constituted a disturbed and volatile family with few other contacts outside their servants (who sometimes worked without pay). This situation supplied the raw material for many subsequent artistic and autobiographical projects for both Evelyn and Cyril. Evelyn's first novel, *The Narrow House* (1921), draws heavily on her parents for the characters of Mrs. Farley, Laurence and Alice Farley's mother, who never fails to ply the tools of guilt, emotionally blackmailing her children, and their father, Mr. Farley, whose years-passed infidelity has exerted personality-shaping force on all the members of the family for more than a decade. The novel traces the fault lines of this trauma in the motivations and personality idiosyncrasies of all the members. *The Narrow House* is joined in depicting the toxic triangle of Evelyn, Cyril, and Maude by Cyril Kay Scott's 1921 novel *Blind Mice*, where the Maude Dunn figure is portrayed as a devious and catty sexual rival for her daughter.

Both Evelyn Scott's and Cyril Kay Scott's autobiographies rework this maternal triangle. Maude Dunn was a challenge to live with, but she supplied both authors with a rich character study to investigate in their fictional and autobiographical writing. Needless to say they hungered for new relationships when they arrived in New York. When Lola Ridge appeared in the Scotts' lives, a woman of Maude Dunn's generation (although representing herself as younger) and everything Maude Dunn was not (ethically principled, not manipulative, established in a vibrant literary community, an accomplished artist, and able to focus on Evelyn as a respected peer), it is no wonder that Evelyn Scott wooed Ridge. Their friendship was conducted largely through letters, but it was punctuated by Scott's intermittent periods of living in New York during 1919 through 1937, when they had opportunities to visit frequently face-to-face. Their correspondence takes on a romantic cast. It is clear from these letters that Ridge assumed a critical role as model and as proof, since many of Scott's other relationships were fraught with misunderstandings early on and ended in feuds, that Scott could have a deeply meaningful friendship with another person, especially a woman.

Evelyn Scott and Lola Ridge were heterosexual, and both were in romantic relationships with men; however, there is a sense of deep affection between them that could be misread if it is interpreted as simply erotic. It is a frank mutual acknowledgment of their sexual selves. Ridge also responded with respect and praise to Evelyn Scott's ruthless and sometimes self-revelatory honesty in her unsentimental work, which deals with a broad range of subjects, including—centrally—the plight of women. It is clear from the letters that Evelyn and Lola's friendship grew early on beyond the familial template in which Ridge was an ideal mother figure. They helped to create for one another a world where their art was legitimated. The earliest letter from Scott to Ridge explains how unexpected a treasure Ridge's friendship was to Scott: "If I had known there was somebody like you in the world a few years ago some of my conclusions about the universe would have been modified and I would have been a good deal happier. When I was a lot more of a kid I wanted a woman friend tremendously, but the mystical kind of idea I had of a bond which would be a recognition of a common defeat was something I had hardly articulated and nobody else understood—and of course I never found the woman."[22] The "recognition of a common defeat" may refer to the idea that women are always on some level sexual rivals and likely to arrange themselves as corners on triangles rather than as points in a dyad or line, or arranged in a circle—and this was certainly true the majority of the time for Scott.

This ingrained rivalry between women is often explored in Scott's fiction. There are no positive female friendships in which women do not undermine each other in the early works, including poems in *Precipitations,* her autobiography *Escapade,* and her early trilogy comprising *The Narrow House, Narcissus,* and *The Golden Door.* The truth of female relationships stemming from her own experience in her upbringing was that women were enemies of each other and rivals for the affections and resources that men afforded them; the only peace that could come, she suggested in her communication to Ridge, is that of a truce. She continued: "My experience with women has always led me to a deeper conviction that they are too thoroughly without faith (due to several centuries of experience) to attempt honesty without insuring themselves against the consequences with sexual weapons. That is a woman may be honest with a man she knows she attracts but not with the woman who is impervious. I was so entirely sure of this that I said to myself once and for all, I don't want any women, ever, ever. I want to live. I want to be strong. And I want to indulge myself in my own particular vanity which is to despise evasions."[23]

Many of Scott's friendships with others, men and women, broke on the rocks of this "vanity." Many people are not so constructed to sustain friendship without any evasions, and Scott struggled to find a middle ground that would allow her to enjoy the benefits of friendships that were more superficial yet politically or professionally to advantage. Early in their relationship, Scott and Ridge established that theirs would be of a different quality, and although rocky at times, Scott was able to operate in a zone of forthrightness with Ridge. This was essential for each of them to provide honest feedback on the others' work, with the larger goal that improved work was better for the other artist than withholding opinion or flattery would be.

Scott asked on many occasions about the progress of Ridge's never-completed book project based on "Woman and the Creative Will," saying: "I am inexpressibly interested in what you are writing about women. How long before I can see some of it?"[24] Scott sought and received criticism of her own work, and she provided feedback on Ridge's. Scott was able to share insights with Ridge about people she was close to and quarreled with, such as her patron, Marie Garland, and her former lover and complicated friend Waldo Frank. Scott was able to try out new ideas on Ridge and get her impressions about people they both worked with, including Gorham Munson, an editor and critic. Scott often submitted her initial impressions about people to Ridge and was affected by Ridge's more temperate positions. In one letter Scott wrote, "Lola I am more friendless than I was the day I hit new york [*sic*] in a literary sense for I apparently do nothing but pile up enemies in places of power."[25] Ridge was the friend Scott could count on in her circle when her complicated personal politics alienated others. In a remark that seems inspired by "Woman and the Creative Will," Scott exclaimed: "One thing I am sure of always is my love for you—your man size courage and woman size understanding and your complex bi-sexual brain, and I wish to God I could see you."[26] Scott was in many ways the realization of a vision that Ridge had prior to meeting her. The two women encouraged one another to move forward against all obstacles as women writers.

Three

"Women with shining secrets in their eyes"

Lola Ridge and Kay Boyle

Lola Ridge's poem "Mo-Ti," which introduces her 1927 collection *Red Flag,* describes an ancient Chinese philosopher who is dispensing wisdom to an audience of young men. The poem explores the implications of the historical exclusion of women from intellectual communities. The persona imagines, "I do not think there were girls who listened" to the philosopher's words "float[ing] out of the night." Ridge chose to focus on the women absent from the philosopher's pedestal, who represent so much wasted potential. The persona wonders:

> Did women—scattering dry words
> as trees dead leaves,
> that are no more communicants of the green sap—
> women with shining secrets in their eyes . . .
> alertly curious eyes
> not baffled because not wondering . . .
> catch a garbled word or so
> and mutely
> quiver along the margins of their silences?

The discourses of women who are cut off from the currents of philosophical thought, separate from the communities where it arises, and without vital mentorship are like leaves separated from a tree. Their words cannot contribute to the larger conversation because they are cut off from the forces that animate the most relevant communities of discourse. Ridge noted that women hold a vast reserve of intellectual capacity, which without development remains a mute gathering of unreached potential. The secrets in women's eyes—without ties to a living community of ideas and without full partnership in a community of thinkers—remain secrets even to them.

These lines recall issues central to Ridge's "Woman and the Creative Will." Cut off from the life force of discourse and current conversations where knowledge is formulated, women historically came to philosophy or art as a twice-told tale. A guiding principle in Ridge's friendships with other women artists was to create a community where these gaps and silences could be bridged. While Ridge would never accept an acolyte, she found in Evelyn Scott and Kay Boyle protégés who were worthy of her wisdom and who created—each for a time—a space where their words to each other were not leaves disconnected from a living tree but germinal seeds. A major result of these friendships and mutual support was the fostering and validation of further creative work.

Lola Ridge played an important role in the early development of the poet and novelist Kay Boyle by serving as an example of an artist who focused on social activism and by enthusiastically supporting Boyle's work. Among the early decisive influences on the young Kay Boyle, one finds next to the central place of her mother, Katherine E. Boyle, first Lola Ridge and then, a little bit to the side, Evelyn Scott.[1] The lives of Ridge, Scott, and Boyle intersected at key—and different—stages in their respective developments. In 1922 Boyle was writing her first poems and working for Ridge as an assistant at *Broom* magazine. Scott had already begun to establish her career with a volume of poems and two novels. Ridge was an established artist, American editor of *Broom*, and author of two appreciated books of socially charged and perceptive verse, *The Ghetto and Other Poems* and *Sun-Up and Other Poems.*

Ridge's vision and commitment to the causes of social justice had a far-reaching influence on artists closely connected with her. Boyle, who since her late teens had been in sympathy with the labor movement in Cincinnati, could not have found a stronger icon of the integration of poetry and activism than Lola Ridge. Ultimately Boyle became a highly visible public activist of the twentieth century, especially with regard to civil rights issues and the Vietnam War protest. In her 1977 article "Report from Lock-Up," Boyle tied her own consciousness as a protester to a long tradition of activists, including Alexander Berkman and Susan B. Anthony.[2] Boyle's activism went back to one of her first poems. In this unpublished poem, "The Book of Cincinnati," she commemorated nearly a dozen of the people who paid high penalties for their outspokenness against violence and U.S. involvement in the First World War.

In 1922 Boyle, prepared with secretarial training and a poetic disposition, came to New York to work for *Broom*, where she steadily took on more responsibility and eventually contributed her own creative work to the magazine. In 1968 she wrote of the 3 Ninth Street offices of *Broom*, which also served as dwelling for Ridge and her husband: "even now, at this moment, when I pass that house I want to stop and draw my fingers along its steps with love."[3] Boyle worked alongside Ridge as she negotiated the unpleasant series of misunderstandings and power struggles that characterized the end of her tenure as American editor of *Broom*.

In fall 1923, now in Paris, Boyle met with Loeb, who at that point had given up his editorship. She reported to Ridge that the meeting went well, but that she spoke her mind: "I told him with heat and bitterness what I thought he had made of *Broom*, and he apologized for almost everything in it and excused his part of it by saying: 'You see, I'm practically out of it. The main reason why I let my name appear on it is because I get paid a salary.'"[4] She nevertheless liked him "without having the slightest respect for him." There was some dispute about how Ridge's exit from *Broom* was understood. Ridge and Boyle were willing to stay and bring out the March issue; however, the transfer to Josephson occurred in February 1923, and at least some of the misunderstandings could have been caused by delays in transatlantic communication. They had multiple misunderstandings. There are interesting accounts of an October meeting that was called among "everybody who has worked for *Broom* or *Secession*, a catholic meeting with Brown, Burke, Coates, Cowley, Crane, Frank, Guthrie, Josephson, Munson, Sanborn, Schneider, Toomer, Wescott, Williams, or such of them as are beyond taking-no-interest-in the immediate future"[5]—a meeting that included everyone but Ridge.

In the early 1980s, Boyle communicated with Malcolm Cowley, trying to get it straight: "I think it should be on the record that Lola was eager to prolong the life of *Broom*, that Harold had agreed to this, and a day or two later cabled, 'Second thought, no.' ... It may seem an unimportant matter, but I feel it is of importance to the memory of Lola that the accurate story be told."[6] Considering how pointedly Ridge is attacked in memoirs by Loeb and Josephson, this desire is understandable.

In 1923, when Boyle first encountered Loeb in Paris, she noted that he stubbornly insisted on putting the writers he associated with into camps. In her remarks one can identify the factions in play: "We who love Alfred Kreymborg and the work of Waldo Frank are still under illusions which only the definite genius of a Matthew Josephson or a Malcolm Cowley can dispel." Loeb saw Ridge and Boyle as "direct descendants of the *Seven Arts*" in need of critical correction by writers such as Cowley and Josephson. "But *must* we be thrust into camps? Can't we stand without cliques? No, says Harold."[7] It is an interesting genealogy. Kreymborg had left *Broom* (which he had founded with Loeb) in February 1922 because, in a dispute similar to Ridge's with Loeb, the two men had disagreed about the inclusion of primarily American authors over European authors.[8] Kreymborg carried forward the editorial mission that had been in place with his previous publications, the *Glebe* and *Others*, to concentrate on new American voices. Kreymborg's departure from *Broom* is perhaps part of the reason why Lola Ridge was vulnerable a year later to the disagreements that took place—she and Kreymborg shared an editorial philosophy that Loeb ultimately contested, and on Kreymborg's departure she was of the minority opinion. Kreymborg presumably had had much to do with bringing Ridge to *Broom*, since the two had worked together successfully on *Others*. When he exited, he took with him a measure of protection as well as his ideology of promoting and discovering new American authors. Left standing alone with her emphasis on American writers, Ridge was an easy scapegoat for the European-based editorial group.

The *Seven Arts* group that Loeb referred to is another part of the mosaic. Waldo Frank coedited *Seven Arts* magazine in 1916–17. It featured American writers who shared an orientation for socially engaged work, such as Sherwood Anderson, Eugene O'Neill, and John Dos Passos. Taking an antiwar stance, the activist magazine and its editors—Waldo Frank, James Oppenheim, and Van Wyck Brooks—as well as the outspoken writings of one of its key contributors, Randolph Bourne, led its primary sponsor to withdraw support, resulting in the demise of the publication. In fact Ridge's peregrinations during this period and the short-run history of the publication conspired to keep her out of its pages.[9] In ways that were sympathetic to the *Seven Arts* project, Ridge in many poems and Boyle in her "Book of Cincinnati" gave visibility to antiwar activists by framing their contributions in verse.

Sharing with Ridge an affinity for the literary camp that roughly followed from Kreymborg and Waldo Frank, Boyle also valued Ridge as a mentor, precedent, and guide. In fact, through the lens of years, Ridge took on a larger-than-life importance, not the least because she was a strong woman poet and editor who had resiliently pursued her craft and found her voice. Of Ridge, Boyle wrote, "I cherished and protected her as tenderly as if she were a small, bright flame I held cupped in my hand. Her work expressed a fiery awareness of social injustice as eloquently as did Emanuel Carnevali's or Maxwell Bodenheim's, but it was always Lola's voice that spoke, a woman's savage voice, not theirs, for all her fervent response to their poetry."[10] In addition to Boyle's mother, Ridge became a primary audience of the younger woman's early poetry. As Boyle described this influence in *Being Geniuses Together*, "Lola's causes became mine, and when I wrote my poems now I borrowed from her conscience and her poetic vocabulary. She gave to my rebellion a wider and, at the same time, a more indigenous setting."[11] She associated Lola Ridge with her own growing interest in Irish nationalism, an enthusiasm that grew as she aged, as well as with her own emerging identity as an American poet and writer.

It is difficult to imagine a better school for a young writer in the early twentieth century than the gatherings Lola Ridge regularly had at the offices of

Broom. There, "every Thursday afternoon, and perhaps one evening in the month, Lola held open house."[12] Boyle met writers such as Marianne Moore, William Carlos Williams, John Dos Passos, Elinor Wylie, Jean Toomer, Waldo Frank, Babette Deutsch, Gorham Munson, Laura Benét, Edwin Arlington Robinson, Glenway Wescott, and Monroe Wheeler. Later Boyle called these writers "resistance fighters" and said, "The resistance was against the established English language, and the fight was for the recognition of a new American tongue."[13] The mosaic expanded to writers who were aesthetically and socially progressive. Once she moved to Paris, Boyle used the shared *Broom* history to meet with Harold Loeb and by chance was introduced to Robert McAlmon, whom she had heard about from Ridge and who became her great friend. McAlmon's connections opened up for her Dadaism and literary Paris, where she spent the next eighteen years forging her own art. It was not until 1941 that she returned to the United States—the year of Ridge's death.

It was with Ridge's vital protest of the Sacco and Vanzetti trial in mind that Boyle contemplated burning a secondhand American flag when she lived at Stoke-on-Trent, Staffordshire, with her estranged husband, Richard Brault, something that she ultimately could not bring herself to do. As Boyle told it in her chapters of *Being Geniuses Together,* Ridge's protest and arrest, dramatic enough, became inflated to a higher level of self-immolation in her imagination: "Lola Ridge had been knocked down in one of the mass demonstrations of protest, and been trampled under the hoofs of a policeman's horse."[14] Boyle repeated the mistaken trampling detail again in a description of some unthinking, unreflective women she met in a Paris nightclub: "[their dancing] heels were as savage as the hoofs of the policeman's horse under which Lola had fallen."[15] This exaggeration indicates the importance of the image of Ridge that Boyle constructed in her mind. In this fable it was essential that Ridge be utterly given to the cause of justice, to the point of sacrifice and self destruction. Ridge's activism and force were not far short of these descriptions, having put her body on the line and having faced arrest, but Boyle revealed her own investment in a romantic amplification of Ridge's activism.

The accounts of Ridge's participation in the Sacco and Vanzetti protests no doubt came to Boyle thirdhand, because by 1927 the once-ardent correspondence and friendship between them had cooled significantly. Boyle did not ultimately deposit letters from Lola Ridge with her papers in academic libraries, and Ridge did not reconnect with Boyle when she traveled through Paris on her way to Baghdad in the 1930s.[16] Their correspondence, preserved in the Lola Ridge Papers at Smith College, dates only through the year 1927. One can speculate about possible causes for the deterioration of the exchange, but the probable situation is that Boyle made many demands on Ridge from a long distance and was going through a tumultuous period in her personal life.

Ridge's focus on her own work and her periodic illnesses also no doubt contributed to the lapse in their correspondence.

There was also a rift aesthetically. When Boyle reflected in 1927 on Evelyn Scott's productivity, she was critical to Ridge of Scott's turn to the historical novel in *Migrations.* She confided that she thought Scott was in retreat from life, having abandoned her earlier focus on the psychology of character as placed in narrow and somewhat surreal narrative canvases. In the same letter, Boyle wrote that what Ridge and Scott had both given her was "a sacred belief in each other."[17] Boyle felt that Scott had not reciprocated the belief that Boyle had in her, especially on the point of their widely different views of Robert McAlmon, whom Scott was ready to break the friendship over. In addition to Boyle's and Ridge's differing views of Scott's work, one also sees in Boyle a movement toward continental European formulations of aesthetics that Ridge could not mirror, being committed as she was to promoting an American literary scene and aesthetic sensibility. In 1929 Boyle signed the manifesto declaring the "Revolution of the Word," which appeared in *transition* magazine, edited by Eugene Jolas. The point of the manifesto was to vivify an avant-garde critical stance and editorial principles; in part it eschewed sociological themes and integrations of poetry with political causes, and it declared forcefully that the "plain reader be damned."[18] It seems these principles would have impressed Ridge as antidemocratic. While too modern and aesthetic in focus to be termed a populist poet, Ridge would probably not have wished to alienate readers who could potentially benefit from exposure to her progressive ideas. She was certainly influenced by trends in modern literature as she reinvented her poetry from early- to midcareer, but as she was distinctly not a joiner of camps or causes in modern literature, she may have found Boyle's endorsements uncomfortable.[19]

In Boyle's imagination Ridge was battered by the horses' hooves at the Sacco and Vanzetti protest, and in fact perhaps that exaggeration symbolizes the end of their friendship. What this layering of the actual history and the imagined history shows is that the idea of Ridge as a self-immolating activist was crucial. She was the focus of a kind of hero worship on Boyle's part that did not mature beyond the stage it had reached when Boyle left the United States in June 1923. Nevertheless Ridge's "passionate voice" and the space she opened up politically and poetically in *The Ghetto and Other Poems* and *Sun-Up and Other Poems* were instrumental in Boyle's early development.

In *Being Geniuses Together* Boyle pointed out that one of the books she traveled with to France was *Sun-Up and Other Poems.* Her mother-in-law, whom Bolye had just met, sorted through her trunk at the docks for a gray suit because she objected to the dress Boyle was wearing. It was important to her that Boyle be "presentable" to undertake the journey from the port to their home in Le Havre—and for this it was necessary to have a gray suit. As Boyle described it, her mother-in-law's hands, along with those of a customs official, with no understanding, passed over the treasure of modern American first editions contained in the trunk in a fruitless hunt for a travel garment: "But the copy of Lola's book, in which her poem about the Negro woman whose baby was tossed into the flames of a burning house, never ceased to sear the pages, was of no interest whatsoever to them."[20] (As a testament to the tendency of memory to merge information, Lola Ridge's astonishing poem "Lullaby" was actually published in *The Ghetto and Other Poems* and not in *Sun-Up and Other Poems.* It was surely the case that Boyle owned and carried both books to Europe with her.)

"The Book of Cincinnati," in which Boyle detailed her time as a supporter of labor causes before leaving for New York, is in debt to Ridge's models of social documentary. Written in heightened, poetic paragraphs, Boyle's poem steps into territory that Ridge's early work made possible. Both poets drew on cadences of Whitman and demonstrated their interest in employing poetics as a marker for memorializing important figures in the labor movement. Boyle's poem exhibits the documentary urge to record labor work, which Boyle felt as a teenager, when she intersected briefly with labor leaders Lincoln Steffens and Duane Swift, circulated a petition protesting the imprisonment of Eugene V. Debs, and saw the contradictions in "Golden Rule" Arthur Nash's antiunion philosophy. At the same time, Boyle's poem takes much from "Sun-Up," also narrated in the first person and chronicling the emotional development of a young girl. "The Book of Cincinnati" was developed concurrently and has overlapping subjects with Boyle's rediscovered novel *Process,* which was written in 1924 and was found in manuscript and published in 2001.

Boyle sent the manuscripts for both "The Book of Cincinnati" and *Process* to Lola Ridge and Evelyn Scott for feedback. Scott sent comments that helped Boyle to rewrite and refocus the novel. Boyle also credited Ridge's remarks on the first draft with her eventual improvement of the novel. Acting as an agent for Boyle, Ridge shopped the early draft of *Process* to publisher Thomas Seltzer, who rejected it. The carbon typescript of the novel was lost until scholar Sandra Spanier discovered it in the New York Public Library.[21] Published by Illinois University Press, it constitutes an important contribution to the study of the modern American novel as well as a crucial addition to the understanding of Boyle's development.

In *Being Geniuses Together* Boyle emphasized often that "women were there as well" for her.[22] No doubt influenced by Lola Ridge's vision of a future world where a woman author could be simply an author if she chose to be without necessary and irrevocable reference to her gender, Boyle carefully constructed a world where she was moved and influenced by both men and women. She eventually developed an authoritarian stance that was difficult for subsequent scholars to sympathize with. She was stridently antiseparatist with regard to the women's movement later in her life, and surely some of her actions are perhaps easily misinterpreted to be antiwoman.[23] Ridge was admitted into an inner circle of influence on Boyle, and she remained an important, if static, icon of inspiration.

Not all the people in Boyle's life got along with each other, and in *Being Geniuses Together* she reported for instance that Ridge had a low opinion of McAlmon, saying that he "was wild and daring and hard as nails. She was inclined to dismiss him as a poet who drank too much." In fact McAlmon's critical reserve and his personal manner alienated many other contemporaries. Recall that he satirized Lola Ridge in his novel *Post-Adolescence,* calling Dora's revolutionary aura into question as a pose. As Boyle said, "I gathered even then that McAlmon had had little sympathy with Lola's earnest commitment to the arts and to the working class, a commitment so dramatized that people felt the necessity of either defending or abusing her whenever her name came up."[24] Thus schisms were apparent even within the mosaic of the "resistance fighters."

In an early letter to Ridge, Boyle's remarks suggest the role Ridge played in her life: "It is somehow necessary to thank you—for that comradeship which has brought me to so many realizations—or rather the confirmation of my individual convictions."[25] Boyle and Ridge discussed plans for starting their own literary magazine from the time they left *Broom* through the end of the year. The magazine, as Boyle imagined it, would "truly be the articulation of youth": the plan began to fade with the increasing length of time Boyle was in France and the strengthening permanence of her stay.[26] Additionally Ridge experienced health problems. As they went back and forth on the magazine idea in letters across the Atlantic, Boyle wrote: "I don't want to do the magazine without you. I am aware how innately it is your child, and while I might partially succeed in bringing it up in the way it should go, the fire and intensity which are so wholly yours would be lacking." She worried about the workload and the difficulty of managing such a project at a great distance. She feared that periodical publishing would impede too much her own creative work and could indeed "prohibit any original output."[27]

Several years later Kay Boyle did put her heart into another little magazine, *This Quarter,* begun by Ernest Walsh and Ethel Moorhead. This period was another complicated chapter of her life, including her separation from her husband, Richard Brault, her falling in love with Walsh, his death from tuberculosis, and Boyle's subsequent giving birth to Walsh's child, which was delivered with Ethel Moorhead in attendance. Without the means and later without the will for Boyle to return to America to undertake the magazine project with Ridge, it did not happen. Lola Ridge moved on to poetry projects of her own, and Boyle became absorbed in a life that involved other primary personalities and the honing of her craft as a short story writer and novelist as well as a poet.

Boyle's indebtedness to Ridge in the earliest part of her career can be seen in "The Book of Cincinnati" and *Process,* which are closely linked in subject and content In her introduction to *Process,* Spanier explains that "The Book of Cincinnati" was a foundational document for Boyle, written soon after she departed the United States for France in the summer of 1923. Both "The Book of Cincinnati" and *Process* demonstrate "Boyle's belief in the dual cause of aesthetic and political progressiveness," which—as the twentieth century wore on and New Criticism became the fashion—became less and less recognized as a valuable approach to writing.[28] In "The Book of Cincinnati" there is also attention to connecting Boyle's personal, family history to the larger issues of labor both locally (Cincinnati being an important location for activism) and in the United States as a whole. One can also see the young poet working with a form of lyrically heightened prose paragraphs, juxtaposed with more formal poetic ballad stanzas, in order to find a new way to fit voice to verse. Boyle created, as one phrase in the first section says, an "intangible rhythm" to describe the urban and somewhat frayed industrial landscape of Cincinnati.

One senses behind "The Book of Cincinnati" the precedents of "The Ghetto" and "Sun-Up." In "The Ghetto" Ridge—by sheer act of vision and voice—made a profound political statement, saying *yes* to the neighborhood she so lovingly rendered in a way that no one had before her. "Sun-Up" in some ways undertakes the same work with Ridge's own underrepresented internal and psychological landscape—that of a woman giving voice to her experience, with political implications in so doing. In "The Book of Cincinnati," Boyle spoke back to a poetic space that her mentor Ridge made possible. Boyle certainly came to the friendship equipped with foundational background and experiences—her involvement from a young age with labor issues and the influence of her mother, who encouraged her artistic development as well as social consciousness—but to find her full poetic voice, Boyle depended on the example of Lola Ridge.

Sandra Spanier has recounted Ridge's efforts to help Boyle secure funding from the Charles Garland Personal Service Fund in order to return to the United States from France. Part of the American Fund for Public Service, the Garland Fund was unusual in the early twentieth century because it made funds available to individuals.[29] Garland's inheritance of a million dollars was ultimately put to use in a variety of ways, including founding the *New Masses.* In addition to making an impassioned case for Boyle on the merits of her involvement in labor causes, stating that "the revolutionary artist is doubly alone,"[30] Ridge sent along a portion of "The Book of Cincinnati," which the fund's referees, Roger Baldwin and Anna Davis, found not to their taste. However, they seem to have damned it for its aesthetic qualities, saying that "while it may be good as art [it] cannot lay claim to help the radical movement."[31] In a situation that all the women in this study might easily have related to at one time or another, Boyle found herself too aesthetic for the political radicals and too political for the aesthetic radicals.

Toward the beginning of her poem, Boyle wrote that "the soul of Cincinnati is sober." She opened her poem by evoking the Cincinnati River, "a mother" who is surrounded by houses with "roofed faces" and "blank mouths." The river has not yet "shattered" them with the weight of her body.[32] This antiromantic view of maternity is an idea that was transmitted and made legitimate through development in Evelyn Scott's work and through Lola Ridge as well. The river is also a "grey pencil stroke on curl-edged paper," a strong and compact metaphor suggesting something of the landscape's fragility as well as its design. The speaker, who at least through some sections in the poem resembles Kay Boyle herself, says she met a drunken man by the river and their "untidy voices" contrast with the sere sobriety of the city itself. In the second section there are subjective glimpses of a group of friends relaxing in a field, discussing the improvements the city will make to the parkland. These public spaces, shielded by high grass, she intimates, are places where couples find some stolen moments of privacy. In these ways she demonstrates her bohemian sympathies as a new woman. In fact Boyle would not allow herself to be confined by convention and used her art as a platform to critique limiting or oversimplified visions of female experience.

In the poem Boyle described her family within the context of her consciousness as a young girl. Details of her mother's appearance are reverently and richly rendered: the feather of her hat is "a blue wave breaking over her eyes." The house Boyle lived in is crowded with generations, including her grandfather and her parents, and the tension and conflicts among them are present in the poem. The poem evokes the shield of security her mother creates for her by describing her being tucked in for sleep: "At night she puts kisses in my palms. I must hold them tight until morning." The ominous presence of the grandfather is felt in the loud noises he makes in the hallway, his influence shaping the reality of others in the house through a negative aura. Her mother makes "songs for me from an old man's words," and he warns the little girl to avoid her mother's fate: "reads too much . . . don't make that mistake." Both mother and daughter work together to forge identities as intellectuals and as citizens engaged in larger debates that take place in the culture outside the home. They depend on one another to create sympathetic space in which to appreciate art and be creative. Boyle follows in her mother's footsteps: "Carefully I step in the places where Mother's heels have been sharp little moons in the road." The acts of leading and following—roles that soon enough became reversed as Boyle gained strength as an artist—reinforced one another and helped to generate a reality acceptable to them even in opposition to male authoritarianism in the home.

The perspective of the poem shifts to her father, who runs his business out of the downstairs portion of their home and whose life is constricted, "the hours nailed in coffin boxes." She knows him "too well . . . his hand turning . . . in the cold, his mind shrinking." His name on the sign outside signifies the small circle of their kinship and their lives, and "Behind my father's name there is an unborn sorrow and a grey-haired pain, a man blown full with courage, sucked flat with fear." This portrait is juxtaposed with the following one in her grandfather's strong voice, which states that his "son is not man enough." He wishes to "keep pain from them, keep from them always pain. Put them behind this wall and set my back against it." Behind these walls, constructed by her grandfather's strong will and her father's failed sense of duty to him, Kay and her mother struggle to keep their souls alive in an environment that is stifled by patriarchy. There is a passage of dramatic monologue spoken in the grandfather's voice when Kay asks him to sign the petition for Debs's release, which he politely though indifferently refuses to sign: "I think no, my dear." Kay's voice replies, "But, an old man, Debs . . . in prison." The poem abruptly turns to the conservative critique, a self-conscious contrast between the loosely poetic paragraph form and the highly ironized stanzaic form with complementary use of rhythm:

> Goose-step, goose-step,
> Stomach flops flip-flop
> If Debs had been president
> There'd be a German General
> In every maiden-lady's bed.

Thus Boyle presented her grandfather's argument for involvement in the Great War—a typical reactionary point of view for many military involvements. Eugene Debs, arguably the most central Socialist Labor leader of the early twentieth century, was prosecuted under the Espionage Act of 1917 for his outspoken activism against U.S. involvement in World War I. In a case that became a cause célèbre for free speech, Debs was imprisoned from April 13, 1919, through December 25, 1921, when he was released after the Espionage Act was repealed. In demonstrating her involvement in his cause, Boyle took her place in the ranks of artists who use their art to promote social consciousness. Her grandfather, not willing to sign the petition even after the war was over, embodies the political fissures within the family.

The next section contrasts by presenting a meditation on Richard, presumably Richard Brault, her first husband, who was a World War I veteran and an exchange student from Brittany. "Richard is a gold beach. / Feet of waves run printless across him." In a series of powerful images, he is described in sensuous detail: "His eyes, / The sharp elbows of his mind / Through his threadbare face." Showing Boyle's aesthetic virtuosity, the poem's form reflects an associative structure that mirrors the mind as it walks among its furniture. Brault's section is stylized, Imagist, and isolated—he does not appear again, and the context for him is not fully realized. The poem does not return to this form again, and perhaps the stylized presentation and the isolation of Richard as an image hold clues for why Boyle's relationship with him was not ultimately successful. Richard is not presented as a person with whom she shared her poetic and political passions but as an image, rather remote, to be appreciated aesthetically. Only someone armed with biographical knowledge would place him from the scant evidence in the poem, but the affection shown him in the descriptions identifies him unmistakably as a lover.

The rest of the poem details some of the ways the Cincinnati labor scene interacted with national labor politics and reveals some of the ruptures in the local labor movement. "The Book of Cincinnati" is as much about naming names in order to preserve the memory of the movement as it is about turning solid phrases and sharp images. The following scenes take place at rallies where communists and socialists stump for their causes. The poem mentions women leaders—such as the secretary of Cincinnati branch of the American Civil Liberties Union (ACLU)—as well as men:

> On the stump, Mary D. Brite, body closed like a fist about the sharp blade of her voice. Sorrow is a throat parched against words . . . speech brims in her hands . . .
>
> Speech . . . through Cincinnati streets walk feet of Child Crusaders, tight bitter words through a loose mouth.

The Children's Crusade was a movement organized by Kate Richards O'Hare to bring attention to the plight of women and children left to fend for themselves while their husbands and fathers served time as a result of prosecutions under the 1917 Espionage Act. The Espionage Act and those who took a public stand against involvement in World War I seem to unite the people mentioned throughout the second half of Boyle's poem. One mentioned by name is a young girl, Elbertine Reeder, the nine-year-old daughter of Walter Reeder, who was serving time in Leavenworth. The Children's Crusaders were marching to Washington to raise awareness, and in Boyle's poem "Elbertine's hands are curled-up leaves blown in your eyes. When she sees the river her hands cry sharply together."[33] The poem captures the poignancy of her plight:

> Progress to Washington . . . President Harding: They may play on the White House lawns.
>
> Grass can be new-washed skin on your palms and forehead. But Elbertine stands like a candle at the gate, black letters on the white banner:
>
> My father is in prison for expressing his opinion.

The simple eloquence of Elbertine's placard, understated and fundamental as it is, marks a powerful use of poetry to enact heightened political awareness.

Other local and national labor leaders are present in the poem, including Nicholas Klein, an attorney and member of the Cincinnati Socialists; Frank Feldhaus, whose company declared bankruptcy in 1921; and Albert Duane Swift, a pacifist conscientious objector who was imprisoned for his beliefs and later became a founding member of the ACLU. Boyle was able to maintain some distance from the figures she portrayed and was quite critical of failures of will by individuals within the organizations. Her poem powerfully evokes Swift's experience in Leavenworth:

> Duane Swift speaks, conscientious objector . . . face an open door:
>
> Leavenworth nights, a long chain linked closer than hot bodies. Days rise bent-backed, bed-rocks to be broken under the sun. Pick lifts into the sky, drops a thin finger pointing earthward. Flat clang of stone against stone, square-headed hammer falls numb on shrill bones. Castrated of response, bodies surrendered upon life.
>
> Set tables are rows of teeth bared in the great room. Hours stretched in the sun breed hunger. Thin soup and one slice of bread . . . heads swing dully . . . Bread . . . hardly uttered . . . Bread . . . wooden spoons lift, sound on the table . . . Bread . . . knocks louder . . . Bread . . . articulate . . . Bread . . . beating seconds . . . Bread . . . more than a hundred more than a thousand voices rising.
>
> Duane Swift, kitchen foreman, passes the false order: One slice each again, once around. Dry tongues move words like withered leaves over the bare floor of night.

The hard labor at Leavenworth turns time itself into the prison from which there is no open door. Fighting the punishments of forced labor, the slow movement of incarcerated time, and relentless hunger, men in this position iterate their being through the demand for bread. Always there is the threat of riot and the impossibility of justice. Later released, Swift goes on the stump to call for the local organization to help found a labor press to meet the challenges: "Democrats have a press, Republicans a press, but the Labor party . . . Now that we're putting it over, comrades, we count on you. Think . . . Russia." In fact Boyle was a member of the Federated Press, mentioned in the poem.[34] Unfortunately the organization does not have the vision to carry the vote, and one voice speaks up on what the group seems to consider a more urgent matter: the need for a new cooler to chill drinks. Then the initiative for the local labor press is tabled in favor of a ball game. Boyle did not flinch from the documentary urge in her poetry.

The poem details conflicting viewpoints surrounding Arthur Nash, a local businessman who became nationally known for cutting the hours of his workers (from a forty-four-hour work week to a forty-hour work week), raising wages, and distributing stock to his employees, all according to the foundational principle of the Golden Rule: "Do thou unto others."[35] The A. Nash Tailoring Company manufactured suits that were distributed nationwide by salesmen who were recruited to work part-time, selling mainly within their friendship and professional networks. Known as "Golden Rule" Nash, this business owner is seen in the poem as evoking the headline "The Bible Text That Worked a Business Miracle." But, Boyle's poem warns, there is more to the story, and it depicts Ann Washington Craton, an organizer for the Amalgamated Clothing Workers Union, contradicting Nash's claims: "Ann Craton, small foot forced in the closing door: 'That is not true. I have been turned away.' Words carried around other corners, pass almost unheard. 'Policemen keep questions from the workers. Through early mornings I have walked pavements to the factory, home on them at evening. To reach the shop at daybreak, cloth-cutters ride the owl car. Golden Rule Nash for longest hours pays the lowest wages.'"

Nash speaks before a Rotary Club, which is much in sympathy with his words, even though Craton makes her rebuttal. Nash finds sympathy from Bishop Paul Jones, who came to Cincinnati after losing his position as Episcopal bishop of Utah because of his outspoken pacificism. Also supporting Nash is socialist and pacifist Herbert S. Bigelow, the head of the People's Church in Cincinnati and a member of the People's Council. When he traveled to speak in Kentucky, Bigelow had been kidnapped and horsewhipped by hooded, disguised men, and warned to leave the vicinity.[36] Thus Boyle's poem shows how people within the movement could find themselves with strange bedfellows. Nash, essentially a political conservative and antilabor, attracts support because his message is based in biblical scripture. The poem later evokes Bigelow's terror during his near-lynching experience, showing him "tied to a tree with his flesh gaping." A section of the poem is devoted to his enduring sense of trauma. Although they are radicals and have each paid a high price for their idealism, Bigelow and Jones are not able to see through Nash's message to the impact on workers.

Boyle's poem then turns to election night, when she hears William Z. Foster, general secretary of the Communist Party USA, who had also had ties to the Socialist Party of America and the Industrial Workers of the World. Although Foster was a national figure, he is not given center stage in the poem, which allows the reader only a glimpse of a meeting where Foster remarks: "Debs is in jail and the country scabs on him. Here, you and I, we're the biggest bunch of boob workers this side of hell." Next on the platform is Lincoln Steffens, labor leader and journalist: "words, footsteps of thoughts that stand tip-toe in his brain. Words, hot on the china-blue plates of his eyes. He, a close hot word thrust on the lips of life." Meanwhile an usher in the back removes the ribbon pinned to his jacket in case the meeting is raided: "better play safe." Foster and Steffens are rendered in slight detail, making surrealist, cameo appearances in the long poem, perhaps reflecting the relatively low level of exposure the young Boyle could have had to them. Figures local to Cincinnati are more actualized and complex in the poem. The appearances of national figures, however, serve to situate the Cincinnati struggles in an national context.

At the Woman's City Club, a progressive organization that promoted women's suffrage and civic causes, Oswald Garrison Villard, the editor of the *Nation,* speaks at a gathering where he and the audience are stoned by marauding American Legionnaires. "Shattering outer doors, up the stairs rising, American Legion, stoning defenders. Protest is blood, like a thin red finger on a temple." A conservative women's organization, the Women's Voters' League, also protested against the Woman's City Club's inviting Villard because he was known as a pacifist because "during the war [he] . . . stood for pacifism and against conscription."[37] At all points in the poem, Boyle went to some pains to show the real human tolls of idealism, which could include imprisonment, physical assault, and riots.

As Boyle herself described it, "The Book of Cincinnati" was a "clear stroke of protest."[38] It ends with an Imagist and surreal return to the river, where Cincinnati clings to its history, identity, and its own contradictions. As a young woman, Boyle worked for and contributed to socialist causes and showed herself to be a critical consumer of the various idealisms that were expressed in the political foment around her. She set herself on a national stage, finding herself able to create a panorama that included national figures. She would only have needed to open either of Ridge's published books of poetry to find poems that feature labor leaders such as Frank Little, Alexander Berkman, and Emma Goldman. It is clear that, although their communication deteriorated, Ridge maintained an iconic force in Boyle's life even as late as the 1980s, when she corresponded with Malcolm Cowley about Ridge's legacy with *Broom.* As she said to Ridge in an August 20, 1923, letter: "You must know, my love, that everything I consider includes you, just as far as you would wish to come in on it. Anything I might consider primarily *needs* you, and it is only my keen realization that you are doing the most important kind of thing in the world right now, and that you are not strong, that prevents me from suggesting any sort of cooperation."[39]

Ridge provided an example of a principled, female artist grounded in social purpose. Kay Boyle took that example forward into the rest of her career, infusing these imperatives with her own motives and goals. Her continuing homage to Ridge, colored as it was with the withdrawal of their living, evolving friendship, was of enduring importance to her.

Four

Important Gifts

Evelyn Scott and Kay Boyle

One of the most important gifts that Lola Ridge gave to both Evelyn Scott and Kay Boyle happened simultaneously: she facilitated their introduction to one another's work and their eventual acquaintance. Long before the two met in person, they became familiar with one another through Ridge. Scott first referred to Boyle in December 1922, when she encouraged Ridge to take a week off at Christmas even though Boyle, who was working as Ridge's assistant, was out sick. The letter is characterized by the solicitous, caring tone Scott had developed, particularly in regard to Ridge's health, her energy, and what she reserved for her own work as opposed to the editing work: "Your description of her [Boyle] makes me feel she is nice for you and I am glad of that but she's got to be well. I feel particularly determined that somebody ought to work for Broom because I didn't and you were a dear not to reproach me or doubt my affection because it really is perfectly good affection even if it doesn't act like it."[1] Evidently the position of assistant had been offered to Scott earlier, and she had not taken it.

Instead Scott pursued her own writing with intense industry and fervor, completing five books in five years, writing several of them simultaneously. Rather than work as an assistant or business manager for Ridge at *Broom,* she traveled with Cyril Kay Scott to Bermuda, where they assisted in taking care of their friends Marie Garland and Swinburne Hale's estate. Prior to this, they had assisted Garland and Hale with their property near Buzzard's Bay, Massachusetts.[2] Scott spent the year writing *The Golden Door* and *Escapade,* and in December 1922 she was just getting to know Owen Merton, a watercolorist who became her primary love interest for the next three years. For the next several years, her unconventional household included Cyril, Owen, her son, Owen's son Thomas (who later became a celebrated writer in his own right, as well as a Trappist monk), and sometimes Cyril's girlfriend Ellen Kennan. Scott may have served as a kind of role model for life choices Boyle later made—or at least Scott may have served as an example of a new woman who followed her heart rather than convention—no matter what.

Indeed Scott's habit of translating her personal experiences and acquaintances into fictive material may well have cleared a professional path for a writer such as Boyle, who put her own life story to rich use in the creation of fiction. Although the two authors emphasized different aspects of women's experience, the fearlessness and determination of Scott's examples of living art no doubt provided an important precedent for Boyle. When Boyle exited her marriage to Richard Brault and began an affair with Ernest Walsh, even as his business partner (who in many ways acted as a jealous lover) Ethel Moorhead was still present and involved, one cannot help but think about the unconventional arrangements of Evelyn Scott, Cyril Kay Scott, and Owen Merton. While the differences between the two women should be remembered, they were both rebellious, unconventional, heterosexual women writers who found their life choices in direct conflict with such Victorian orthodoxies as survived in the early twentieth century.

The project of Scott's fiction tended to uncover the untenable nature of traditional family structures and highlighted the paralysis of the new woman still caught up in the pressure to act and think conventionally. There is an essential struggle for freedom that is not realized by the female protagonists of Scott's early fiction and autobiography. Autonomy and selfhood are centrally compromised by the effort of rebellion against society. In Boyle, however, one sees in her early novels *Process* and *Plagued by the Nightingale* female protagonists who are better able to negotiate their rebellion against social pressures to conform.

In some ways, as Marilyn Elkins has pointed out, the literary influence of Scott on Boyle and vice versa is both "apparent and not apparent."[3] Elkins has noted in both writers prose immediacy, impressionistic style, critique of social norms (particularly as applied to women), lyricism, and focus on the body. At the same time Elkins has made important distinctions such as Boyle's reluctance to cast her female characters as victims and her realization of their individuality. In contrast Scott's women are often subject to and subjugated by their circumstances. Yet, Elkins notes, Boyle seemed to "fill her first novel with echoes of Scott's work" (80). Both Boyle and Scott confronted the female protagonist caught in a "narrow world" and set about exploring the implications of that world.

Boyle attributed the inspiration for one of her early poems to her reading of Evelyn Scott, although the specific source that sparked Boyle's poem has not been identified. Given the timing of the correspondence related to this subject, Boyle would have had available to her Evelyn Scott's book of poems *Precipitations* and her first two novels, *The Narrow House* and *Narcissus.* Conveying messages through Lola Ridge in the spring of 1923, Scott reported that a mutual friend, Ellen Kennan (who became attached to Cyril Kay Scott), had sent her a poem by Boyle inspired by her reading of Scott. Scott stated, "I am proud again to have been an association in a mood so esthetically austere and so really lovely. It's like a very perfect ivory carving of a bird. I wish I had seen other things by her."[4] She also received Boyle's address but was somewhat hesitant to begin a new contact, especially from her location in Bermuda, remote from New York: "I feel somehow I ought not to take a risk that might spoil the possibility of a friendship when we meet."[5] The qualities she valued most in the poem were its "harshness" and "loveliness," qualities she also identified with Ridge's work and her own: "You see Lola I suppose if I have an ideal esthetically it is of the combination of the harsh consciousness, harsh because of its definition, emerging from the undefined and carrying with it a kind of intimation of its source that is even more unescapable than the definition. Her work, to judge from one small specimen, is less poignant less matured in consciousness than yours, but it has a good deal of your flavor—only don't tell her that, for I don't mean she imitates, only that one reason you like her is natural rapport and one reason I should undoubtedly like her (IF my judgment is right) is this identity of a quality in her with a quality in you which I consider precious."[6] This is Scott's articulation of Ridge's principle that women writers should ideally proceed in their work without fear and in freedom. Scott's iteration was in particular sympathy with a Freudian naturalism that portrayed her characters as subjected to their social environments and their own drives and needs.

Scott especially admired Ridge's poem "Sun-Up," which Scott felt captured the terrible and unsentimental beauty of a female consciousness forever damaged by her environment. The qualities all three women shared—lyricism, an appreciation of beauty as it intertwined with the horrible, and the fearless portrayal of harsh truths—sustained the exchange of appreciation and criticism for a time.

Later, writing from France, Scott expressed a wish to meet Boyle, who was in reasonable proximity to her in Harfleur.[7] On a subsequent occasion, later in the spring, Scott reminded Ridge to convey her appreciation for the poem again: "I hope Kay Boyle heard I appreciated the poem—I mean I hope you told her I'd like to know her."[8] One is reminded in these exchanges how important the issues of audience and feedback were to Scott and Boyle, both of whom were working in some isolation. Both also felt that Ridge was an important member of their imagined audience, and in part Ridge's strong philosophy of women's writing helped to shape their respective ideas of themselves as they worked within this group. It worked both ways: letters from both Scott and Boyle for years prompted Ridge to tell them how the "woman book" was coming along. Her project was important to how Scott and Boyle understood themselves. They were working in proximity to a woman writer who—to some degree—was philosophizing about their parallel projects.

Ridge strongly encouraged Scott and Boyle to meet in person, especially once Scott and her entourage were relocated—first to Bou Saada, Algeria, and then to Coullioure, France, where they remained from spring 1923 through early 1924. While still in Bermuda and in a depressed mood, Scott replied to Ridge, "I would like to know Kay Boyle, but I hope I shall. Some of these dreary days of rain I have wished I was having tea with you and one or two others maybe half as nice."[9]

Scott and Boyle each entertained the idea that they would meet, and when they finally did, there was a complicated response on each side. They came together during the summer of 1924 in Paris, and true to Kay Boyle's much later 1968 description in *Being Geniuses Together*, the two women found challenges to a close face-to-face friendship. When Boyle was recuperating from a period of illness she thought was tuberculosis, Scott invited Boyle to visit, but Boyle later wrote, "into the intellectual and sexual turmoil of her life I would not go."[10] During that time Scott was going through her tense and tumultuous relationship with Owen Merton, which soon came to an abrupt end. Cyril Kay Scott still was present in her life but had assumed a generally paternal role. As Boyle explained, "The reality of our friendship resided in our letters, and this may have been because each of us was writing not to a stranger but to another facet of herself. In Paris we were abruptly two separate human beings, women with actual faces, voices, and we must look into each other's eyes and decide whether or not we believed in what we found there, whether we were comforted or discomfited."[11]

Looking back, Boyle remembered she was struck by Scott's age ("was she ten or fifteen years older than I"), her rather ordinary—or at least anticlimactic—appearance ("She had neither the saintlike head nor the burning presences of Lola Ridge, nor Lola's shining aura of belief"), and the nervous and somewhat desperate emotional demands she made. As Boyle wrote later in *Being Geniuses Together*, "in which direction could she possibly go, I asked myself, in the intellectual uproar of her life? She had exchanged her dreams, her unseen world, for something I could not name."[12] These words and Boyle's assessment were written after the friendship had run nearly forty years, and Evelyn Scott had died in 1963, poverty-stricken and entangled in paranoid delusion.[13] Boyle's key observation, that Scott demanded "surrender" with a "terrible, terrible hunger, of everyone she met," offers a glimpse into a life that was, even in the middle 1920s, marred by obsessive tendencies.[14] Nevertheless each woman served the other as a source of companionship and perhaps as a negative example.

The balance of feedback for work was skewed. Scott was generous with her responses and guidance, sharing the knowledge she had gained from her advanced position as an author, with Boyle in the role of mentee. Scott later felt slighted by what she perceived as a silence about her own work that fell over their correspondence, and indeed Boyle's remarks to Ridge show that Boyle grew disillusioned with Scott's work when she began to publish more historically oriented fiction with the 1927 appearance of *Migrations.*

For her part Scott gave generously of her time and her critical intelligence to bring a different perspective to Boyle's developing work. As Boyle reported, Scott's brilliant and "ruthless" criticism of Boyle's first novel caused her to rewrite it from the beginning. Incorporating feedback from Ridge and Scott, Boyle worked through her early apprenticeship as a writer and emerged with a more mature art. According to Boyle, the gist of Scott's criticism was that (in a metaphor strikingly similar to the first missive Ridge sent to Scott) "a veil hung between my work and the reader, and that I would have to tear that veil away before my writing could have value."[15] As Ridge had written to her then unknown admirer in 1919: "Thank you for believing in me. I shall try not to disappoint you. I feel happier in the work I am now doing. I see more clearly. There are seven veils before the eyes of the creator—but you too must know this. This last year one of mine has parted. You have helped in this. Your aid gave me a great stimulus."[16] Evidently the metaphor had traveled through the friendships to inform not only Scott but, through her, Boyle as well. The metaphor was powerful enough to prompt Boyle's reworking and to remain in Boyle's memory decades later.

Writing to Ridge, Scott summed up her first meeting with Boyle in a lukewarm tone. Scott was glad that Boyle liked her, "and if I didn't rave it is because experience has begun to teach me not to rave oersoon in order not to curse later. I mean I saw at once she was a sensitive, intelligent, and talented girl, but just how much of a rapport for friendship that would constitute I couldn't tell in those two days."[17] She allowed that she trusted Ridge's instincts to uncover new talent, concurring that Boyle's writing put her "in much, much more than the merely talented class."[18] She valued especially Boyle's ability to define and present characters in "their differentness as well as in their identity."[19] There was a wariness between Scott and Boyle in person that disappeared in their quite effusive and deeply personal correspondence. Particularly in letters from the period in which each was going through heart-breaking crises—Scott with Owen Merton and Boyle with Ernest Walsh—they achieve an intimacy as Boyle discussed with Scott the details of her pregnancy and her overwhelming emotions at Walsh's death.

Scott provided an effective model for Boyle's prose style. Shortly after leaving the United States with her husband, Richard Brault, for Brittany, Boyle had begun to write the novel she called variously "Source," then "Process," then much later "The Imponderables." Since the novel was lost for decades before it was rediscovered by Sandra Spanier and published as *Process* after Boyle's death, Boyle's memory of the novel had deteriorated by the time she referred to it in *Being Geniuses Together*. By June 1923 she was reporting in letters that it was underway.[20] While she was in the middle of writing *Process*, Boyle received Evelyn Scott's *Escapade* as a present from her mother in early December 1923. Although looking backward Boyle seemed to recall only the limitations of *Escapade*, in 1923 she described it as "one of the most exciting and altogether tremendous things that has happened in America. . . . I was mad with a tense wild recognition for weeks after finishing it (it came early in December), and I am so deeply thrilled with its beauty and strength."[21] In *Being Geniuses Together*, however, Boyle said she had learned from *Escapade* "to mistrust a woman's analysis of her own motives."[22] She wished to write instead of an imponderable psychological knowledge, of subjects that were beyond the measuring and weighing that signifies the value of most things or acts. She said she wanted to evince in her work an "unseen world" where spirit, ethics, and the indefinable value of things are evoked. In Evelyn Scott's creations, Boyle said, "I could find no vision of that world," and she grew impatient with Scott's narrowness.[23]

It is true that the persona in *Escapade* is in an antitranscendental situation for most of the narrative, simply trying to negotiate peace and privacy for herself against the extremely poor odds of her poverty and domestic situation, which includes her young son, her lover, and her mother (written into the story as Aunt Nannette). To the extent that Scott's novel evokes "imponderables," it does so within a framework of manic and dystopian intensity. Despite the two writers' aesthetic differences, which seem to have intensified over the passage of years, the friendship persisted. Scott provided Boyle with something she needed, and Scott deeply respected Boyle and her art. It was rewarding for Scott to have been involved in the development of a talented writer.

Scott was unfailingly supportive of Boyle's work. They shared books, Boyle loaning Scott James Joyce's *Ulysses* and William Carlos Williams's *Great American Novel*.[24] Scott further theorized that Boyle was able to create "relational truth" in her writing as well as painting lovely images. As Scott said to Ridge, "I know you have a wonderful sense of potentialities, but I had not expected her to be that good. Her admirations at present are all for the immediacy and form be damned school (I don't mean form as a subjective atmosphere) so I hope she won't kill her own advantage by stressing the turgid or the violent or the too delicate moral noncomittalness at the expense of this other thing she has. She probably wont though since she is beginning as herself."[25]

Scott encouraged Ridge to steer Boyle away from Alfred Stieglitz—at the center of his own circle, which emerged from the heyday of his 291 studio in New York and of which Scott had found herself at the skeptical fringes. It was an instance of Scott's meddling and perhaps a precursor to a later, stronger strain of anti-Semitism that emerged in thoughts she expressed in letters. Ever since Boyle had shown her work as part of a children's art show in Stieglitz's gallery, he had been an icon for her. "Do save Kay Boyle from it," Scott said to Ridge. "She seems to have the usual youthful feeling about that old Rabbi."[26]

Boyle wrote to "My Dear Mrs. Scott" on August 11, 1924, sending her the poem "Harbor Song" and explaining that it would appear in *Poetry* in a censored form, "much mutilated because H.M. [Harriet Monroe] can't 'risk' the word 'Buttocks,' nor the 'Whore Street' affair. Isn't it appalling?"[27] This was an excellent topic to discuss with Scott, whose autobiography *Escapade* and her novel *The Golden Door*, the third in her trilogy, were censored by her publisher, Thomas Seltzer, in anticipation of a Sumnerian attack on the works. In *Escapade* Scott was strongly encouraged to remove too-explicit discussions of toilet arrangements, passages in which she was unrepentant about being with John (Cyril) as an unmarried woman, and sensual descriptions of motherhood, including breast feeding.[28] To Ridge, Boyle wrote, "I was glad to have E. Scott's address and wrote her a little note, which she answered at once and which I shall answer this afternoon. I was awfully happy that my poem meant something to her."[29]

Boyle tried to find a way to balance her need to develop as an artist in isolation and her need to connect with other mentors and writers. In August 1924 she wrote to Ridge: "I don't honestly want to meet Evelyn Scott or anybody. I have nothing to give anyone at present and until I am recharged I want to be alone. I have come definitely to the conclusion that when I want to write I must go away from everyone as you did. Close all the doors of my life."[30] After more poetry had been sent to Scott and they had a chance to meet, Scott reported to Ridge: "I saw Kay Boyle in Paris and she was damn sweet to come up specially to see us. I've read some of her poems and they are full of really lovely passages (sometimes I think she's a bit under your influence, Lola, do you mind) for I don't think that matters but does her credit since everybody is influenced somehow."[31] The question of influence was one that Scott would return to from several sides in her letters, seeing herself influenced by her partner, Cyril Kay Scott, as well as by Lola Ridge. From Ridge, Scott may have drawn a force to not swerve from difficult subjects, and she certainly drew a strong current of belief in her as a writer. When Scott wrote her best-received book, *The Wave*, in 1929, she dedicated it to Ridge.

By December 1924, Boyle was sending the manuscript of *Process* to her two friends for remarks. The response from Scott was nearly immediate and offered high praise. In addition she suggested that Ridge take up the book in the role of an agent with Scott's own current publisher, Thomas Seltzer. Scott wrote a cover letter to be presented with the manuscript, a letter that does not survive. As Scott explained to Boyle, "If anybody is capable of talking convincingly about an enthusiasm, Lola is. If they are favorably disposed, her added comment will be all to the good, and if they aren't you can find out more accurately through her than in a perfunctory correspondence just why they aren't."[32] Scott was confident in both Boyle's work and the strength of Ridge's advocacy.

Boyle was buoyed by Scott's positive response to her work. She worried when sending it that she did not know if either woman would like it, but after working in isolation she was heartened to hear Scott describe *Process* as a "classic" characterized by its lyricism and the "the modern sense of the beautiful." Scott especially valued Boyle's ability to "preserve the persistent oppositions as in a fugue of individuals, individuals who are not simply the novelist in fancy dress, but who, though the novelist has taken them to her and they stem out of an identity in her emotions, keep their own consistent melodies."[33] She encouraged Boyle to continue developing her ability to create characters who were individuals, concluding that "you are, or you ought to be, our coming novelist—our very best."[34] Boyle told Ridge that, if her friends had this sort of reaction to her work, concerns for publication were secondary: "If Evelyn feels this way, and if you get something out of it, I can't really care whether it is published or not. I mean, if the presentation of a inevitable expression is made . . . then I have succeeded."[35] In spite of all this support from both Ridge and Scott, Seltzer did not accept the book, but Boyle maintained to Ridge on April 1, 1925, "I get much more kick out of having you and Evelyn reacting to my things than anything else."[36] By October 1925 Boyle had rewritten the novel in light of the remarks from both friends. Although she later relegated *Process* to the category of apprentice piece and worked in earnest on subsequent projects that were published soon afterward, Boyle found the community and support to begin within the framework of these friendships. Visits between Boyle and Scott continued off and on during 1925, when they could both make it to Paris. The two friends conspired on how they might get Ridge to join them in France for a short visit or a more extended stay. Boyle wrote to Ridge, "But you do see how possible and how logical it is, don't you Lola? You could divide your time between us and get wholly rested and see marvelous things and you would be doing us all the greatest favor you ever did anyone in your life. . . . Evelyn is writing you too."[37] Lola Ridge did not make this trip, even when it would have been possible for her to accompany Boyle's husband, Richard Brault, on a return passage from the United States to France early that summer. After trying to engineer a way for the three friends to be together and in light of Ridge's refusal to come to France, a chill temporarily entered their correspondence and a lapse of several months opened up. In fact, while Scott and Boyle continued to correspond and visit, the three friends never met together.

Scott visited and lived in the United States during several different periods before Ridge's 1941 death, but Boyle stayed in Europe until her return to the United States in 1941, missing Ridge. Scott maintained correspondence with both women, but after the original sharing about Boyle's early work with Ridge and her encouragement that they meet, the letters grow mostly silent about Boyle. Boyle often asked Scott to transmit her good wishes to Ridge, but their conversation did not center on these friendships once Boyle moved past her apprenticeship. Still a central figure in Boyle's imagination, Ridge took on an iconic status, and their friendship did not evolve over time. Scott tried—with her heart in the right place—to do something to help Ridge and set up an impromptu benefit fund for her, which Ridge received as meddling.[38] Despite these misunderstandings, their friendship endured. Boyle and Ridge drifted apart.

In the meantime Evelyn Scott suffered a devastating heartbreak at the dissolution of her relationship with Owen Merton, which coincided with the estrangement Kay Boyle initiated from her husband and her intense affair with Ernest Walsh. One of Scott's options as she went through the crisis, which included several suicide attempts, was to stay with Boyle. It is not clear if she accepted her friend's offer.[39] The two did grow closer; it is clear in correspondence to Lola Ridge later in 1926 that Boyle shared the details of her attachment to Walsh with Evelyn Scott. Scott ended up in New York, and as Boyle later said in a March 4, 1926, letter to Ridge, "I think of you as the impalpable angel who nursed Evelyn last summer in the hellish heat." She also informed Ridge briefly of her relationship with Walsh, "of which Evelyn knows much."[40] On October 16, 1926, Walsh died of tuberculosis, and in the spring of 1927 Boyle gave birth to his daughter.

Beginning in late 1926, the correspondence between Boyle and Scott takes on a personal tone, reflecting a deepening of their friendship. Boyle reached out to Scott from the depths of her grief: "You should be here with me because I love you. I want to talk about my baby and yet I don't want a baby, I want Michael [Ernest Walsh] I want him reborn again because he was something to have gone on with and a child is sad because it is an ending of something beautiful even though it is the beginning of itself."[41] She was able to share fierceness with Scott, bringing authenticity to her suffering: "With you I do not have to be gentle or false, from you I can demand everything and you must give it to me."[42] She shared in vivid detail the vicissitudes of her pregnancy, secure in the knowledge that Scott, of all people, understood and had shared details of her own pregnancy with the world in *Escapade.* For Scott too her story had not been *escape* but *escapade*—with the connotations of something undertaken without the full view of consequences that would evolve with time.

Boyle wanted to share with Ridge the details of the life she briefly had with Walsh, but it was difficult to have her know him simply through descriptions in letters. Inviting Ridge to contribute to *This Quarter,* Boyle continued to assist with editing of the magazine throughout her pregnancy, working with Ethel Moorhead, who stood by Boyle throughout her pregnancy.[43] The two women could not continue because of the tensions of the situation and their personality conflicts. In the last weeks of her pregnancy, Boyle contemplated a return to the United States, but she met with opposition from her mother and sister—a breach that caused Boyle a great deal of pain. She reached out to Ridge, who responded with letters (that do not survive) and small gifts of money. But Boyle and Ridge no longer had the rapport that Boyle had been able to establish with Evelyn Scott, who was in closer proximity and who was herself going through titanic upheavals in her unconventional life. The moral judgment of Boyle's family encouraged her to think toward an ad hoc family and lineage for her child, consisting of artists who had meant so much to the development of her art and spirit: Emanuel Carnevali, Ethel Moorhead, and Lola Ridge. To Ridge she wrote that she needed her: "I'm in a lone hard country without love. . . . BELIEVE IN ME."[44]

Boyle shared with Scott the difficulties of her arrangement with Moorhead in the wake of Walsh's death. Scott had sought some comfort after the breakup with Owen Merton by rejoining Cyril Kay Scott for a time in Bou Saada, Algeria. Richard Brault, Boyle's estranged husband, offered support, and Boyle eventually moved in with him for a time in Stoke-on-Trent, where he got a new job. She asked Evelyn Scott if she was going to Cornwall: "I do want to live near you before we all die young. We mightn't get along, Evelyn, but at least we'd disagree intelligently." As she went through the pregnancy and birth of her daughter Sharon, she shared with Scott that she recalled passages of *Escapade* during her confinement and that "somehow you and your experience is bound up in this experience of mine."[45]

The two argued fiercely about the writer Robert McAlmon and about influences in general. Scott had disapproved initially of McAlmon because of her protectiveness of Ridge, but also because she was not successful in manipulating him sexually. In return McAlmon disliked Scott, just as he evinced disdain for Ridge. Boyle was loyal to McAlmon throughout her life because she respected his writing and perhaps as well because he offered her help after her pregnancy and childbirth, giving her money when she had few options and no other means to escape the deteriorating situation with Ethel Moorhead. Scott and Boyle's rift over him was quite bitter, but ultimately their friendship survived in a cooler manner after the quarrel.

McAlmon saw Scott as an example of a literary careerist and artistic mediocrity. In *Being Geniuses Together* Boyle quoted from a letter McAlmon wrote to William Carlos Williams when they were defining the mission of their little magazine, *Contact*, published between 1920 and 1923: "But when a person like Evelyn Scott, with an analytical intelligence, writes pretty imagism, and other verses that would do for a 'textbook of modern poetry' she is writing verses because that's the thing to do, and not because they share the quality of her perception, or apprehension of experience.... But as I said in a letter to you before departing, it isn't lack of contact that condemns most writing.... It's lack of an individual quality that makes the stuff worth reading, and presence of too much desire to be a 'literary figure.'"[46]

Later McAlmon wrote in a chapter of *Being Geniuses Together* that Evelyn Scott's *The Wave* was "probably the world's dullest book, with its horrible 'spiritual' messages beneath its hack pretenses. Probably she believed it recreated history, but her intensities and significances always made me feel squirmy. She'd be more restful if she would just admit her mediocrity."[47] The intensity of his remarks suggests some professional jealousy: in 1929 Scott achieved the height of her literary reputation with *The Wave*, which was a commercial and public success. McAlmon understandably distanced himself from Scott because she approached him as a conquest.

Scott accused Boyle of clouded judgment with regard to her support of McAlmon and had evidently brought up the matter of other Boyle mentors, such as Stieglitz.[48] It is a mark of Scott's insistent personality that she felt she could try to persuade Boyle to subscribe to the aesthetic positions she espoused in her letters. Boyle wrote to Scott on October 22, 1927 that her interest in Scott's work "was based on *Escapade* which I thought was as direct and simple a piece of writing as anything I had ever read. My love for you is something else besides."[49] On November 29, 1927, Boyle wrote to Ridge that she was disappointed because Scott misunderstood the friendship she offered, but that the connection between Scott and Ridge had "given me what is important as a sacred belief in each other." Boyle also reported to Ridge that Scott had written: "If you want our friendship to break on Bob McAlmon—well here goes."[50]

Although this was a heated disagreement, the two women managed to get beyond it. Time passed, and Scott and Boyle continued to support one another through that disagreement; especially noteworthy was Scott's support in 1933 of Boyle's application for a Guggenheim Fellowship, which she received. In her recommendation Scott said she felt that Boyle had already written "prose classics" and was a writer who has "fully justified herself as an artist."[51]

Despite the aesthetic differences that erupted between the two women in the late 1920s, Scott and Boyle were supportive of one another until Scott's death in 1963. Boyle could be counted on as a friend throughout the lean and difficult years Scott and her husband, Jack Metcalfe, lived in the Benjamin Franklin Hotel in New York. Boyle's later remarks about Scott in *Being Geniuses Together* may be seen in part as reflecting Boyle's later experience of Scott as emotionally debilitated by paranoia and obsessive personality disorders. As Boyle wrote in her memoir, "I had come to demand a great deal of women, and more of women writers than I was able to express. It was an actual pain in the heart when they failed to be what they themselves had given their word that they would seek to be. I think I never forgave Evelyn for this."[52]

Because *Escapade* was a decisive influence on Boyle's early writing, it is useful to examine it alongside Boyle's first novel, *Process,* which was written in 1924 and 1925. In the middle of composing the novel, Boyle read *Escapade,* and she found it to be a liberating text. In it Scott modeled an attunement toward experience that led to insights about knowledge, the making of an artist, and the consequences of an unorthodox lifestyle. Scott's early prose works, including *The Narrow House* (1921), *Narcissus* (1922), *Escapade* (1923), and *The Golden Door* (1925) constitute a sustained, naturalistic examination of women's social roles. The autobiography *Escapade,* which Boyle referred to as a foundational text for her own development, is a separate narrative strain from the trilogy comprising the other books in this period, but it presents another dimension to the same overall project. Scott shifted her focus more than once during her long career, but during the period 1920–25 she was a naturalist who sought to present characters objectively in their restricted social environments. Her books closely examine traditional attitudes toward marriage, family, pregnancy, and children. There is also implicit in her work the question of whether or not women may be able to live psychologically whole lives within the contexts of societal expectations. Her books depict conventional lives as morbid and self-deceived; the consequences of rebellion are extremely difficult to bear, but resistance also provides the rebel with a modicum of dignity and independence unattainable in any other fashion. There is no heroic transcendence in her works of this time and whatever personal freedom and fulfillment the characters attain is perceived as one step on the way to a full life and psychic wholeness—never achieved but theorized.

Like Boyle, Scott was precocious in her involvement in political and feminist causes. As early as age fifteen, she had immersed herself in the suffrage movement as well as radical philosophical writing. Her reading "'inspired [her] with simultaneous ambitions to become a writer, a painter, an actress and a disciple of Pavlova, Tolstoy, Nietzsche, Bergson and Karl Marx all at once.'"[53]

Callard mentions that "at fifteen Elsie Dunn wrote a letter, including her age, to the New Orleans *Times-Picayune,* advocating the legalization of prostitution as a means of controlling venereal disease."[54] Scott's involvement in political organizations fell off as her position as an anarchist and later more generally as a Christian socialist (without any particular group affiliation) developed. Her mistrust of any organization grew stronger as time went on and became a feature of her later obsessive imbalance. However, her early attunement to the plight of socially marginalized people and to the poor informed her writing.

Through a series of deliberate moral choices in which she maintained her absolute justification throughout her life, she broke irrevocably with tradition when she left for Brazil with her lover in 1913, a situation she documented in *Escapade.* For Scott there was no question but to leave behind her upbringing in an attempt to construct a new foundation for her spirit and mind. She later strongly defended her going to Brazil and entering into a common-law marriage with Cyril Kay Scott (leaving behind his spouse, her enraged parents, and a scandalized community), by saying that his marriage had been an unhappy and superficial marriage. In 1960 she described her relationship with Cyril and the legitimacy of her child with him unequivocally in the following way: "WE ARE IN EVERY WAY LEGALIZED—ADHERENTS OF LAW IN EVERY REASONABLE SENSE, but we are unorthodox of course. Church and state separate."[55]

Scott was not only acting on her own emotional behalf when she broke with conventional values; she was executing a plan of emancipation from a fading and idealized culture that she found reprehensible. That she spent so many of her later years and so much of her energy explaining her actions to others is an indication of the extent to which her program to free herself of convention was only partially successful. Particularly as she pursued her father's estate after his death, she sought to make these genealogical relationships clear and to establish identities for herself and her family through the 1940s. Seely Dunn began a new family after divorcing Maude, but Scott believed that, as his daughter, she would inherit something on his death. Her hopes in this regard did not materialize. Poverty remained a shaping feature of her life and the subject of the artist and remuneration was a recurrent theme in her later work.

In *Escapade,* Scott insisted on her own responsibility for the elopement, and one source of her greatest irritation was the tendency of others (including her mother, fictionalized as Aunt Nannette) to place the lion's share of blame automatically on Cyril (fictionalized as John).[56] The narrator struggles to realize moral autonomy, and the challenges are not only from the outside judgments of others but also from a fractured sense of self. Her selfhood is deeply contingent on how others perceive her. She invites her mother to visit because she has an admittedly vain wish to be at the center of someone else's world while at the same time realizing how her arrival will complicate their lives. On more than one occasion, in surrealist fashion, Scott asserts that unless she is directly perceived by her partner, Cyril, she does not exist. Her pregnancy and the complication of self and other that arises from nurturing a new life within her also underscores her contingent, eroded selfhood.

Callard speculates that *Escapade* was transcribed from journal notes, and the vivid descriptions of her natural surroundings, written years after Scott lived in Brazil, support that theory. Scott admitted that *Escapade* was a difficult book to write and that she had tried to fictionalize her experiences several times, but she is quoted by Callard as having decided, "I had to write it, and write it just as it was" (23). One senses that Scott's overall goal in the autobiography was psychological accuracy and a fearless vulnerability. The book describes in detail the deterioration of the family as they endured increasing financial hardships and even came close to starvation. In a tremendous gamble designed to provide a way of life in which Cyril would not have to travel all the time and they could be together, they invested seven hundred dollars in a homestead ranch in the state of Bahia. The ranch failed because they did not reserve enough savings for costs incurred subsequent to their investment in the initial stock; the labor proved too strenuous for Cyril; and their main livestock purchase, 130 sheep, died in large numbers from an unidentified disease. They found themselves without a cent, grateful for the cabbages they had planted and saved from ants and surrounded by beautiful mountains that looked more and more cagelike. It would take money to escape such a remote location, seven miles from their nearest neighbors. Evelyn Scott believed that they would die there and was consumed by terror at the thought of what might happen to them—two unprotected women and a small child—if Cyril died.

Their main challenge, however, was emotional. Scott unflinchingly portrayed the turmoil of the family as they faced extreme circumstances. Her mother became shrill, and Scott described her more than once as a "mad woman" whose only comfort is to recede into the chaos of insanity.[57] Cyril coldly informed Evelyn that if he did not fear consequences, he would kill her mother, and Evelyn also thought about killing her. All the human relationships suffer to the breaking point, including the bond between Scott and her son, telling him "I cannot be your mother any longer. I will make us a mother, a big God who will be father and mother both. Then we can hide ourselves in the shadow of him" (254). Wanting to apologize to her son for bringing him into such a merciless world, she decided that suffering is not ennobling, as she once thought, but distorting, making people hideous. Compare this scene to the fraught motherhood Scott constructed in her poem "The Tunnel."

One of Scott's targets in *Escapade* is what she termed the tendency of some to leverage self-sacrifice for an emotional and moral advantage. Much of her energy was spent in asserting herself against the perceived malignant opinions of others. Isolated at least through the first third of the text by her inability to speak Portuguese, her feelings of helplessness in navigating Brazilian culture, her pregnancy by a man who was not her legal husband, and their increasing poverty, she imagined herself to be vulnerable—with cause. As a foreign woman with no legal ties to anyone with power in her environment and without even a passport, it may be more understandable to see why she initiated contact with her dysfunctional, disapproving mother even when her arrival would shatter the couple's privacy and color their lives with her active paranoias. Her mother blamed Cyril for Evelyn's situation, not only the social consequences of their escapade but for her ill health after the pregnancy. As time wore on and Maude did not hear from her husband or receive the return fare to the United States he had promised to send her, she grew more desperate to assign blame not only for Evelyn's situation but her own.[58] In one of the passages that is most sympathetic to her mother's point of view, Evelyn reports that her mother says: "At least you chose the thing you wanted and you have each other, while I have no one—nobody on earth! And I am dependent on you and John for everything, for the very air I breathe!" (211).

Cyril is sympathetically portrayed throughout the book, even when the group was at the extremities of their emotional states with each other. One of the ironies of Scott's situation is that much later on Cyril—apparently jaded by subsequent events and relationships—wrote his own account of their time in Brazil, *Life is Too Short,* published in 1943. His account is so different in detail and mood from Scott's that Scott concluded erroneously the manuscript had been tampered with.[59] He reported in 1943 that the major motivation on his part for their elopement was to go to the tropics with an agreeable companion, and "Miss Dunn was the only woman I knew at the time who would consent to go to the tropics with me. I was glad it was to be someone who wouldn't bore me."[60] This statement contrasts to a moment of love between them that Scott detailed late in *Escapade:* "He looks up at me, smiles, and I love him and wonder who he is" (232). Cyril criticized Scott's account as solipsistic; it is true that it centers on her consciousness and is rendered in a style that flattens the characterizations of others. That any love survived between them in that emotional desert is a welcome sign to the reader.

When leaving the United States with Cyril, Evelyn felt they might earn a living doing something together, and that poverty, she imagined, could be "more completely shared" (5). Instead Cyril frequently had to work away from home, sometimes for weeks at a time. Unescorted by him, she perceived herself as vulnerable to continual male threats. Some of her mother's paranoia seems also to have tainted her perceptions and her world; there are few sympathetic people among the indigenous Brazilians depicted in Scott's book. Few of the Americans Scott described are sympathetic either. They are often selfish and shortsighted, but Scott did not exclude herself from the same exacting judgments she exerted over them. She was most consistently sympathetic in her descriptions of her many pets, which she recognized as an emotional luxury. She saw that her attachment to animals was an expression of a possessive love that did not always work well when shared with other human beings: "My love is a kind of benevolent tyranny and I can indulge it best with pets" (154).

Scott's fears that the entire family would be wiped out if something happened to Cyril are highlighted in the several dreams that close part 6 of *Escapade.* In one dream she is dancing with Cyril, and he mysteriously disappears, leaving her dancing with only an empty shirt and trousers. In another dream he fatally wounds himself in the neck with a penknife, and she discovers a postcard indicating that he has left on another adventure, this time to Asia. The symbolism of the dreams varies, but the message is the same—they express the profound fear that Cyril is dead and that Scott and her son must find their way without his protection and love. When he is ill, she wonders: "If John should die! I want to die also, quickly, at once, so as not to face what may happen to Jackie and Nannette. There are no doctors here, no medicine, but, worst of all, there is no money with which to buy freedom from the necessity to do things for which you are physically unfit" (194). When Cyril left them for several weeks in order to secure a job with a mining company, which will be their deliverance from the ranch, a local "witch doctor" spreads rumors that Cyril has deserted her. Immediately some of the livestock disappears, and he fills her "ears with tales of horrible things that happened to women who were left alone up here" (255). As luck would have it, the increased manganese mining in response to the needs of World War I had opened up an opportunity for Cyril. He secured a position, and the family became able to escape their escapade. Her mother's faith in Cyril as a man who could deliver them is justified: "It seems she knew all the while that John could liberate us. She did not anticipate a lifetime in this place" (256). Scott constructed a world and a subjectivity where modern feminism staggers under the imperatives of the deadly environment. This may not agree with her feminist ideology, but it is congruent with her drive to be ruthlessly honest. She did not cast herself as physically or mentally able to seize their situation and craft a different outcome. *Escapade* investigates various aspects of dependence, even as it celebrates Evelyn's emergence as a writer. Writing, then, became one of several possible ways to assert a measure of control over their situation.

In some ways *Escapade* is an investigation into what one can know subjectively. The narrator says that "a belief which does not spring from a conviction in the emotions is no belief at all"; she must be confirmed in her knowledge by the experience of the flesh as well as the mind (9). Specifically Scott gained new knowledge based on experiences of pregnancy and pain. She felt herself to be an outcast socially, spiritually, and physically. To the extent that she was condemned for her choices, she welcomed the sense of being that sprang from having evoked a response in others. As her narrator states, "Yes, I want to be an outcast in order to realize fully what human beings are capable of" (9). Scott had a particular desire to find a knowledge paid for through hardship and suffering. "I wanted to go to the end of myself, to the end of something obscure in my consciousness" (25). What she showed through the journey is that an early idealism about what she could know faltered when she was faced with hardship after hardship. Early on she was able to ask "I wonder who I am. Who is this being I am alone with every day" (41). The hard-won truth of this quest was, she posited, that the "only escape will be through the mind—into a world unmodified by our experience" (214). She wrote, "I must make others realize what I alone seem to know, that all of us are subject to the obscure attacks of misfortune, that we have nothing to waste in unnecessary struggles which we ourselves precipitate" (186). At the center of the knowing Scott posited was her experience of pain. Physical pain is "timeless, absolute" in that it cannot be shared with others and it does not allow space for individuality, personality, or expression (54). Scott's descriptions of the physical pain of a difficult childbirth (her labor lasted five days) and several subsequent surgeries are intense and provide the structure of interiority that marks the book. That she could not share the experience of pain with anyone else was the basis of her feelings of profound isolation.

Escapade suggests the only real deliverance from the trap of their isolation, no matter what physical escape that they negotiated, was through writing. Both Cyril and Evelyn were writing (she said it was as though they were saying their last words on paper), and the autobiography ends with a piece derived from a work Scott titled "Shadow Play," which was written during her stay in Brazil and which she had shopped separately to *Broom* before its publication in *Escapade.* Scott described sending poems to American journals. Some of them were rejected by an American editor who, knowing her age, told her she should live more before she tried to write poetry (223). Her mother, however, believed Evelyn was a writer, but it seems as though she herself was a little unsure of her vocation: "I wanted to be a writer but I had nothing to write about" (30). "If only I could write! But I had no thoughts" (2). The enactment of the autobiography belies this uncertainty about vocation.

In "Shadow Play" Scott created a suite of characters—some of whom are modeled on animals—who debate what sort of a society they can create. The humans find themselves excluded from the natural order, on the outside of the widest of social circles and experiencing an infinite separation from the animals. Throughout the play, characters ask ironically "What's God?" The book ends with darkness descending on the stage, a complementary bookend to the blazing light that illuminates the text's beginning. The play is clearly the child of Scott's thoughts and strivings in a survival situation, and in it she contemplates the questions of nature, life, God, gender, and mankind. Juxtaposed with the rest of *Escapade,* the artistic, imaginative product becomes the logical conclusion of the basic arc of the text.

Kay Boyle thought *Escapade* expressed a "cold and lovely personal truth."[61] She praised its straightforward simplicity, but she, like later readers, was puzzled by the ending in farce. Nevertheless Boyle found a model in Scott for a modernist ethos. The detachment that is at the heart of Scott's project translated into an objective stance in Boyle's novel *Process.* Scott provided one powerful model for how a woman writer could translate her life experience into art. Like *Escapade, Process* is about family that through its life choices participates in much larger ideas. The relationships between people are drawn precisely and economically through light, detached touches. At the heart of the book is the question of how much people are willing to compromise their stated ideals. This problem—the ways people fall short of their ideals—is at the heart of Scott's writing as well.

Set in Cincinnati, *Process* opens with a view of the Tyler Davidson Memorial Fountain, which sprays in all four directions. Cincinnati, the center of the world Boyle created, is an industrial city seen within its natural setting of the river and surrounding hills. The novel is also about the connections and directions of the various characters—how they make sound connections or fail to connect with each other. Boyle was gifted at creating highly charged situations with a few deft strokes. At the beginning of *Process,* the main character, Kerith Day, modeled on Kay Boyle, is driving with a character we later learn is her mother, Nora. Their relationship is more of equals than mother and daughter and is characterized by concord rather than discord. In fact it takes a long time for the reader to ascertain what their relationship is because their manner toward one another is without hierarchical posturing. They are at peace with one another, and Nora appreciates that they are able to do just what they want to do, mutually satisfied: "going on easily and stopping simply when one felt like stopping. I never really wanted anything more,"[62] which is in contrast to her rather strained marriage with her husband, Harry Day, whose primary loyalty is to his father and their business and who has not made time to take care of their relationship. Nora encourages Kerith to use what opportunities she can to escape the narrow world of their family home and business, a garage the family lives above. She does so without also inducing guilt over abandonment—Nora's kind wishes for Kerith seem uncomplicated by a sense that her own life is also tied to the narrow world she wants Kerith to escape. Where Evelyn Scott found only selfishness and envy in her mother, Kay Boyle constructed a remarkably healthy relationship between her fictional self and Nora.

Much of the novel concerns how people can, or fail to, reach each other. Nora observes, "Relationships are so rarely complete, rarely."[63] One of the true connections in the book is between Kerith and her Ford automobile, which she puts to use in taxiing speakers about during labor rallies. She is fond of her car, although she maintains that society should be strong enough to turn away from cities and industrialism in order to reinvent labor relations from the ground up. After a meeting, she tests the limits of her driving ability by stopping just short of a passing train—exulting in the responsiveness of the car to her will, and in her passengers' momentary fear. Earlier in the novel she was stopped and given a ticket for having her high beams on; she drives rebelliously through a pedestrian arcade as revenge for the citation. But, for all her daring, in the first scene of the novel a motorcyclist passes them moments before a fatal crash. He waves at them, and when Nora asks Kerith who it is, she replies, "Youth escaping."[64] In a few minutes they catch up to where he has crashed and broken his neck. Whether or not Kerith can escape the narrow world of Cincinnati and her family is a central question of the book.

Kerith's relationship with her father never fully materialized. As she puts it, "We never happened to each other."[65] Later, when she decides to take a job away from the garage, and her father encourages her to stay, trying to make an economic argument about lunches and transportation when she works at home for board, she feels that she has brought him a final, decisive betrayal, one that he has anticipated her whole life.

A striking contrast between Scott and Boyle is their respective critiques of gender. Whereas in *Escapade* John is allowed the role of savior, and the mother/aunt is a shrew, in *Process* Nora has sense and strength while her husband is weak and subject to the will and censure of his father, who is clearly the head of the household. Kerith's grandfather, whom she tries to persuade of the unfairness of the Sacco and Vanzetti trial, doubts that in America men could be tried in a cage. Formerly a lawyer, he asserts his disbelief that this well documented event ever took place. He has authority in his household and resents the independence of thought that others show. Boyle's novel portrays him as simply asserting his will and faith that no court in America could treat defendants in that way. The famous court case riveted the attention of the world over just such violations of defendants' rights.

Kerith Day has two potential suitors. Brodsky, who is nine years older than she, suffers from rheumatism and is old before his time. An intelligent but somewhat cold man, he espouses ideas about the separation of mind and body. He believes that any possible escape from their environment or situation is through the mind. Kerith develops her own views to a certain degree in opposition to him, believing that only through her body in tandem with her mind, can she really know things. In this respect Kerith Day is similar to Evelyn in *Escapade,* who also believed that "true being is behind and beyond words" (204). Brodsky and Kerith visit a black man and offer to buy some potatoes, which they roast on the spot. In conversation with the man, Kerith asks straightforwardly, "You *are* free, aren't you?"[66] The matter is not so simple. The man replies that he, like everyone else, has taxes to pay—and, unlike many other citizens, he can expect to have occasional visitors who exercise white privilege, showing up and asking personal questions. Kerith feels for a moment almost included in his gaze, but then he protectively withdraws it. Brodsky speculates that "I don't believe there can be any real material freedom. Somewhere we all have to conform."[67] The degree to which any person can remain independent while being part of a community of others is at the heart of Boyle's investigation.

Kerith rejects Brodsky but not entirely. As a contact, he is valuable to her. Because of his connections to the chamber of commerce (signifying that his politics are probably more conservative than hers), she secures her job away from the Jesse Day and Son garage. She strings Brodsky along, even as she grows closer to her second suitor, Soupault, who eventually proposes to her—after a fashion. When Kerith and Brodsky make their final split, he says he has not been blind to what has gone on between Kerith and Soupault—and that the only way he can account for her behavior toward him is "will to power." He has brought her a turtle as a gift, which seems a fitting symbol for his own relationship to his cumbersome body and his self-contained, intellectual spirit. "The bitter little poisoned face lifted, straining, as though he would strain himself out of his own psyche, and into a new set of conditions."[68] The turtle cannot escape himself no matter how strong his will. Boyle, like Scott in *Escapade,* used descriptions of animals as a way to comment on human ideas and relationships. This interpretation of the turtle speaks to Kerith's developing politics, which separate her irrevocably from Brodsky.

Feeling that the problems with labor are foundational to industrial civilization, she is particularly inspired by the story Soupault, a World War I veteran and exchange student, tells her about French soldiers who turned their backs on France and marched with the Germans. Only a few did so, and they knew they would die, but they nevertheless turned against the political body that sent them into war. It is important that these soldiers were not merely deserters; they did something far more radical. Knowing they would be shot, they nevertheless marched against the flow and turned their bodies in protest to the entire concept of war. Kerith remarks, "When we can all come to that, things will happen.... Not before."[69] For his part Soupault, who strikes Kerith as a cynic with regard to the effectiveness of political action, remembers silently the butcher shops that were turned into makeshift morgues, "the cadavers ... hooked up by their jaws in moonlight."[70]

Kerith and Soupault make a pact to escape Cincinnati together. Their agreement seems remarkably tepid, and one cannot really say that they are in love—they just seem to have coinciding needs. What excites Kerith is the discovery of herself, of her voice, and her political potential as a radical.

She quits her job with the jewelry manufacturer R. C. Tarney because of her supervisor's mishandling of an employee death related to poor working conditions. Tarney was also an idealist but a conservative. A member of the Rotarians, he tells Kerith about a retreat they have made in the Colorado Rockies, a remote location with plentiful game, but at the same time he asks her to research plumbing because they want to add it to the cabins. Although his idealism is admirable to Kerith and she sees that this type of activity is one response to industrialization, she recognizes that it is "a far cry from the humble withdrawal" from cities and industry that she idealizes.[71] When a worker named Mary—covered in the gold dust that ironically symbolizes the poverty of her position and the deterioration of her lungs—comes to Tarney to quit, he placidly advises her to exercise more. After Mary's death he asks Kerith to take up a collection from Mary's fellow workers for her wreath and says he'll augment what she collects as long as it does not go over eight or ten dollars. As she puts it, at that moment her work there is "*done.*"[72] She draws a line she will never again cross and makes a commitment to herself that she will never do that sort of work again. Whatever her future compromises or the failure of her ideals, she feels with body and mind that she will never again allow herself to be put in that position.

In an epiphany Kerith states: "I am the miracle ... I am the perfect ego released."[73] Earlier Nora had told her that she was her own source of centeredness and energy, a being ready to make her own way in the world. In this quest Kerith resembles most the Evelyn of Scott's *Escapade,* although Kerith's journey is not a brutal fight for survival, and she has the support of a loving mother. One can see how *Escapade* made a way for an important first novel such as *Process,* because both books engage the female experience with philosophical questions and use a naturalistic, direct style to present such ideas. Marilyn Elkins suggests that in her early works Boyle was in some sense "writing back" to Scott, and surely this is true of *Process.*[74] Both Boyle and Scott created heroines who would work against great odds to remove themselves to a new set of conditions.

Near the end of *Process* Kerith and her fiancé, Soupault, are in a temporary arrangement. Soupault's self-containment is a source of deep irritation to

Kerith. When she slaps his face for his political apathy, he laughs at her and says "this doesn't change my mind."[75] His detached individualism is shared by all the main characters and ultimately, they drift apart as if incidental to each other. Four individuals, Kerith, Soupault, Nora, and Kerith's father walk together, but the novel describes them as "dark slow points moving in an infinite world"—moving in the same direction only for a time, to separate again soon. Her father must immediately return to the garage, and one is left to understand that this is his choice, even if it seems like no choice.[76]

When one reads these early works of Scott and Boyle together, one appreciates the importance of first audiences and the ways in which—for a time—these authors said yes to one another's creative projects. They both internalized and were informed by the priorities and principles that Lola Ridge's poetic project set forth, and there is a strong sense that Boyle situated herself to a degree in response to these two older mentors in both her earliest poetry and prose. After 1927 Boyle had diminished contact with Lola Ridge and less contact with and regard for Evelyn Scott's work. Throughout her long career, however, Boyle retained characteristics of philosophical insight, fearless self-examination, and social relevance fostered in her relationships with Ridge and Scott.

Five

"The mind spins from the mind"

Charlotte Wilder and Evelyn Scott

Charlotte Wilder was the third child and oldest daughter in a family of gifted writers. When mentioned at all, she is now remembered as the younger sister of playwright and novelist Thornton Wilder. Her story is told briefly and in general terms in Gilbert A. Harrison's *The Enthusiast: A Life of Thornton Wilder* (1983). More attention is paid to her in *The Selected Letters of Thornton Wilder* (2008), where she is still, and rightly so, of secondary interest. She is also mentioned briefly in both biographies of Evelyn Scott as well as in Katherine H. Adams's *A Group of Their Own: College Writing Courses and American Women Writers, 1880–1940* (2001) for her involvement in the Federal Writers' Project.[1] As a poet in her own right, Wilder has remained unnoticed in contemporary criticism. Her collections of poetry, *Phases of the Moon* (1936) and *Mortal Sequence* (1939), are now rare books, listed in no more than one hundred library catalogs worldwide. They have not been the subject of any recent critical inquiry, but in their own time they were favorably reviewed in periodicals such as the *New York Times Book Review*, the *Saturday Review of Literature*, the *Southern Review*, *Scribner's Magazine*, and *Poetry: A Magazine of Verse*. These books, particularly the experimental collection *Phases of the Moon*, warrant attention for their craft and their contribution to modern American literature.

Charlotte Wilder and Evelyn Scott's friendship was among the most important and life-changing relationships in each woman's life—and also among the most tragic. It is not clear precisely how Scott and Wilder first encountered one another, but the record of their correspondence begins in medias res during the summer of 1932. Late in her life Wilder recalled in a letter that they met in 1930; they were both residents at Yaddo, a writer's retreat in Saratoga Springs, New York, in July 1931 but may or may not have made a connection during that brief time. They also overlapped there in the fall of 1933 and were definitely well acquainted by that point.[2]

During the early to mid-1930s, Scott and Wilder had a lot to offer one another personally and professionally, and they exchanged encouragement, advice, philosophical conversation, and discussions about writing craft, as well as helping one another professionally. Through Scott's contact with Charlotte, Wilder's oldest brother, Amos Niven Wilder, incorporated a brief discussion of Scott's *Escapade* in his study *The Spiritual Aspects of the New Poetry*, published in 1940.[3] Although Scott's novels and other works were widely reviewed, this was the first scholarly treatment of Scott's writing, and she was exceedingly appreciative, even for a short mention.[4] Charlotte Wilder also provided supportive commentary on Scott's work in progress and inspiration for her writing.[5]

For Wilder in the early 1930s, Scott represented a dedicated and successful artist, one with a large writing and publishing network that she was willing to share with her friend. Scott possessed an uncompromising intensity and believed in Wilder's work with all her heart.

In December 1933, approximately a year and a half to two years after Scott and Wilder met, Scott introduced her relatively new friend to Lola Ridge, whom Wilder admired. Also recommending Wilder in a letter to Ridge's husband, Davy Lawson, Scott stressed how easy it was to be in Wilder's company and assured Lawson that Wilder would not cause the couple any hardship or stress. This was significant because Ridge continued to battle illness, and Scott was concerned that Ridge reserve as much strength as possible for writing. Wilder was, according to Scott, the one bright spot in the social landscape at Yaddo during the fall of 1933; Scott had felt claustrophobic in the group. Wilder's interest in Scott's work and Scott's admiration for Wilder's lyric poems were a sustaining basis for friendship until mental illness—particularly Scott's progressing mental difficulties—clouded their futures and created problems for them both.

Charlotte Wilder was born in 1898 in Madison, Wisconsin. The Wilders resided there until 1906, when her father, Amos Parker Wilder, left his job as editor of the *Wisconsin State Journal* to become U.S. consul general in Hong Kong. The family, consisting at that time of older brothers Amos Niven and Thornton, Charlotte, younger sister Isabel, and their mother, Isabella, sailed for Hong Kong to join Amos Parker Wilder. Within six months, Isabella and her children relocated to Berkeley, California. The family spent many years separated in such ways as her father traveled extensively for the diplomatic service, and Charlotte was often separated from her parents and siblings as a result of the family's complex travel arrangements.

Charlotte Wilder lived in Berkeley from late 1906 until after the birth of her youngest sister, Janet, in 1910. Then the family, with the exception of her oldest brother, joined Amos Parker Wilder in Shanghai, where he had been transferred in 1909. Wilder and her brother Thornton attended the China Inland Mission Boys and Girls School at Chefoo (Yantai) in Shantang Province, China. In 1911 Isabella and daughters Isabel and Janet traveled to Italy to be near Isabella's younger sister, Charlotte Niven, and their mother, Elizabeth Niven. Charlotte Wilder eventually returned to California in 1912 to stay with friends of the family in Claremont. Thornton joined his older brother, Amos, at the Thatcher School in Ojai, California. In 1913 Charlotte, her mother, brothers, and sisters were reunited in Berkeley, where she attended Berkeley High School, graduating in 1915. The family then reunited with the father and moved to Mount Carmel, Connecticut, in 1915. Charlotte began attending Mount Holyoke College.

While a student at Mount Holyoke, Wilder did war farm work in the summer of 1918.[6] She participated in the cabinet of the YWCA and sang in junior choir as an alto.[7] She was already writing sketches as an undergraduate, and some of her work appeared in the *Mount Holyoke Monthly*, where she served first as an editor and then editor in chief.[8] In 1919 she graduated from Mount Holyoke with majors in English and zoology and physiology. She received a Sigma Theta Chi award and the Alumnae Association Poetry Prize for 1918–19.[9]

During 1920 and 1921 Wilder traveled in Italy, where her aunt and grandmother lived, and Wilder worked in Milan at a YWCA.[10] In 1921 Wilder lived in Boston, where she worked as a secretary, then as a governess, and then as a proofreader for the *Atlantic Monthly*.[11] In 1922 she was a junior editor for the popular magazine known as the *Youth's Companion*.[12] She entered Radcliffe in the fall of 1924 and earned her M.A. in English in 1925. After briefly working as a secretary in Milton, Massachusetts, and teaching at the North Bennet Street Industrial School,[13] she joined the faculty of Wheaton College in Norton, Massachusetts, in 1926. In addition to teaching composition and literary criticism, she was director of publicity and had dormitory duties. She left Wheaton in 1928 because of the heavy academic service demands the job made on her time.[14]

Wilder began teaching at Smith College in the fall of 1928, around the same time her career as a published writer began in earnest. She placed poems and sketches in the *Atlantic Monthly*, *Poetry*, the *World Tomorrow*, and *Commonweal*. Her article "In a Southern Mill Village," which appeared in the August 1929 issue of the *World Tomorrow*, chronicles her travels in the Carolinas, where she described the lives of mill workers. While researching this piece, she was arrested on June 9, 1929, in Gastonia, North Carolina, on suspicion of unionizing.[15] This arrest came several years before the Wagner Act (National Labor Relations Act of 1935) protected such activities. In her sketch, Wilder described the Brandon Mill Village near Greenville, South Carolina, the mill itself, and being mistaken for an agitator rather than a journalist.

In July 1931 Wilder visited Yaddo for the first time. Subsequently her works appeared in *Poetry, Saturday Review of Literature,* and the *Nation.* She had begun writing the poems that later became *Phases of the Moon,* published in 1936. Obliquely autobiographical and surreal, they combine elements of lyric and prose poetry.

In 1933 Wilder resigned from Smith College to pursue her writing career full-time. Moving to Greenwich Village in New York, she worked variously as a copy editor for *Atlantic Monthly,* as a writer for the Federal Writers' Project, and as a journalist. During another period at Yaddo in the fall and winter of 1933–34, Wilder worked intensely on the poems that became *Phases of the Moon.*

Subsequent to this residency at Yaddo, Wilder began a peripatetic phase of her life. Among other places, she lived in Christodora House, a settlement building in the East Village, then moved to Free Acres in Scotch Plains, New Jersey, where Evelyn Scott joined her as a roommate for a period in late 1934. At Free Acres they rented a small cottage and lived near Gladys Edgerton Grant, a mutual friend and poet. Wilder and Scott then moved to 30 Grove Street in Greenwich Village in the early part of 1935. In later years Wilder and Scott were neighbors again in Greenwich Village, but more and more Scott's travels took her away from New York. Charlotte Wilder lived for the longest period at any single address at 102 Greenwich Avenue, from the fall of 1936 until February of 1941.

Wilder's writing career continued to be promising in the years after her resignation from Smith College. In addition to working for the Federal Writers' Project, where she contributed to the *New York City Guide,*[16] she continued to place poems and sketches in periodicals. There were periods of time when Wilder knew economic privation, and she accepted financial help from her brothers, Amos and Thornton, as well as from friends. She was also unfailingly generous to the even poorer Evelyn Scott. Wilder even offered money that she herself had borrowed.[17] In 1936 *Phases of the Moon* was published by Coward-McCann and won the 1937 Shelley Award (shared with poet Ben Belitt), a national recognition.

Phases of the Moon was especially innovative, seeming particularly so because most of the verse that Wilder had published in magazines was more formal and lyric in style. In this book Wilder developed a theory of her own sexuality. The poems are marked by a luminous and deep appreciation of women, and she made no attempt to disguise her own gender or the quality of her appreciation for people of the same sex. In an afterword, however, she specified that her desires were shaped by her abstinence from sex and the frustration that resulted. Wilder attempted to map a position between heterosexuality and homosexuality—a position that seemed somewhat oblique to contemporary readers.

Those who reviewed *Phases of the Moon* were largely mystified by the form of the poems and frustrated by their indirect treatment of themes, but reviewers nevertheless found the book to be an expression of concentrated talent and intelligence.[18]

William Rose Benét (a good friend of Scott's) reviewed it in his column, "The Phoenix Nest," in the *Saturday Review of Literature.* He commended the insight of the book but also remarked, "To be absolutely frank I have found it a bit cryptic throughout." He appreciated its innovative form, content, and psychological insight. "I myself wish that Miss Wilder could be clearer. But then I wish Mr. W. H. Auden, for instance, could be clearer."

William Lyon Phelps, a long-time professor of English at Yale as well as a journalist, mentioned the volume briefly in *Scribner's Magazine,* admonishing that it was "not to me fully articulate; of course one does not expect it to be as clear as a primer, but I think her emotions have not found adequate expression. It may be well for her to forget theories of 'inhibitions' and just write; every one believes that Christina Rossetti was a virgin, and it did not seem to stifle her genius. Miss Wilder has a splendid mind, and I have high hopes of her future."

In the *New York Times Book Review,* Eda Lou Walton drew special attention to the two formal poems in the volume and ended her review by praising these lyrics highly, while saying "the other poems are in a form comparable only to that used by Marianne Moore, a kind of heightened prose with certain of the effects of verse." For Walton the form of Wilder's prose poems did not work in her favor because "there is some lack in communication here." Walton's is the most perceptive of the major reviews. She observed, "Obviously the poet's personal struggle as here given is against loneliness, is concerned with the conflicting desires startled into being as she moves, detached and unclaimed by close personal relationships, through her world. . . . But that state of mind is sometimes just a little too incoherent, a little too personal, a little too directly the result of the precise experience which brought it into being to be the truest art." Walton's advice later in the review that Wilder should concentrate on the lyric form may have influenced Wilder's choice in her second volume to focus on more rhymed, patterned verse. Many of these poems were written earlier than the material in *Phases of the Moon.*

Assessing *Phases of the Moon* for the *Southern Review,* Morton Dauwen Zabel stated, "It is a barely disguised history of physical and emotional frustration, and aims toward sublimating the consequences. This problem entails the ultimate in self-analysis and discipline." He complimented the lyric poems, saying they show "both formal beauty and a delicacy of perception that should have instructed her more safely in a task which her present method has rendered not only mortifying but impossible."

These critics all sensed that there was a hidden world of feeling below the surfaces of the poems, and all of them struggled to one degree or another to pinpoint what that something was. Wilder was grasping to articulate her sexuality, which at the time of *Phases of the Moon* was—at least for her—unsayable in a direct way. Nevertheless, given the personal subject matter of the volume, Wilder showed herself to be a courageous woman writer worthy of the admiration of Lola Ridge. Although a specific record of Ridge's response to Wilder's work does not survive, one sees the affinities that Scott no doubt recognized when she arranged the introduction of Wilder and Ridge. It is also known that Ridge supported Wilder's application for a Houghton-Mifflin fellowship, surely a mark of Ridge's support and admiration.[19] Wilder understood that the task of her art was to approach the truth of her sexuality and to do so as much as possible without fear. Wilder admired Ridge's verse and counted herself fortunate for having made her acquaintance.[20] In Ridge, Wilder found a model of a writer who was uncompromising in her vision and whose emotional intensity was similar to Wilder's own.

Phases of the Moon is an experimental work of prose poetry in a long sequence. The poems are arranged to accent line breaks, with short lines interspersed with long ones. The way Wilder emphasized line reflects the vers libre and Imagist traditions. Shifts within poems invoke internal monologues and form a type of psychological montage. Some lines threaten to become paragraphs and shift over into the category of poetic or heightened prose without at the same time giving up their striking images and Imagist intensity. Wilder is not in the Whitmanian tradition, however, in spite of the lengthened lines. There are no catalogs or exhortations.

Wilder's poetry evades narrative. Although there is a general theme developed in the sequence, there is a distinct focus on image rather than story. The speaker is not a prophet. She is a persona steeped in Freud, investigating the writer's relationship to narcissism, and she is introspective in voice, interpreting signs and symbols in everyday exchanges with others that may or may not be fraught with meaning. She reveals sensitivity to nuance, image, and the pull of interpersonal misunderstandings. In poem after poem she is weighted with emotion that cannot be expressed successfully to the object(s) of her affection and love. That sense of isolation and frustration of being a subject with a message that is impossible to deliver gives her poetry its unity.

Phases of the Moon opens with an epigraph about Wilder's mother, dated 1915 and commemorating the role her mother played in fostering her children's imaginations and artistic ambitions. The scene is Mount Carmel, Connecticut.

Her mother, also a poetic spirit, looks out of a small, square window at a night sky, saying: "'As I grow older, more and more I come to love *the moon*." The incandescence of the moon is contrasted with the square shape of the window, juxtaposing the natural with the man-made, the frame and the pictured, the limitless and the limited. Through their mother's notice of it, the moon becomes an aesthetic object. The children around her "saw it"—and thereby her mother teaches her children to see the moon poetically, its distance and presence, its fullness and brightness, and the darkness of the world. As with many books of poetry, especially first books, *Phases of the Moon* is a book about the genesis of a poet. Its title pays tribute to this initiation to poetry as well as suggesting psychological or mood-driven phases that are dwelt on through the poem sequence.

Only four poems from *Phases of the Moon* appeared individually in advance of their publication in the book. Most of Wilder's poems in periodicals were lyrics and were eventually collected in her second volume of poetry, *Mortal Sequence*. Poems from *Phases of the Moon* that appeared in periodicals include "Isolation" in the *Nation*, "After Anger" in the *Saturday Review of Literature*, "Song for Her" in *Voices*, and "To Beauty" in *Poetry*.[21] In contrast nineteen of the lyric poems that eventually found their way into *Mortal Sequence* were published in periodicals, with a significant number appearing before *Phases of the Moon* was published.[22] The experiment that *Phases of the Moon* represents was a significant departure from what Wilder herself developed and presented in advance of its publication. The earlier poems that found their way into the 1939 volume are largely formal lyrics with end-rhyme schemes. By moving in her book publication from more experimental to more formal verse, her career mirrors those of Evelyn Scott and Lola Ridge.

In spite of the epigraph that depicts her mother's contemplation of the moon, *Phases of the Moon* is not dedicated to her mother or any other family member. (Wilder did dedicate her second book of poetry to her mother.) *Phases of the Moon* is instead dedicated to her friends Evelyn Scott and Ernestine L. Friedmann (1884–1973). These two women represented different and important spheres of influence in Wilder's life. Ernestine Friedmann, who worked in various capacities to further women's labor issues, including her work as secretary of the Bryn Mawr Summer School for Women Workers and as supervisor of the Barnard Summer School for Women Workers in Industry, was head of the Industrial Department of the War Work Council of the YWCA. She also worked for the Works Progress Administration (WPA) as a trainer of teachers and later was a professor of economics at Rockford College in Illinois. As a labor leader and worker for social justice, she organized and facilitated the education of thousands of women. Charlotte Wilder admired Friedmann and considered her a dear friend, one she could count on for help when she was in a tight spot and someone whose vision of social justice complemented her own. In a late letter Wilder mentioned that their friendship went back to her time at Wheaton College, and in fact Wilder worked at the Barnard Summer School for Women Workers in Industry during the summer of 1928.[23] At one point when Charlotte Wilder was in financial need and uncertain of her future in New York, she mentioned Ernestine Friedmann to Thornton Wilder as a friend who had offered her a place to live in Washington, D.C. It never came to that, but their friendship was of that caliber.[24] Evelyn Scott and Ernestine Friedmann—and the spheres of professional and creative influence they each represented—hover over Charlotte's first volume of poetry as muses and perhaps as models for the female figures Wilder developed in the volume. But the poems would be misread if they were taken to be addressed literally and directly to any one person or persons. Wilder instructed the reader that "the names given in the text are fictional . . . the epitomization of all those—and they are many—whom she has loved, or resisted."[25]

Phases of the Moon is notable especially for its engagement with conflicted and subterranean lesbian themes. Wilder's investigations reflect her own deep sense of struggle. Living in Greenwich Village during the 1930s, she might, one imagines, have found viable models for homosexuality, but she did not. She created partially veiled ways to address it. In the afterword, titled "Words of Annotation," Wilder explained her approach to subjectivity in the volume, explaining that the pronoun "I" is a mutable construct and that there is no one object of desire denoted in the pronouns "she," "our," or "we." With regard to the sexuality expressed in the poems, she stated:

> Readers made acquainted by modern science with aspects of the psyche heretofore uninvestigated, need hardly be told that complete abstinence from sexual experience—over a protracted span of time—results in states of consciousness curiously remote or violent: the former marked by a pervasive sense of detachment, and fundamental ennui; the latter, by attitudes of acute defendedness. When spontaneous emotion, banked against outlet (the intangible withholding that figures itself as an iron restraint), is first permitted to issue—often in response to welcoming perceptiveness in a person of the same sex—there comes, associated with it, an uncontrollable volume of angry and bitter feeling (the discharge, anachronistically, as in a void, of feeling long thwarted and denied, intensified to a force naturally proper to the sex-impulsion): irrationally projected against the other; bewildering to the one suffering it, inasmuch as the genuine emotion is compounded solely of devotion and gratitude.
>
> At the close of the narrative suggested, we are left on the threshold of a future in which expanding experience, re-orientating the individual with

> respect to human relationships, effects a cathartic resolution of the particular conflict that troubles the pages here.[26]

Wilder described the situation of an involuntarily celibate person, including the sense that what is blocking contact with others is an "iron restraint" and that the emotional consequences are out of proportion, misdirected, and complex. Her defensiveness, anger, frustration, and isolation come from a situation where intimacy is blocked—except as it is redirected to sympathetic yet romantically unavailable friends of the same sex, and then more frustration and anger are created. This passage reveals the hard labor of a person who is struggling with taboos. Wilder explored isolation, frustrated desire, transference of desire to female objects, and anger, but the claim that cathartic resolution follows seems both too hopeful and ultimately unrealized. The book may be read as an attempt on Wilder's part to exorcise these desires or to claim publicly—with restrictions—a nonnormative sexual identity that falls short of a vested lesbian identity. In letters written after the publication of the volume, Wilder cautioned family to not read it as the final word about her interior life.[27] Transgression, limited in this case to admitting prolonged celibacy and a circumstantial direction of desire toward women, reveals a wish to retain a space for subsequent identification as a heterosexual and to keep the autobiographical "I," as represented in the literature she created, fluid and adaptable. The passage strains the limits of what is permissible for the speaker to say, and including the afterword shows Wilder's own awareness of how her conflict marked her art and how it might present hurdles for readers without access to her distinctive psychological landscape. Seeking justification of these assumptions in modern theories of psychology would not have been difficult because it was popularly believed that sexual abstinence in women was linked to nervous disorders.[28]

The poems are in part an attempt to explore and resolve the conflict of desire and object, and some of them are posed from the viewpoint of a female persona who is focused on other female figures. There is a strong will in the poems toward a "cathartic resolution," but the majority of the poems in the sequence investigate the conflict rather than mapping the peace that may follow it. The section of *Phases of the Moon* that draws most strongly from this schema is "Monologues of Repression," which includes "The Virginal Inference," "Denied," and "Repression's Violence." The overall structure of the volume is from isolation to connection to qualified affirmation. The volume is infused with densely coiled psychological conflict.

Wilder did not have a fully realized romantic relationship that resolved these issues for her; she did not successfully pair off with someone who could help meet her needs as an artist and as a person—and who might have helped to make, with her, a unified front against public opinion or to help her overcome her past or her culture or her own reservations, which may have blocked her open expression of these feelings. Loneliness—being isolated and fundamentally misunderstood—is evident in her work and is one of her major themes. She tended to pour feelings into relationships that had no hope of a grounded, romantic future, which perpetuated her isolation, making it more pronounced and inevitable.

Although she had important literary influences such as Charles-Pierre Baudelaire, Rainer Maria Rilke, T. S. Eliot, and Marcel Proust, it should be emphasized that Wilder's poetic contribution is distinctive. As she was sending *Phases of the Moon* to publishers, she despaired of its acceptance because of how different it was from other works in the American tradition. She wrote to her mother in 1935: "I am going to have a very hard time placing this book of poems—it is too experimental. Both my prose and poetry have been experimental because it was natural to me. I had to get 'on to' my material that way—but now it leads me to forms that are traditional again. That is, not tied up subjectively—so oddly enough, coming back to the traditional, represents a freer place, that I was not able to handle before—so I have a book of traditional poetry partly done. . . ."[29] This letter refers to both *Phases of the Moon*, recently completed and under review for publication, and her subsequent collection, *Mortal Sequence*, which comprises short, lyric poems following traditional forms in terms of meter and rhyme scheme.

Evelyn Scott had contacted Random House in the spring of 1935 to promote Wilder's manuscript, and she received a rejection from an editor stating that they found the style "highly elliptical."[30] Wilder's successful introduction to the public in periodicals was for the most part through poems in traditional forms, and *Phases of the Moon* was a significant departure. Wilder had had an important insight: that because it shields subjectivity, formal poetry permits a freeing distance from one's material. Two of the elements that mark the verse in *Phases of the Moon* are psychological immediacy and a deft ability to convey fine and shifting shades of mood. Wilder suggested that the forms themselves help to mitigate the subjectivity of the poetry. In *Phases of the Moon*, because the forms do not function primarily as a mediator between her subjectivity and the public, they seem to create a more transparent experience of the private self. It was only after conducting her large-scale experiment in free verse, which in some ways felt like exposure, that Wilder went full circle back to forms that she had begun with earlier in her writing career. Their structure may have protected her sense of self more than vers libre. How to present her material, honor its complexity, and protect herself emotionally were perennial issues for her.

Phases of the Moon begins with one of the three formal lyrics in the volume: "Invocation," written at Yaddo in 1933. This complicated lyric poem makes broad and significant claims for poetry as an art:

To name the real: if we but knew
    The real containment of a tree:
The thrust of branches from the bough
    Is, like the waning of the sea

Or granite's single-season hold,
    But gesture proffered to the Shroud,
Whose resolute will-lessness compels
    Obedience even of a cloud.

Sun of the night: if we but saw
    Your planet circle, silver-bound,
Of Being and its elegy
    Illumine our unquickened ground

To something more than shaken lights;
    Or drifting desert spaces, where,
Unshadowed by the lift of moons,
    The fires of oblivion flare.

Poetry attempts to name the real, but that naming is conditionally held as an ideal never reached—to name the real actually, the poem suggests, would destroy it. The parallel between the inability to name what is right in front of one and her own strategies of naming sexuality elliptically and indirectly are important. Her insights about the purpose of poetry seem to be informed at least in part by the dominant pattern of communication that is shaped by her sexuality. Naming the real is likened to an achievement on a scale with the drying up of the sea or the radical truncation of geologic time—immense and revolutionary. There is a suggestion of the transcendental in the use of the word "Shroud." Robert Frost's well-known poem "Desert Spaces," also about the isolation of individuals not only in nature but in their own mental topographies, first appeared in the *American Mercury* in 1934, and there is certainly a striking—and probably spontaneous and coincidental—echo of it in the fourth stanza. Nature itself is a mystery in which our isolation becomes supreme. We can merely gesture at it with inept words. We mourn in advance our inability to express our experience and reality with precision.

"Isolation," the next poem in *Phases of the Moon,* begins the dominant free-verse pattern of the volume. It is about the vacancy left behind in a house by fleeing ghosts or the auras of visitors. The poem does not explicitly say that the presences are those of the dead, so it could be either kind of aftereffect, but the vacancy is absolute. The persona is alone and feels the affective changes in the atmosphere of the place. She senses the spirits' departure by degrees. She asks what presence do the dead or those who are no longer here have? What ground and reality does the "I" have? And she creates a haunting poem about their retreat from her rooms:

> The days of that month . . . were blood
> drops, one by one . . . coldly gathered. . . . hanging
> Pendent
> to the twist of midnight. . . .
>   they were dew
> reflecting in the pearl shimmer
> of their rounds
> evanescent sealed static images:
>
>   the presence of those I loved
>   who left
>   stayed for ten days . . . I was in their
>   rooms; every inch was their
>   movement . . . the ninth, it began to seep
>   out . . . as warmth leaves a house, through
>   the windows and door-slits . . . and,
>   one certain hour, toward twilight: I knew
>   they would never come back; this was not their
>   place any more; I doubted
>   it had been . . .
>
> that evening, the sunset . . . was a sword:
> it approached . . . and, bending fluidly upward,
>   laid only two parallel blade-cold surfaces
>   on my eyes' surfaces.

Wilder was able to pace the images through the use of ellipses, asides, and the placement of words on the page in order to juxtapose tone and perspective. The form tends to showcase the phrase rather than the line. The days that pass, in their containment and similarity, are described first as menstrual, then seminal. The heart of the poem is about the fading absences of absences. The ultimate isolation, the poem seems to suggest, is when the memories and felt presence of ghosts evaporate, and we remain with a doubt that they were here at all. The final image is excruciating and visceral, creating a remarkably felt sense of violence, violation, and tension. The sunset acts as a cauterization of what the persona can see and know about herself, her environment, and others.

Wilder explored many individual subjects in her prose poems. The volume invites readers to consider the whole sequence as it explores aspects of her main theme in a logical progression; yet it does not totality compose a cohesive narrative. Many of the poems have a unity unto themselves and explore themes that are self-contained, especially in the first subsection, "Of The Earth." Some of the poems do not appear to touch directly on the main preoccupations of the afterword: sexual repression, aggression, and same-sex attraction, but many take up the related subjects of the failure to communicate and the isolation of individuals. Such poems include "Of One Almost Insane," "For a Distant Friend and Poet," and "In a Flutter."

"Of One Almost Insane" is an incisive snapshot of an old man caught at the threshold of madness while considering his lost youth. The poem tracks his glance first at one extreme angle and then another, capturing a sense of instability and internal chaos. His glance becomes like a wild ray of light, a watchtower lamp erupting into incoherence as it crashes. The man's isolation "in bowed and corruptible coughing, over the rod of his sobs" is absolute. For this individual the descent into madness is both a chronic condition and a threshold he will inevitably cross within a short time. In a few words Wilder created a portrait of a mind filled with tangled and choked thoughts, a person who is immobilized by an unspecified, internal, and unresolvable conflict.

"For a Distant Friend and Poet" may allude to Thomas Wentworth Higginson's poem "The Horizon Line." The two poems share the memorable phrase "thronged earth," which Wilder includes in quotation marks, and the poem is about communicating across time. Higginson was one of the first two editors of Emily Dickinson's verses and a good poet in his own right. By alluding to him, Wilder expressed appreciation for his poem as well as her affinity for Dickinson, whom Wilder commemorated in a poem named after her in *Mortal Sequence.* In Higginson's poem, the "magic distance" of the horizon can never be brought nearer to the observer, "On the thronged earth one inaccessible thing."[31] Wilder's poem describes communication with her subject across time. Time is a "continuous segmented coil / ticked toward"; yet the two, separated by time, share the "same sun," and are able to cross-fertilize ideas in spite of conventional barriers.

"In a Flutter" depicts a backyard scene through the collective voice of wrens defending their territory against intrusion from the poet and her companion. The human beings in the poem are standing in a brush pile and have thoroughly disrupted the birds:

(scolding me)

get away from our nest, from my porch . . .
you . . . monster in green, in the brushpile,

standing compact on soiled sneakers, bending
and breaking; you, in the human shape,
thieving . . . in the brushpile
that's rightly our brushpile . . . cracking twigs
from—staccato—splitting boughs . . . so
the bark peels . . . you, intruder on the
footpath,

(flying over) . . . with the hands, snapping
off dry twigs . . . of the thicket, our
thicket . . . interwoven rummage heap with dusk
in the pocket-holes, I dive into . . . angled
boughs, we poise upon . . . go along,
you disturber . . . we're distraught:

you, it's you this is for . . .
can't you hear? our agitation; your dismissal:
O well . . .
O then . . .

what a day! what a morning! . . . Joy,
in the flight; round the golden ring, up
the yellow stairs . . . what a wonder under-glance
to the blue over-floor . . .

where's the other? there she is . . . (see the demon?)
what a mate!

tilt the sky, with the cry,
(let her rasp) . . .
we, the wrens.

The poem playfully depicts the scolding outrage and brief attention spans of the birds. Their collective subjectivity sees the poet as an intruder, a monster. The poem emphasizes their cacophonous protest and their darting thoughts between disturbance and joy in being and in flight while trying to defend their sense of territory. It is a humorous study in perspective: "what a wonder under-glance / to the blue over-floor." Wilder wrote herself and her companion into the poem as helplessly different and infinitely separated from the main drama and conversation of the wrens.

The first section also includes "Puritan," a poem for her father, who, after a long illness that included debilitating strokes, died on July 2, 1936, a few months after *Phases of the Moon* appeared. In "Puritan" she took the role of a prodigal daughter to her aging father. The poem describes a walk they took together, which is meant to symbolize her reconsideration of his broad attitudes toward life. Her steps in his presence are "narrow," "considering," "even and cautious," and the poem describes him as her "arch-enemy tyrant" and a "bruised outraged ancient." "O my father . . . somehow, from love that is an awakening / in me of identification, I come back." This poem emphasizes a tense attempt at truce with her father in the declining years of his life and suggests a broad rift between them that did not completely dissolve the love they shared.

"Sterile Love" is about a love that is frozen at its beginning and fraught with misunderstandings. It describes a relationship blocked by unnamed forces and unable to flourish. The opening image parallels a passage Wilder later used to describe her shattered life: "we are at odds . . . / upon the film-tissue of a spreading unseen / connection—our sense of each other—prick / shreds of ice-splinters, that frost / makes . . . delicate brittle and cross-hatched, crystal / fine minute clash of needles." The poem creates a distinctive tableau where attraction and repulsion are both present and acknowledged. As the two figures interact, they may be at the threshold of an erotic encounter. Desire is there; then reserve thwarts it. The poem focuses on the "over-under-and-through human and supernatural blending," but ultimately "distance wraps us." The poem implores "oh, let us be nearer: / though never . . . ," and at the verge of connection, the persona moves backward, distancing herself from the other:

> the relinquishment backward: nothing said, nothing
> heard; the slow drift through the bodies of no-need-for-
> speaking; a ground rested upon . . . the support and
> the burden . . . and between, rushing upward, poured
> upward . . . the column, spray . . . the fire-
> wonder . . .
>   no, no, never that:
>   our lost meeting, unknown
> to us

The romantic poems in *Phases of the Moon* describe this impelling toward the other and the repelling back from the unspeakable, taboo nature of the connection. This forbidden aspect of love, "no, no, never that," is contrasted to the impulse and desire to draw nearer nevertheless and to settle perhaps for the closeness of a misunderstood friendship rather than a love relationship. The phallic, explosive imagery of the last paragraph of "Sterile Love" illustrates remarks in the afterword, where Wilder described the frustration of desire "banked against outlet" finding its way to expression regardless of impediment and causing anger, frustration, and misunderstanding when it is so expressed. Wilder's skillful use of line breaks within her form increases the tension of the description and brings into balance some of the opposing ideas (for instance "support" and "burden," "rushing upward poured / upward," and the compound construction "fire-wonder" split beautifully over a line).

"Of Naomi" is poignantly addressed to the object of affection in a series of intimate, sexual images that reveal appreciation of her beauty: "if I might set the world in order around you, / that already begins to shrivel and brown, the flesh- / delicate magnolia texture of your petal—." The love the poem commemorates is like other things that stand in and of themselves and for themselves, "of an essence immutable," as salt is savory. The object of desire becomes the centered, ordering structure of existence. The expression is not of an evolving relationship in a social field; her "terrible head" is "beautiful as an olive-smooth / signet . . . is a clear leaf, etched to no purpose, / on my white page." The desire is captured, hovering, before any reciprocation or development between them can spoil the effect.

Wilder commemorated an admired fellow writer tenderly in the poem "Narcissus," which is also the title of Evelyn Scott's second novel, published in 1922. In Scott's *Narcissus* she recast as fiction her life in Greenwich Village during a period when she was living with Cyril Kay Scott but having an affair with Waldo Frank. The second in a trilogy, the novel is a close study of the ennui and impulsiveness that characterized her relationships to men during this period, and Scott drew from autobiographical material in her depictions of the sparring rivals for her protagonist's affection. In Wilder's poem the writer is at work, apart from any audience, in a space of "no flattery but the grant of alone- / ness"; her shoulders are "spent," reflecting the stress and effort of creation, and the poem describes the "delicate irritability of her brow." Wilder's poem emphasizes isolation, the writing woman

> drooped forward, to a desk—that, polished brown
> holds the gleam of a shield's mirror—to the paper,
> her paper; as the pen to her fingers: here . . .
>
> in an invocation, that the mind spins from the mind: a
> translucent testicle-organ of her own tissue and its
> wraith pulse . . .
>
> though truly annihilated by the waste of an effort
> that must make a self, from herself: an embodiment
> in the word and—the umbilical cord cut—in the
> stature of the tale:
>
> in letters, stroking back at her an identity sweet as
> allurement; and a signature nearer than breath . . .

black-stamping the page . . .
is the I:
from which she writhes and turns, like a man . . .
burned by the ropes of his own flesh.

This writer's work is excruciating self-genesis. Especially if her material is autobiographical in inspiration or nature, the woman writer has a particularly fraught relationship to her material, as was true for each of the authors discussed in this book. The work itself was isolating, joyous, and wrenching. The artistic self had to be fertilized, gestated, and birthed from the same raw energy and exercise of craft. The persona in Wilder's poem is a perceptive observer of the whole process of creation in her fellow artist and friend. The paper is a mirror and also a shield in which the created self is alternately exposed and protected. The process of writing the self is fused with the process of augmenting the self through creation.

This discussion of Wilder's poems from *Phases of the Moon* covers a small sample from a complex volume of poetry. Themes that emerge from her writing include her investigation of the schism between what is known and lived and what can be said to others and to the public. She developed the subject of isolation of individuals who are separated from human communities and exist in a vacancy or void of understanding. Isolation is caused in various ways by time, death, mental illness, nature, generational gaps, unconventional sexualities, and the process of creating art. Wilder's poetry seeks to bridge isolation through her thoughtful meditation on the topic and by mapping out her subjective experience of it, but without reducing these images and thoughts to a strictly autobiographical account. Clearly Wilder's work warrants further attention from readers. She courageously mined her own psyche with as much honesty as she could to create a fresh approach to poetry—a difficult, austere vers libre in *Phases of the Moon.*

In "Words of Annotation" and in letters, Wilder indicated that she struggled with how much to reveal about herself in the book: "The author has gravely considered—and dismissed—the question of the right of 'taste' to exercise its censorship upon the materials of art: not merely that taste which is conventionally imposed, as a habit of decorum; but, more profoundly, that from which it is derived—a quivering inmost sense-of-privacy, seemingly born with the soul, which forbids a public dramatization of the ego, or a naked exploitation of situation involving other people."[32] She negotiated this position on taste with her readers and particularly with her family. On publication of the book she received a supportive telegram from Thornton Wilder cheering her for her accomplishment and specifically acknowledging her struggle with her subject.[33] The sense of natural privacy must be sacrificed, according to Charlotte Wilder, when obeying it would distort the disciplined creation of the art. The artist works with the materials of her subconscious and the artifacts of her life. In her case she sought to "liberate the psyche from its load of subjective encumbrance, and, in expression, purify the 'I' of autobiographical detonation."[34]

Phases of the Moon was briefly mentioned by Louise Bogan, *New Yorker* poetry reviewer and poet, shortly after it was published.[35] Bogan's column was followed avidly by Wilder, Scott, and Ridge, and Bogan's own poetry was deeply respected by the group. Bogan said that *Phases of the Moon* "actually attempts to solve a personal problem by the awkward and unfashionable means of introspection," which she admired. "In a period all too full of public speech, it is refreshing to come upon some private affirmations." Through her brief remarks, Bogan permitted Wilder the space to engage her materials on her own terms, recognizing that her work was authentically felt. After Bogan's remarks, Wilder wrote her a letter thanking her for the sympathetic mention.[36] This contact initiated a lifelong friendship between Charlotte Wilder and Louise Bogan. They visited frequently, wrote to one another often, and shared interest in other poets, particularly Rilke and Yeats. In 1937 Wilder introduced Bogan to Evelyn Scott, a contact that Scott tried unsuccessfully to exploit in placing her unpublished volume of poetry *The Gravestones Wept* nearly twenty years later.[37] Bogan stayed in touch with Wilder through the long years of Wilder's hospitalization in the 1940s and beyond, and when Evelyn Scott died, Wilder contacted Bogan, who was able to intervene on behalf of Scott's grieving and mentally ill widower.[38]

In the years after the publication of *Phases of the Moon*, Wilder settled in a walk-up apartment at 102 Greenwich Avenue and worked on at least four writing projects,[39] one of which became *Mortal Sequence*. In addition to that published volume, manuscripts for poems and a fragment of autobiographical writing survive in the Wilder papers.[40] She worked for the WPA Federal Writers' Project until that appointment ended in 1939; she typed others' manuscripts as opportunities presented themselves and applied for but did not receive a Guggenheim Fellowship.[41] This rejection was a particularly difficult blow because she needed the money. Lola Ridge and Evelyn Scott had both received these fellowships in the past, Scott in 1932 and Ridge in 1935. Kay Boyle, whom Wilder did not meet, received a Guggenheim in 1934—something Wilder may have heard about, since Scott was her first recommender.[42] It is clear that during the years after Wilder gave up her teaching career, economic hardship shaped her living situation, and she was often not getting by financially.

In addition to the pressure of making ends meet, Wilder endured the increasing mental deterioration of her closest friend, Evelyn Scott. This aspect of Wilder's life was carefully documented by Amos Niven Wilder, Charlotte's oldest brother, who created several documentary transcripts of correspondence received by various family members, including Charlotte, particularly letters to her and her family from Scott. The assembled information makes clear the additional burden of Scott's emotional difficulties on Wilder. Scott was suffering from paranoia and obsessive complexes, which grew worse over time and ultimately blocked her ability to continue as a professional writer.

Amos Wilder—a poet as well as a biblical scholar, literary critic, and educator—gathered information that helps to document Charlotte Wilder's illness as well as highlighting her artistic achievements.[43] He quoted at length from letters he received from his sister and separately from Scott in December 1940, which detail perceived political harassments and conspiracies surrounding them. Though Charlotte Wilder and Scott had shared residences at various times some years before, during 1939 and 1940 Scott was splitting time between her son's apartment in Greenwich Village and a rooming house in Saratoga Springs, near the campus of Skidmore College, where she taught for several semesters. Her son, Creighton Scott, had an apartment approximately a mile away from Wilder's residence at 102 Greenwich Avenue. In a December 1940 letter to Amos, Charlotte mentioned that Evelyn was no longer in the neighborhood and that it was a relief because intrigue and tension surrounded her.[44]

As Amos Wilder noted, the remarks made by both authors reflect the anxieties of many people who worked as artists at the time in New York, but Scott's response to political and social pressures are extremely strained and show pronounced marks of paranoia. For instance the absolutism of this remark to Amos Wilder shows a totalizing worldview: "I am writing to you without Charlotte's knowledge, because I am very much worried that she may suffer from a state of affairs, largely a mystery to me, but indubitably I think, attributable to the evil ways of this present world. . . . I think her own family ought to be aware that she is definitely in some degree of danger from sources that are assailing me."[45]

While Scott was never involved in public political demonstrations or protests, her thinking about politics during the 1930s was philosophical, had depth, and was central to her project as a writer. After she published a strong anticommunist statement in the preface to her 1937 novel, *Bread and a Sword*, she believed she was being singled out for retribution by communists in publishing and reviewing. She had the opportunity to flesh out her political ideas in correspondence with anarchist Emma Goldman over a long friendship that lasted from the mid 1920s until Goldman's death in 1940.[46] They disagreed on the efficacy of revolution, but shared beliefs in individualism, feminism, and free love. Looking forward, one of the most enduring themes of Scott's later writing was her critique of communism. She eventually resolved that practically any "ism" was totalitarianism and repudiated all hints of it and of propaganda in her letters to her associates, many of whom became more and more distant from her as her mental crisis escalated and her letters lengthened to screeds of ten or twelve pages.

Scott struggled to give a name to her political position. At one point she remarked to Theodore Dreiser that she was a "Christian Socialist," a term that she did not reuse in later descriptions.[47] Both her biographers, D. A. Callard and Mary Wheeling White, have pointed to the loneliness of Scott's path and how she positioned herself as a rebel against almost all the major political movements of the first half of the twentieth century. Scott's remarks were later dominated by the outraged tone of a cornered and outnumbered individual. Scott's quest for community in her isolation was no less urgent than Wilder's.

Callard's Freedom of Information and Privacy Act inquiry, made during research for his 1985 biography, is informative. As he has pointed out, Scott had several associations that could have attracted government investigation of her activities, including her friendships with communists and her close ties with Emma Goldman (and her active lobbying for Goldman's readmission to the United States).[48] His search for any information on actual surveillance turned up only one letter, written to the FBI on November 27, 1940, from Evelyn Scott herself. Given Scott's proclivities for writing long and frequent letters, Callard had expected there would be a thicker file. In this letter Scott documented a conversation with someone she believed to be a foreign agent of an unspecified sort. This person, she said, informed her that the war would escalate to include the United States and that it was doubtful she would ever see her husband (Jack Metcalfe, then deployed in the RAF) again. Conveniently this possible foreign agent also suggested that he had a safe place worked out and that she should join him there. In a fragile state of mind and in the atmosphere of war excitement, Scott took this person at his word and wrote to the FBI. Callard suggested that there was some sexual innuendo and that the "agent" was probably an unstable individual himself, a crank unconnected to any foreign or domestic agency, who was attempting to take advantage of Scott's vulnerable situation as a woman living alone.

There was a sense of heightened drama surrounding Scott, and her anticommunism had escalated to a level where she was discussing possible espionage and foreign interference with government authorities. She also mentioned in the letter to the FBI that she was talking to WPA officials about possible subversion in that organization.[49] While Scott did not work for the WPA, Charlotte Wilder did. The names in Scott's letter were redacted by the

U.S. government, but it is possible that Scott named Wilder in describing what she believed went on in the WPA, or that Wilder provided some contacts to Scott that she then identified to the FBI.

At about the same time as this November 27, 1940, letter, Scott also wrote a long letter to Amos Wilder in which she went into considerable detail about perceived communist activities, raising his concern. Writing to him without Charlotte's knowing in order to alert him to pressures and difficulties that they were facing, she went into detail about perceived persecutions by known communist writers and critics such as Louis Gannett, William Soskin, and Horace Gregory, who insinuated that she was to be targeted (shut out of publishing and/or reviewing) because of her vocal anticommunism. She expressed worry about rumors "indefinite sources" were spreading about her, including rehashings of the elopement detailed in her 1923 autobiography *Escapade* and—new to her—rumors that she and Charlotte Wilder were connected "in a perverse relationship."[50] This misunderstanding seems conceivable. In December 1940 Scott and Wilder were extremely close friends, having lived together at various times in 1934 and 1935, and Wilder's *Phases of the Moon,* while careful to limit its identification with homosexuality, could easily be interpreted by outsiders to be a book in which its author is obliquely identified as a lesbian. That Scott was frantic about rumors is characteristic of her frame of mind at this point in her life. She emphasized to her friend's brother: "This is so grotesque and vile an interpretation of a sisterly friendship, that I would not have given the suggestion attention but for some happenings Charlotte has not mentioned to the family. They concern efforts made by strangers of obviously Lesbian bent to pick acquaintance with her."[51]

Charlotte Wilder's December 1940 response to Amos Wilder was to minimize the implications of her having been interviewed by the FBI. She faulted herself for not talking to the family about what she and Scott were going through. She had been visited and interviewed by someone, but in the letter Charlotte explained that she discussed the situation with her publisher and felt that whatever the motives for the interview, the interviewer had moved on to other targets. She said that once Scott was out of their neighborhood, the difficulties diminished. Wilder did not address the rumors about them as a couple, but it is possible that Amos Wilder did not find them of sufficient importance or credibility to pass on to her for comment.[52] To Scott she said, "The sheer physical terror that was aroused by the convergence of frightening incidents in Grove St. was an awful thing to have to bear. I agreed with you, that there was drawn out a convergence of destructive forces on you that are too much for one individual, without financial security, or even supporting family background, to continue to counter, except for the intermittent and comparatively ineffectual sympathetic gestures of friends, alone."[53]

From both women's accounts it is apparent that there was an inquiry and some harassment. It is also probable that Evelyn Scott connected the events in a broader way than they warranted. She began to see a unified pattern of harassment going back to her first visits to Yaddo in the early 1930s, where she was exposed in a small, closed environment to those she perceived as strident communist ideologues and felt like an outsider when she would not concur with their views. Even removed as Scott was in Saratoga Springs, the controversies and negative energy surrounding her were a large part of the scene Charlotte Wilder contended with through the winter of 1940–41.

In February 1941 Wilder was walking with her mother in Greenwich Village to a restaurant they frequented when she suddenly ran back to her apartment, locked the door, and let no one in. Her mother reported that Charlotte "ran away calling out that she had changed her mind—that her 'inner voices' told her not to go."[54] Authorities called to the scene eventually took the door off its hinges. Evelyn Scott's son, Creighton, who lived a few blocks away, called the Scotts' family physician, May Mayers, who—discovering that the ambulance was heading for Bellevue Hospital, quickly recommended a different course because she believed that going to a mental ward at a public hospital might unnecessarily traumatize Charlotte Wilder. Arrangements were made for her to go to New York Doctors Hospital, where she was under the care of psychiatrist Carl Binger. Later she was transferred to Payne Whitney Psychiatric Clinic, where she remained for several months.

What followed for Wilder was a protracted period of hospitalization in several different facilities. She was moved to the Westchester branch of New York Hospital in White Plains[55] and subsequently spent much of the rest of her life at the Long Island Home in Amityville, New York. After undergoing a frontal lobotomy in 1947 at the Brattleboro Retreat in Vermont,[56] she was allowed some independent living and freedom to move about in the early 1950s, living in a Greenwich Village apartment from 1950 through 1953 and vacationing in Maine, but she returned to institutions after a difficult episode of stomach ulcers. Her physical ailments were exacerbated by poor diet and emotional stress.[57] After hospitalization in 1941, she never published again, but she kept up (with some lapses) correspondence and visitation with a few close friends and family for the remainder of her long life.

During a period outside the hospital in the early 1950s, Wilder wrote some reflections on her experience, two pages of which survive. Looking back on her life from the vantage of approximately eleven years after her admission to Doctors Hospital, she wrote: "My life is a smashed crystal—I don't know any other way to describe it. It is like the lens of a huge telescope that an explosive bullet has struck; the glass has not fallen out, but the entire surface—even the inside—shows an infinite cross-pattern of a mosaic of cracks without a center. This situation, of course, started, as it happens virtually with birth; but the inciting cause of the present situation began in what my notes tell me was 1940—about eleven years ago."[58] In these two pages she then described an arresting figure, a Danish singer named Povla Frijsh in a green satin gown, who sang in Sage Hall at Smith College during Wilder's tenure as a professor there. Wilder attended the recital alone and was so riveted by the performance that she felt the rest of the campus radiating from that center point. She evidently felt, in addition to strong attractions to women, the strongest of conflicts about this event: "I am the sort of woman who—not married as it happened—almost falls in love with other women; not a homosexual, in the abnormal meaning of the word, I am what might be called a psychological homosexual; always more interested in women than in men, and able to idealize them—*when I have reason to think they warrant it*—on a plane so elevated that it might even be called an enchanted, entranced state of mind. I was thrilled by her."[59]

Povla Frijsh represented an object, removed and inaccessible, toward which Wilder could direct these emotions. Evelyn Scott was not able to reciprocate romantically because of her own preoccupations and proclivities, including a pronounced and aggressive heterosexuality. Wilder's conflict about these issues was so extreme in 1941 that she entertained the idea of entering a convent in order to escape the pressures she felt.[60] She was in the process of making that commitment when she ran back to her apartment and locked the door.

During the early years of her hospitalization, Wilder attempted to exert some control over her situation in institutions by turning away visitors or refusing to accept gifts.[61] She would invite visitors and then refuse to see them, which for people traveling to Amityville from New York City involved some investment of time and expense. Some guests were repeatedly turned away. There is a record in correspondence of her anger and frustration. She refused to accept the diagnosis of "nervous breakdown," denying her illness with force many times, especially to her family, whom she saw as preventing her from leaving the institution.[62] It is difficult to now recover the full details of her illness, but her remarks to loved ones constitute a heartbreaking record of her own understanding of her situation.

Wilder kept in touch with a few people by letters and visits that she allowed. The two writers with whom she kept in closest touch were Evelyn Scott and Louise Bogan, with some lapses in the correspondences, especially in the early 1940s. She also wrote letters to family members, who sent her literary periodicals, about which she commented from time to time. She continued to read major works of literature, but she did not write long letters of exegesis about what she read as she had in earlier years. She found that institutional life and psychiatric treatments considerably dampened her desire to write.[63] Struggling with mental illness, the end of privacy, the stigma of being institutionalized, alienating personal relationships with other institutionalized individuals, and physical and mental fatigue, Wilder seems to have had a view of the end of her writing career by 1945. On the way to accepting this situation, she said that she had brought her artistic project to a close, perhaps referring to her unpublished poetry.[64] We do know, however, that Wilder continued to write sporadically after this time, but nothing further was published.

Wilder experienced intense insecurity about her mail. The mails provided her only connection to literary people; yet her letters were read as part of her treatment regimen so her physicians could better know her frame of mind, and her outgoing letters were often sent first to her family for forwarding. To Evelyn Scott she wrote, "I am haunted by the fear that if I stop writing to you I will lose some kind of essential touch with you, though persons here laugh at me for doing so. I will persist, and far oftener, though there is no way of knowing if you <u>really</u> get my letters. Yours—the one of some months ago—I find in it an under-meaning that is yours; the top so unlike that I explain it by refusing to believe it came from you. I got the messages."[65] There is a strange similarity of Wilder's delusions to Scott's persistent idea that weapons of war were being used to attack her mind, generating voices she from time to time complained of hearing. The two friends may have reinforced these ideas for one another.[66] Added to the normal difficulty of remaining close to friends through letters was Wilder's lack of privacy. Her letters often seem cryptic or coded in response to their multiple and—as she perceived—hostile audiences of readers.

Through the years Scott repeatedly wrote to the Wilder family to plead for Charlotte Wilder's release. Scott, however, was increasingly not in a position to evaluate the situation fairly. She did not have any sustained contact with Wilder in person after 1940, mostly because she had moved from the United States to Canada and finally to England, where she stayed until 1952; Scott based her judgment of Wilder's situation on letters she received from her, which were often short and lacked context,[67] and from occasional updates from Isabel and Thornton Wilder. Scott wrote to Amos, Thornton, and Isabel Wilder many times over many years, trying each time to persuade them that Charlotte Wilder was sane. "But as Charlotte's letters to me, while often just scribbled notes, gave every evidence of being sane, I have been hoping and hoping to have word that she was soon to be free."[68] Thornton Wilder responded to Scott patiently that the situation for Charlotte was much more complicated than her letters might suggest. He pointed to serious memory lapses, her refusal to communicate with medical personnel, and a persistent paranoid delusion that people were assuming the identities of and impersonating loved ones and friends.[69]

The preoccupation to which Thornton Wilder alluded— that there were people who shared the names of her loved ones and might be impersonating them for gain—was one Evelyn Scott shared, and it became part of her complaint of persecutions through the 1940s and 1950s. Because the two women shared several delusional ideas, these notions became amplified. That they shared delusions seemed to confirm their reality further. Had their social networks been broader, the effects of these shared delusions might have been diluted. As it was, during these years, the social circles of both writers became drastically truncated.

Wilder's friendship with Scott suffered setbacks as Scott's obsessions about her own career, her attempts to get back in touch with her estranged son, and her political absolutism dominated her letters. In September 1951, in what reads as a healthy response to Scott's tone, Wilder broke off the correspondence for a time—after a rapid series of letters between them: "I just am not going to go on having ulcers because you crack down on me from London, England, about every ten days or three weeks. If you don't like my ideas, you don't have to know what they are."[70] Regarding Scott's insistent tone and paranoia, Wilder remarked, "I came back from a silence of almost ten years, and found, in you, a person whom I do not recognize. You are not the Evelyn I used to know; and, probably I am not to you. The only way we can have a correspondence is for us to write each other as though we were courteous strangers."[71] They carried on, and Scott continued to insist that Wilder was wrongfully held in institutions, a victim of psychiatric medicine, a branch of her self-fashioned understanding of totalitarianism.

In the unpublished poetry Wilder wrote in the years before her hospitalization there is a lyric poem written for Evelyn Scott and sent to her in 1940. It addresses the subject of isolation that Wilder had developed so strongly in *Phases of the Moon:*

For Evelyn Scott

Pacing an arid distance, I had come,
Forcing impeded footsteps through a maze
Dry as extinguished summer, on a loam
Riddled with winter-frost's corroded rays;
Thus—in a bitter leisure—I drew near
Something discerned as space within the wood,
Opening softened contours on a sphere
Luminous as a jewel's amplitude,

Blue, with the heightened after-flame of mind,
Kindled by cold, to crystal; and I found

Nearer, the gentle flowing of a kind
Pulse of attachment. I was thereby bound,
    Evelyn, in my being, to your art,
    And, in my love, delivered to your heart.[72]

The poem maps some of the emotional crisis and background Wilder faced at this turning point in her life. It describes the loneliness of a cold, solitary, and confusing life journey across "an arid distance," her footsteps forced "through a maze" in a cold, desert climate. The persona sees an oasis—an aura that represents refreshment and a source of beauty. Her friendship with Scott constitutes the beauty and community of a "kind / Pulse of attachment." The poem ends with a poignant couplet celebrating Scott's artistic accomplishments and Wilder's tenderness toward her. The poem highlights the strong need for artistic and personal community, and it also expresses the way in which at their best Scott and Wilder created a space in which they could each be artists. It is a sad legacy that mental illness damaged their talents but a testament to their friendship that they remained in such ragged contact until the end of Scott's life in 1963. Wilder was able to honor her friendship with Scott, which no doubt presented many frustrations over the years, and also to maintain some distance from her ideas, although their interaction in the late 1930s and 1940 clearly exacerbated Wilder's own mental crisis.

Wilder remained in institutions until her death in 1980. She invites our attention now as an example of a gifted poet and writer whose reputation fell into obscurity largely because of her decades-long confinement and her consequent cessation of writing. The works she produced prior to hospitalization were experimental. She created fresh poems in the modernist idiom, and they contribute to a fuller understanding of what constituted potential subjects of poetry at that time. Both Scott and Wilder were deeply and tragically affected by the events of Wilder's life in the winter of 1941. It speaks to their individual desires for artistic community that, despite impediments, they continued to be part of one another's life, attenuated as their contacts became.

"Reflecting bright pain"

The Later Poetry of Evelyn Scott

In 2009 Elaine Showalter mentioned Evelyn Scott as a brief but illustrative example of how invisible an American woman author can be.[1] Although a discussion of Scott's work would have been edifying in several areas Showalter addressed, Scott continues even now to be one of the most overlooked authors in American literature (as she has been since the late 1930s, when her literary reputation began its precipitous decline). Nevertheless her work was accepted by some of the best known publishers and some of the most significant journals of her day. Her novels were published by Boni and Liveright, Henry Holt, and Charles Scribner's Sons, and her poetry, short stories, and criticism appeared in periodicals such as *Poetry,* the *Dial, Poetry Journal,* and *Others.*[2]

Scott's third volume of poetry, *The Gravestones Wept*—a collection of fifty-one poems begun in 1931, completed in 1960, but unpublished until 2005—is significant because it records some of her experiences in the interwar years and beyond. The collection is a record of her most important professional and personal struggles in the later part of her career and contains significant stylistic choices and a way out of Scott's early imagism.[3] Along with Lola Ridge and Charlotte Wilder, Scott went through new, free forms of poetry back toward formal verse later in life. A look backward toward Romanticism seemed one possible way to infuse one's art with a sense of tradition, order, and the past.

Is Scott a major, mysteriously overlooked writer, or has she been consigned to her rightful place in literary history? Did a system of aesthetics that routinely undervalued the contributions of women nevertheless justly evaluate her work? Alongside other works in her oeuvre, *The Gravestones Wept* suggests not. Any assessment of the writings of Scott, Ridge, or Wilder must put them into a nonmodernist rather than a postmodernist critical framework, as each woman moved through early and energizing modes of poetic expression toward more ordered works.

In 2005 a significant addition was made to Evelyn Scott's body of work with the publication of *The Collected Poems of Evelyn Scott,* which included the previously unpublished collection *The Gravestones Wept.* Between 1931 and 1960 Scott reshaped and edited the volume four times. Thus the book received the benefit of Scott's attention and thought over a longer period than many of her works that did see print in her lifetime, in part because there was always pressure to make money from her writing right away. For many reasons the manuscript for *The Gravestones Wept* lingered, and Scott continued to rework the material through life changes such as a brief and regretted conversion to Catholicism.[4] In *The Gravestones Wept* Scott continued modernist investigations of themes and subjects that are present in her earlier books of poetry, *Precipitations* (1920) and *The Winter Alone* (1930), both republished in *The Collected Poems of Evelyn Scott,* and in her many novels and two memoirs. *The Gravestones Wept,* however, is more comprehensive and detailed in scope than her earlier books of poetry, perhaps because it evolved over a longer period of time and was a record of her spiritual growth as well as of her developing mental illness.[5]

Scott's first book of poetry, *Precipitations,* was an important and original contribution to the modernist conversation and the Imagist movement. Its female subject reflects on her own sexuality, motherhood, the city, race, and nature in unorthodox ways. Scott's second collection, *The Winter Alone,* shows the influence of Scott's travels to Bermuda and Beziers, North Africa, much as *Precipitations* is unimaginable without Scott's Brazilian and Greenwich Village experiences. The primary thematic development in *The Winter Alone* is a sustained investigation of the disillusionment of renewal in spring. There is an increase in *The Winter Alone* in instances of direct address to the reader, in calls to action, and in the use of exclamation marks, trends that continue and proliferate in her later poetry. Scott used these devices to create an urgent, even strident, tone. These tendencies eventually evolved into full-blown protest poetry in *The Gravestones Wept.* They may also be markers of the mental strain she worked under throughout these years.

The Winter Alone was not widely reviewed. There are mentions of it in newspapers such as the *New York Evening Post* (which noted that the author of *The Wave* had come out with a volume of highly subjective poetry), the *New York World,* and the *Boston Transcript.* Lengthier treatments by Dudley Fitts, Eda Lou Walton, and Babette Deutsch provided a range of qualified praise to negative responses. A contributing factor to such assessments of *The Winter Alone* may have been the proximal success of Scott's novel *The Wave.* Scott may have flooded her market and been somewhat difficult to classify as a poet after ten years of sustained critical attention for her novels.[6]

The Winter Alone contains notable poems, but one in particular reflects the subject of this study. The tribute "To Lola Ridge" is notable for the sense of conflict it captures around her idealism:

Blue moths that circle the moon,
The soft stern eyes,
Reflecting bright pain
As sweet lakes reflect the brass of battle.
In them, Mars sees himself,
While mildest virgins bathe secure.
She, whose courage always flings a thousand banners,
Is of all gaudy vanities withholding, and demure.
Her hands are burned transparent,
Like clear alabaster,
By her long shielding of a solitary flame.
A brutal vegetation barred her way.
It gored the air.
It tore her thighs and breast,
And feet so light
Their very running was our rest
When Darkness wrote her fame.
The bitter brambles drew her blood.
The blazing thickets made her smart.
Not one arrow flung upon her
by the blinded
Pierced her shining heart.

The poem highlights the physical pain that was part of Ridge's daily existence and against which she formed her asceticism. It also emphasizes Ridge's stance as a loner, a rebel, and one filled with courage against powerful foes. The poem includes imagery suggestive of the Sacco and Vanzetti protest as described by other writers, such as Katherine Anne Porter and Kay Boyle. Scott's poem captures the sense of urgency around Ridge and the immanent violence that surrounds someone of such independent and dangerous thought. Somehow Ridge is both a symbol of a haven and a site of war. She yearned for peace but never at the cost of justice. Held within this personality were the seeming contradictions of protectiveness and protest, peace and war. She would do what is necessary within an austere ethics to demonstrate justice, and, Scott's poem suggests, she was ahead of her time.

A few years before Scott's poem to Ridge appeared in *The Winter Alone,* Ridge published "Sonnet (To E.S.)" in her 1927 volume, *Red Flag.* Ridge's poem also focuses on the poet's eyes as expressive organs that speak toward her poetics:

Your eyes are candid, but they sheathe a light,
A ray unbroken of vast distances,
That wear no shadow on their nakedness
Save the recurrent shadow of the night,
And like those shapes that wheel in torpid flight
Above some steaming shambles of the waste,
O merciless and yet defenseless one,
You range . . . a living target in the sun.

No furtive move of palpitating thing
Eludes you, avid, questing without haste . . .
Nor feint of life that covers up her wry
Illicit children, nor the fragile wing
Of death, arisen in a jeweled fly . . .
Evades the cold extortion of your eye.

Likening Scott to a vulture, which all artists who use their life materials and experience for art must be in some sense, Ridge's poem focuses on the clarity and unsentimentality of Scott's sight. The two writers consider one another targets of the critical community, and they thought the enemies that each fought were common enemies. Mostly though, they shared a sense of battling against contemporary critical opinion, and they exerted themselves in highly original creative lives. Their isolation is profound but not total because they recognize in one another a sincere and precise determination to pursue her art.

After publishing *The Winter Alone* and during the period in which she was composing the poems in *The Gravestones Wept,* Scott returned to the novel as her primary form of expression. Although her novels continued to be reviewed well, she never again achieved the recognition she received for *The Wave* in 1929. As the years continued, she had fewer and fewer financial and emotional resources with which to promote her work. Her novels *Breathe upon These Slain* (1934), *Bread and a Sword* (1937), and *Shadow of the Hawk* (1941) are a three-part examination of the plight of the artist in society, a theme in which Scott felt a keen personal interest. These novels, as well as her poetry of this period, reflect an increasing tendency in Scott's work toward identifying injustice and voicing social protest. For instance in her 1937 preface to *Bread and a Sword,* Scott lamented the ways in which art was being used to promote politics, especially fascist politics. She stated that, in an age that does not promote artists or provide their basic needs, artists are more likely to be desperate and to be bought or swayed as to their perception of truth. The artist who produces propaganda—and her definition of this term would have been broad enough to include any art that has an insincere political dimension—is no longer an authority on his or her own work and becomes instead a "'technocrat" (xiii), whose function is to promote the state's agenda. She posited that there are material rewards for producing art useful for the state. Furthermore, Scott maintained, the machine has become a model by which the success of everything else is measured. Even the pursuit of science has been shaped by commercial concerns so that the "free scope of [scientific] investigations" is curbed to promote profits (xv). Thus, in all realms of knowledge, truth is shaped by economic forces.

In examining *The Gravestones Wept* one can see the story of the second half of Scott's career in capsule form. She used poetry to mark her responses to the events of World War II and to lay out the problematic issues involved in being a woman artist in the twentieth century. Over time Scott developed a stronger and stronger tendency to voice protest, to address her audience directly, and to move from open forms to closed ones. One can see the articulation of an antitotalitarian politics that valorizes individual development and talent. The volume also contains important tribute poems to Lola Ridge and Charlotte Wilder, and one feels the precedent of Ridge's "Sun-Up" in Scott's "Woman Cycle," the long, autobiographical poem that opens the volume.

The Gravestones Wept begins with a quotation from Jack Metcalfe's novel *Sally* (1936).[7] These lines from her husband's novel describe a young girl who lives among graves and is completely at home there. Because of their humid environment, the gravestones weep condensation—a completely natural and indifferent act; yet to say they weep is to say that they feel on some level. The gravestones with their inscriptions are emblems of the dead; the imagination of the artist assigns them a closer kinship to what they represent than to mere stone. The young girl living in the graveyard is alive; yet she walks among the dead. In this way she is a more obvious type of the hybrid of life and death that we all are. This scene, provided as an epigraph to the volume, aptly indicates the major theme and evokes the primary mood of these poems.

Part 1 of *The Gravestones Wept* focuses on Scott's private evolution as a woman writer: her choices, the roles she played in her family, and the consequences of her choices. The poems show her sensitivity to social injustice and set forth criticism of an impersonal society, in which the devaluation of individuality limits meaning in people's lives. Scott sought solutions for these dilemmas in powers that are larger and greater than she. The central contrast in part 1 is between solitude or solipsism and the appeal to some type of transcendence or escape from her day-to-day world. In poems such as "Woman Cycle" and "What Bourne?" she examined personal details of her life and the struggles she experienced as she tried to balance her conflicting responsibilities as wife, mother, and writer.

Like Ridge's "Sun-Up," Scott's autobiographical "Woman Cycle" is a free verse voicing of a young, female consciousness, who details Scott's perceptions of her own childhood from the point of view of a forty-year-old woman (Scott's age in 1933, which she assigned as the poem's composition date). With slight variations and shifts in emphasis, this long, sequenced poem covers Scott's life from the time she was an adolescent until maturity, looking forward into the future. The poem emphasizes key images and ideas through line and strophe breaks, capturing the poet's life as a thoughtful adolescent moving toward a disillusioned adulthood. The poem begins in her grandmother's garden in the South, with spring arrived early. The first image sets the tone for the poem:

> But the water in the fountain basin
> Was like brown autumn
> The year round.
> There six goldfish stagnated
> And delicately burned the shadows
> With their dreaming fins.

This is an image of a beautiful, decadent, and stifled way of life. The light of the goldfish is internal, inscrutable, and secret. The predominant imagery in the poem as a whole suggests that the young girl is alienated from others, specifically her family and later "the poor," who exist for the persona outside the gate of her grandparents' house but of whom she has an acute awareness. She is also alienated from nature, which is out of tune, with seasons arriving early and the moon offering no comfort, and from herself as her body and mind mature and develop in inscrutable ways, making complex demands on her. Her home life with parents and grandparents is represented by the still goldfish—it is an ornamental, forced, and closed system doomed to self-exhaustion and prone to self-delusion. "Woman Cycle" documents the young girl's struggle to find meaning independent from others and chronicles her partial failure to do so.

In stanza 6 of "Woman Cycle," the narrative voice changes from a third-person recounting of the girl's experiences, a stance that provided Scott with some distance from her subject and with some freedom to judge her own actions, to a third-person choral voice that apostrophizes the fate of the girl to the moon:

> Quiet the young heart!
> Make it beat less!
> Will the girl be a slave forever?

Is she bound to her nameless hopes?
When dawn rises higher than darkness,
Her elation leaps with it,
In pain of delight!

The moon is heavy on the garden.
Foliage wastes, swamps smoulder,
The world is brass.
What is in her that refuses resignation?
She is tired of her body.
It might as well be given away.
Shall she consign it to mankind?
Or shall the business end with gas, a rope,
Her father's pistol?

Pity her, Moon,
As you shed your light
On forgetful Creation!
Deliver the too-alive!
Teach her for the last time.

The moon is a symbol for the way in which nature turns its face from the events in the girl's life. The moon provides continuity for her, but it is also a blank object to which she may assign her interpretation of the world or events. The apostrophe is a pervasive element in *The Gravestones Wept.* Frequently Scott made exclamations for various purposes, but in "Woman Cycle" they deliver urgency and evoke a sense of prayerful demand while at the same time risking stridency. They strongly evoke the girl's confusion about herself and surrounding events. Scott was suicidal on more than one occasion in her life, and the fatalism of this passage is indicative of her early struggles with depression.

In a reversal of the Wordsworthian proposition that poetry is emotion recollected in tranquility, "Woman Cycle" proclaims: "The flesh has lied! / Joy, recollected, / Is like the memory of a crime!" The things in her life that were joyful were fleeting and involve emotional expense to recover and remember. Even the spring, it turns out, is a blooming forth from death and a prefigurement of the next cycle of death. From this recognition comes wisdom. The progress toward this wisdom is confession.

"Woman Cycle" is unusual in *The Gravestones Wept* for its length (262 lines), for its often transparently autobiographical subject matter, and for its free verse form. While there are many other free verse poems in the volume, there are also a surprisingly large number of metered and formal poems. Of the fifty-one poems, seventeen are sonnets—from a writer who did not publish formal verse in the earlier periods of her career. Most of the poems employ end rhyme in unconventional variations. Also several of the longer poems are narrative poems. At no time before *The Gravestones Wept* did Scott write narrative poems; her work in previous volumes is entirely lyric. Taken in light of her previous books of poetry, which were stridently, self-consciously avant-garde, these developments are significant. They suggest a merger of the poetic and prose strategies Scott employed throughout her writings. Scott's prose in her early novels and *Escapade* was often described as lyrical; her later poetry, when not formal, reflects prose modes she developed in her later novels.

The presence of formal verse in a post-Imagist landscape suggests a desire on the part of the poet for control, order, and stasis. The fact that sonnets predominate in the last section of *The Gravestones Wept* contributes to a sense that order is being sought and is achieved as a project of the whole work. Scott's need for order, evinced in the forms of the poetry, roughly follows a chronological development. The shifts in subject matter of many of these poems add more evidence that she was concerned with the disorder of society, her lack of control over her own life, and what she perceived as the meaningless flux of the modern era. It also coincides with her personal experiences of mental instability and spiraling poverty, which developed and intensified over time.

The last poem in part 2, "What Bourne?," recapitulates themes in "Woman Cycle." "What Bourne?" investigates the persona's being through her roles as mother, daughter, lover, and wife:

> O, illusion of self adored in another,
> Was myself the moment of love given—
> The man loved, child loved, the mother, father, friend?
> Has what I am now been wrenched from my flesh?
> Is it I, bleeding, I tear up by its roots
> From the ancient soil of the past,
> With a wail of stricken senses,
> *Mine, yet mine no longer?*

This is a crie de coeur from someone who is losing herself in a primary struggle for integration. Something of what Kay Boyle noticed in Scott may be seen in this poem and in others in the volume. Scott diffused her energy and attention in multiple roles as writer, mother, wife, and lover—roles that often were in direct conflict with each other. Boyle wrote in *Being Geniuses Together* that Scott's visit with her in Paris in 1924 was not an "easy visit" for the following reasons: "One was aware at every instant of the nervous complexities of Evelyn's marital, and sexual, and professional lives, and in the smoke-filled, crowded hotel room I found it impossible even to hear what was being said. Perhaps I had lived too long in an almost unbroken inner silence, and now in my own confusion and insecurity I trembled for Evelyn's shattered depths. Was she wife, lover, mother, or none of these things, or all of them? It was difficult for me to determine, although all the elements and all the protagonists were there."[8] The pressures that were brought to bear psychologically on Scott as a writer and as the protagonist in a complex series of layered relationships with (at the time of Boyle's meeting with her in Paris) Cyril Kay Scott and Owen Merton, in addition to her responsibilities as mother to her son, were crippling but probably also artistically invigorating. In these remarks Boyle was reading backward, creating an interpretation of Scott that included their forty-year friendship and Scott's denouement in poverty and paranoia. Scott became a negative example for contemporary women artists who were also sacrificing much for their art and who faced similar pressures.

In a quest for stability, in light of the dilemma of being that her artistic fracturing engendered, Scott shifted to apostrophe in "What Bourne?":

Wind of the morning,
Rippling over the city roofs to the sea,
Where dark salt fountains spurt and break,
O, slake the thirsts of this mortality!
Sweep us away
From sight of house-tops, streets and throngs,
To solitary shores
Where rugged rock withstands the shock
Of marbled, silvering attacks,
As quaking mountains pile their snowy racks
Upon ineffable graves!

Let us enter nothing, not as meager bones and dust,
But by spending ourselves upon annihilation generously,
Like the turbulent, terrible waves!
Here hope frets us to extinction:
Better to be tossed, torn, rent with blows
That wrest apart submissive mind and heart!
These are not living who mere ignominy saves!

The move from confusion about identity to a cry for annihilation is one Scott returned to again and again in *The Gravestones Wept.* If identity, if selfhood, fails, is rent, and cannot withstand the pressures placed upon it (as mother, wife, writer, and artist), then there follows her collective call for nothingness. Only personal apocalypse can answer such a struggle. In terms of theodicy, it is significant that Scott called to nature to bring her a measure of fulfillment and justice. Scott edited this version of "What Bourne?" from earlier versions in which she cried out to God by name.[9]

Thus the first section of *The Gravestones Wept* deals with Scott's struggles of psyche; with her roles as writer, mother, lover, daughter; and with an emotional appeal for order and affirmation to a higher power (transcendental nature, previously God). Other poems in this first section emphasize philosophical issues such as the nature of evil ("To a Snake in Eden"), the validity of science as a worldview ("Scientific Commonplace"), the futility of modern life, and the predicament of modern civilization ("Old American Stock," "On Behalf of the Inarticulate," and "Pike's Peak"). "Old American Stock" focuses on a rustic who finds himself out of step with the times as the poem invokes as background the strident optimism of the 1939 World's Fair, which through its "Democracity" display offered the first popular model for superhighways and suburbs.[10] In the poem the World's Fair is contrasted (and loses in comparison) to the county fairs with which the rustic would have been more familiar and which emphasize the local rather than the global.

"Old American Stock" and "On Behalf of the Inarticulate" are poems in part 1 that incorporate answering, privileged voices, and thereby illustrate an important technique in Scott's later poetry. The voices, denoted by italics in the poems, add a new dimension to the lyric style. They appear to have more authority than the questioning voices, adding an element of spiritual or transcendent involvement as they create a limited sense of dialogue. Many more poems, beginning in part 2 and continuing throughout the volume, also incorporate similar answering or choral voices in italics. As a result poems that might be only declarations of opinion become more complex. By using this device Scott suggested that there is an intelligence or will standing beyond ordinary reality. This privileged voice suggests a larger coherence and order to the world. The closest identification of this power in Scott's work is nature. Elsewhere she called it "creation," "will," and finally, in the last poem in the volume, "Liberate Omnipotence."

In contrast to part 1, which deals primarily with Scott's relationships with others, part 2 concentrates on a forceful critique of the modern, technological world. Scott identified as natural that which emerges from itself, as opposed to things that are made or designed. The natural order, while neglected in our era, is where renewal and ultimate meanings reside. Apocalypse and disaster will result, she suggested, if we continue to forsake the natural order. Industrialization has promoted conformity above individuality. This tendency toward normalization is devastating for artistic expression, not to mention political independence. In this section Scott outlined the main conflicts between nature and technology, creativity and conformity.

Behind this critique is a strongly romantic worldview that seeks renewal through an apperception of nature. For Scott technology's effects could be seen in the way a large, industrial city dwarfs the individuals who live in it or in the ways in which living in a machine age warps people's sense of their own autonomy and individuality. Living in an age of machines, according to Scott, separates one from nature and from one's own ability to reflect. At the time Scott was writing *The Gravestones Wept*, especially during the 1940s, an optimism for the saving power of machines and technology was strong and what we might now consider one-dimensional or even overblown. Rather than seeing an exaggerated faith in technology as merely foolish, Scott considered it a pernicious trend, one that threatened society and individuals at the most basic levels.

For Scott the tendency of technology was to erase individual differences and promote conformity of action and thought. In such an atmosphere, she maintained, art cannot flourish. Through the poems in *The Gravestones Wept*, she decided to become an active critic of what she saw as a way of life that blunted the abilities of individuals to create and appreciate art. Every poem Scott included in part 2 has to do with the conflicts between mankind and postindustrial society.

Part 2 begins with "Nineteen-Forty-One," in which the cacophony of civilization is contrasted to the euphony of nature. The poem is separated into two sections, and then an answering voice concludes the poem. Scott set forward two scenes. The first, "Street," describes an empty street and a brief silence, punctuated by birdsong. The bird's note is a pure representation of nature. It brings to the persona's mind a "breath from wide, green living lands / A million miles and years away." This peaceful scene is contrasted to "Neighborhood," which presumably takes place in the same location as "Street." "Street" refers to the landscape or locale. "Neighborhood" represents human inhabitation or community. The neighborhood is described as loud, disorganized, and annoying. Cats mewl, dogs bark, radios blare, children cry. The sunset reflected from windows is an "angry" hue, in contrast to the growing dusk. Overhead, we are told, "The ignored stars began to ripen." The primary contrast in this poem is between street and neighborhood, but a secondary contrast emerges and is emphasized through the final, answering stanza. Finally we are told by the privileged voice that above is the mystery that "*no man can understand.*" Peace, tranquility, and purity are a "million miles and years away." Some answer, or some greater peace, lies outside the meaning that human beings know in their communities. Important themes that emerge from "Nineteen-Forty-One" are the seeking of peace from travail, the saving power of nature, and an assertion that mystery is contained within nature. The mystery, according to Scott, is both self-evidently extant and incomprehensible to the human mind.

"Nineteen-Forty-One" is followed by "Deus ex Machina." A failure of transcendence, the betrayal of some expected deliverance, is explored throughout this section. Written in 1939, "Deus ex Machina" also incorporates an answering and privileged voice. The poem depicts an apocalyptic cityscape in which all things, human and divine, go awry. As in "Nineteen-Forty-One," darkness is an active force. Here it "devours" the fields. The first forty lines of the poem describe a Christ story with a difference: the dead find no peace; the wise men find the star that was to lead them strangely darkened; the land is not fruitful; the shepherd forgets the wandering lamb; Mary loses her child; and in general chaos and disaffection reign. The conclusion of this section is that "all now blindly die / As they were blindly born." In other words, there is a wasteland. Darkness is an active and symbolic force, extending from the night itself to a metaphysical blindness that is the failure to see enlightenment. The last section of the poem answers by bringing the scene up-to-date, from a windswept desert of Christ's time to the skyscrapers of a modern city:

At last, the morning!
The sun rises late,
And shines down searingly
On vomitings of hate—
On factory monoliths and city towers!

The true source of the trouble, the poem implies, is the life human beings have chosen to live: separated from nature and isolated by a misplaced faith in machines. The sun rises late because it is too late to save humanity; the buildings of the city itself delay its presence, casting things in perpetual shadow. At the end of this apocalypse is a final judgment—the sun shines down "'searingly" as a punishment and a final unveiling of what the city has wrought—suggestive of a final apocalyptic trial by fire. Here Scott adopted the vatic mode in order to posit disaster, ecological and spiritual, as a final outcome of modern civilization. A deus ex machina is traditionally a god or device contrived to resolve a plot. In this case Scott emphasized that no god can redeem mankind and that the machines themselves have become the gods—that literally, God has been supplanted by the machines.

Later in part 2 we find "Lost World: The First Defeat," which acts in part as an answer to "Woman Cycle," the first poem in *The Gravestones Wept.* In "Lost World" time is the element that defeats youthful enthusiasm and idealism:

Slow Time, the python-strangler of the heart,
Has crushed this thought to dust.
My senses have been shed as husk,
Where was life here? What joy, what bane,

Stirred in me grandeur that ennobled death?
What made of the very transience of my breath
A paradoxical sublimity?

Wisdom and peace, the poem maintains, do not come with age. In fact the wisdom of age is that "the old are delusion consummate." She asks God to "say why the generations are new-born / To question and to end as we, / Forlorn?" An important intertext to this poem is Wordsworth's "The world is too much with us; late and soon," which describes the alienation people experience from nature when they are absorbed in '"getting and spending." He so advocated a unified life that he exclaimed he would "rather be / A Pagan suckled in a creed outworn" than have a fractured view of nature. Scott's poem departs from Wordsworth's in the respect that she does not advocate superstition, even though it might reconcile life, thought, and belief. Instead she wished to find a new location of and perception of the divine:

Let us outdistance desecration!
Let us, who are the voiceless, celebrate the spirit's wakening,
And rededicate the mystery around us
Who are but textbooks on matter,
Whose mathematics multiply extinctions!
O, God, we ask that when they seek us in the morning
And we are not there,
We may be everywhere. . . .

In her call for distance to analyze her spiritual situation, Scott expressed a desire to escape into the holy through death. The final note of the poem is to "rededicate the mystery around us" by opening oneself to the truth that remains hidden in illusions.

Part 2 as a whole provides a tight nexus of themes central to *The Gravestones Wept.* The section communicates a strong condemnation of what she saw as an overwhelming tendency to exclude art and spiritual truth from life. Conformity seems to result from technology. This group of poems offers evidence of Scott's being located securely within her own time and place, involved in the moods and issues of the modernist moment, if finding herself tragically and personally implicated by them.

The third section enlarges further on themes, images, and symbols developed in parts 1 and 2. Totalitarianism is pervasive, the political realization of industrial paradigms. The human spirit suffers restrictions because of the promotion of conformity through political systems. All human events and urges are part of an eternal pattern of human history—redemption can perhaps be achieved through feelings of loss or sadness. For Scott feeling regret and loss was better than feeling nothing. We get a clearer idea of Scott's cosmology through her depiction of the relationship between chaos and order in her poems about nature. Although part 3 is a less tightly organized unit than parts 1 and 2, it places historical events Scott lived through in a larger context of cyclical, dispensational time. Part 3 includes poems that, while altered from the original versions, directly refer to her brief conversion to Catholicism during 1941. Scott achieved through this section a sense that all particular human events are part of an eternal dialectical cycle; to this she brought a Hegelian sense of predetermined historical culmination. Although all events are part of an endless resounding of the same, for Scott these experiences were building toward a cataclysmic final event.

"Wax Works," the first poem of the section, suggests figures in the poem are like figures in a wax museum, that they are transitory, as if made of wax, or that their accomplishments on earth are as transient as works made of wax. The poem has a manic, kaleidoscopic tone as it presents Neville Chamberlain, Adolf Hitler, Franklin Roosevelt, and Joseph Stalin as players on a stage where their actions are determined by chaos and confusion. The farcical tone of the piece enhances the sense of the overall meaninglessness of the players' actions and lends carnival fiendishness to the twentieth century's forays into fascism. Each historical figure is shown in cartoon relief, doing something or behaving in some way broadly characteristic of him.. For instance Chamberlain is sporting an umbrella during a rain of bullets; Roosevelt beams a false smile to the public; and Stalin is shown as a figure brooding over revenge. Hitler is depicted as a Gabriel figure blowing the "horn of morning," but this portrayal is followed by the privileged voice, who indicates that the call of Hitler is not unique to his time and place but a music that has been heard from time to time throughout human history. To develop further the sense that all history is repetition and continuity, the poem describes how overhead, the "bloody ball" (the sun) has projected its light on similar tragicomic events at different times.

"Wax Works" depicts soldiers of World War II on land, sea, and air behaving as soldiers have always behaved: at least in part as the drones of the hive. German soldiers replicate in some fundamental way Caesar's march on the Rubicon and Hannibal's contemplation of Rome. The privileged voice enters once more with a broader perspective:

But from ten thousand Greeks
And from the twenty thousand at Verdun
There rises still, orchestrally, the moan of time.
And of an earth grown colder at its core, aborting rhyme.
There is something here not spoken by those others

Who have split the atom, but who cannot make men brothers.
There is something here for the listening ear
That will outlast the rasping gusts of human fear—
Something for tomorrow to outlast death
In a regathering of all this wasted human breath.

Several things are of note here. The ancient Greek army and soldiers of World War I are mentioned in a single breath. For Scott these elisions of events and time illustrated that all war is testament to the same elementary human struggles. The "moan of time" and the "rasping gusts of human fear" refer to the eternal rustling of human history. The climate described here is hostile to poetry, "aborting rhyme." The voice says there is "something" here, however, that can be accepted as wisdom, something to outlast death. The indefiniteness of this "something" is an essential component of the hope. The overall effect of invoking this indefinite and remote "something" is to experience suffering as deferred meaning in one's life. The reward is not present but forever anticipated. From Scott we have the promise that pain leads somewhere, even though nature is aloofly indifferent to the affairs of men. The "something," we are told, may be perceived by one receptive to its message. Receptivity depends on readiness to perceive and an awareness of the phenomena.

In a more far-reaching diagnosis, "Our Era," written in 1937, describes a world in which freedom has died, and the spirit itself, once as free as birds, has been chained. Scott's use of the term "Spirit" in this poem and in others, has strongly Hegelian overtones. For Hegel, Spirit represented the positive and negative becoming of being as human history. For Scott, Spirit carried this meaning and could further represent the way in which individuals participate in the absolute evolution of history. Scott diagnosed Spirit in our era as diseased; we are like cattle pressing down a narrow path, to use her image, presumably heading to our own slaughter. The highest actualization of Spirit for Scott was in artistic production, and in our era even the imagination itself "mutely drudges," a slave to baser purposes. We are reduced to "birth, copulation, and death" (to use T. S. Eliot's formulation in *Four Quartets*); in Scott's poem: "And as the worm, the bat, the tiger / Forage, mate and die, / So I and my diminished race." For Eliot the altered perspective revealed in "Burnt Norton" (1935) ultimately led to peace: far removed and above the specifics of life is a perceivable pattern, a reconciliation. For Scott the larger perspective did not lead to peace but to judgment."Spirit can scarce crawl," "These are the saddest days of all," and members of the human race are no more than animals in their pursuit of basic needs. "Our Era" is centered in the human perspective with no intervening voice of hope or unity to moderate it.

Part 4 begins with "Survival," a sonnet about exile and banishment. "We living," the poem explains, are forever separated from an understanding of "the plan" or the principles that order our universe. We want desperately to know, however, and our hubris expresses itself in the manufacture of "girders, joists and joints"; mechanized degradations of and attempts to subsume the natural world. The sestet mentions Laocoön, a resident of ancient Troy who was punished by Poseidon for being skeptical about the Greeks' gift of the wooden horse. When Laocoön expressed his doubts about bringing the horse into the city, Poseidon sent two enormous sea serpents to strangle him and his two sons. In Scott's version Laocoön must struggle with the serpentlike coils of machines, brought forth as if to strangle his skepticism. Her message is that skeptics of the new age are punished as Laocoön was, by the things they cry out against. Some natural order, perhaps even on the molecular level, "proves itself in silence" within "these steely coils." Technology, however, obscures the sense of creation or an underlying will ordering the universe. "Survival" means bare living in exile from nature's truth and an awareness that mechanized human endeavors obscure and sully the natural order.

In "Archaic Art," later in the section, there are several examples of complexity in nature, to which, the persona explains, there is no analogue in the soul. First the poem describes a seashell, feminine and sexual in its unfolding depths. The privileged voice in this poem is nihilistic, suggesting that humans' propensity to find meaning in the sound heard within the seashell is futile and empty. Second the poem describes a feather, a symmetrical and intricate symbol of flight and freedom. The persona finds it similarly empty of meanings or correspondence in her own experience. Then the crystal is offered as a penitent monument to mathematical abstraction, but in the end that perfection is a sham and does not represent the order of nature. Finally philosophy is characterized as a barren, abstract endeavor because it fails to consider the alternative states of existence, such as the emotions, which cannot be subsumed by reason. Just as Cain and Abel struggled with one another, Reason and Feeling are in turmoil for control of the self. The privileged voice signals that out of this conflict and the failure of meaning will spring a new beginning truer to the natural order than the present one. The poem moves toward renewal and rebirth through the struggle to integrate reason and feeling.

"Convoy of 1944 Recollected," written in 1955 (one of the latest composition dates in the volume), is about some of the darkest days of World War II for the Allies. Written from Scott's perspective in England, the U.S. ships that accomplished the June 6, 1944, D-day landing of troops on Omaha Beach and Utah Beach in Normandy arrived as figures of salvation and mystery. On the arrival of these troop ships from the west:

There emerged, as on the last Day,
From the rain-sooted torrent of sunset horizon,
Sail and funnel, streamline and tanker,
To possess, like ghosts sped from eons of shipping,
The colossus of empty ocean and wave.
And as the dying blaze on the sea
Became populous with a suddenly-revealed host,
What stood forth to us silently
Was as wonderful
As though the napkin laid over the Grail had been lifted;
And again we saw Power benign,
Even as in the dreams of the most ancient of mankind.

The last section of the poem sets the convoy in the perspective of ten thousand years of history. As if in answer to the betrayal of power throughout time, the arrival of those troops in 1944 seemed like a deliverance and a sanctification of power. Elsewhere Scott described arriving on her voyage to England alongside a large American military convoy in 1944. She noted her relief at the large number of ships appearing at sunset and the sense that this convoy would usher in a conclusion to the war and a return to normal life.[11]

"The New City in Rain," is one of several sonnets following "Convoy of 1944." All these poems offer brief glimpses into renewal, the theme to which the volume ultimately turns. "The New City in Rain" focuses on an evening rainstorm in New York, alluding to traffic, the bridges, and the phosphorescence of a searchlight. Thunder and lightning are imaginatively described as a "flashing door" that "wind shuts, / Opens and shuts, again, on recalled pain." The sonnet ends with the freshening of everything that the rain brings in a city that epitomizes the modern depersonalization and embrace of technology. The title evokes New York City as well as intimating that it is a new version of itself after the storm and that it is transformed by the covering and cleansing properties of the rain. The sonnet suggests, through the glistening scene of the city, that the people in it might themselves "arise from hell into clear rain." In these final poems of the volume Scott looked toward this sort of renewal and offered a hope that modern people, in spite of the iron cage of technology, could seek ecstatic renewal and be touched by nature.

In a rewriting of William Blake, Scott ended the volume with a celebration poem titled "Pantheist's Paean." It focuses on a persona who is near the shore's edge, where she feels ecstasy about the order of things:

Like the joy of a child
Is my thrill to the might that is free

Yet bound:
Its laws resounding
In the beat of the empty sea,
Traced in the poet's destiny,
The crystal's pattern and the clod!

Taking Blake's "Clod and Pebble" a step further, Scott saw a reconciliation of self and society in the poet's destiny and in the natural order. Scott moved from experience to a type of innocence that incorporates the disillusion of experience. A final apostrophe declares:

O, let us,
On arousing to the daybreak's sweet disaster,
Give obeisance to man's natural master.
This shocked enchantment,
Frigid smell of brine,
And radiance climbing
Like a rosy vine, from gushing shadow,
Have provoked me to such gladness
That my heart and mind
—no less than lion and lamb!—
Exult contentedly, in gratitude,
I am! I am!
And marking, in a plume of surf along the shore,
The strand of Paradise,
And in pellucid depths above,
The Lake of Heaven,
Ask nothing more than to participate
In an accord
Like the hushed praise of the Jews' Lord.

A boat glides by on ruffling keel,
And surely beasts and creatures kneel,
As Light speaks, stilly and unheard,
The strangely simple, lucent Word
Of Order, silent and immense.
O, Liberate Omnipotence,
Could I, I would but live and die
In Thy serene and awful Eye;
Guided like cloud and wave on water,
I would again become Creation's daughter.

Scott's persona evinces joyous surprise over her unexpected discovery of "Order," which has been the quest of *The Gravestones Wept* from the beginning. *The Gravestones Wept* is an orchestral attempt to salvage Scott's sense of self, to put right the fracturing of modernity, and to transcend the ravages of war. "Liberate Omnipotence" became her invocation, much revised and edited, of God.

Also included in this volume are tribute poems to Lola Ridge and Charlotte Wilder, who played key roles in Scott's sense of artistic community. Composed shortly after Lola Ridge's death in 1941, "To Lola Ridge: Poet" fits neatly into this book about vision, seeing, and power:

> Celestial mariners whose stars none see
> Must ponder mortals as you meditated me.
> Gay and unasking giver, ill yet strong,
> Nun-lover of the earth, aloof yet warm,
> Child-sage whose spirit was immunity to harm.
> No furtive pang of loneliness could lure to lies
> A heart that knew no grudging mood,
> A mind that, with chaste, sweet solicitude,
> Bestowed its insights, burningly precise and pure.
> Too frank for consort with evasive meek,
> Her wisdom's feast was spread on wayside stone
> And ripped by many a harpy beak.
> She embraced simply sorrow's taste of iron. . . .
>
> Her eyes, so lucent, luminous and grave,
> Still out-gaze time and change,
> Their gallantry eternal:
> The eyes of vision, steadfast, brave!
> Such valiant eyes—the very eyes of Good!

The poem brings together many of the contradictions that made Ridge a formidable poet and critic, complimenting her mind and exclaiming over the effect of her eyes and vision. Scott felt as though she had really been *seen* by Ridge and that her art had been considered and understood by a first-rate, if underappreciated, critical intelligence. That Scott and Ridge both focused on sight in their poems to one another is key. In "To Lola Ridge: Poet" Scott again lauded Ridge's particular grace and explained that she was misunderstood in her own time. Now deceased, Ridge becomes almost sainted in this poem, personifying the transcendental quality of the Good. This elegant tribute to Ridge expresses simply and straightforwardly her importance in Scott's life and work. Surely Scott's task as an artist must have become much lonelier at the departure of her friend, who was in some ways the first audience for her work.

Also composed in 1941, "They Know Not What They Do (For Charlotte Wilder)" expresses the complexities of the unfolding story of Wilder's illness and what Scott interpreted as her unjust incarceration:

There is a hate born in the tender breast
The brute of sluggish caution never knows:
A gift of hope that hopelessness bestows,
Indriven by the hand that would be blest,
It goads the gentle to a fierce unrest,
Inflaming kindness with a pride that grows
Until abused benignance kindles snows
And crowns the meek heart with a fiery crest.

So on the winds of time is sown the seed
Of dragon's teeth, while force makes mercy bleed.
Mere glut of meat sates mobs protesting wrong,
But not sweet charity that suffers long,
As from wrath nourished by an outraged love,
Years rouse the eagle in the frenzied dove.

This poem suggests that Wilder has been crucified and that in time a different perspective about her sacrifice and suffering will unfold. In Scott's view Wilder's life was controlled by institutions and a medical program that largely failed to acknowledge her as an individual or preserve her as an artist. This poem expresses the sense of anger and helplessness Scott felt as she continued to crusade for her friend's liberty.

Something of Scott's fierce independence, sense of vocation as a writer, and determination to overcome an array of obstacles, not the least of which was her own disintegrating mind, suffuses *The Gravestones Wept.* Over a long career, Scott wrote a large body of interesting work that covers a wide range of registers and idioms and is remarkably difficult to classify in terms of period, style, or genre. While there is certainly a range of aesthetic success in her work, the large number of truly innovative and strong works should afford her consideration by many readers. *The Gravestones Wept,* even with its anachronistic apostrophes, nonmodernist invocation of the Romantic poets, and Luddite warnings about technology, should be categorized as one of Scott's major achievements—her last successful publication, and a culmination of her poetic and prose careers. When one considers the totality of her work, even Scott's failures are instructive, and her personal and visible struggle with paranoid delusion marks her later work as one of the most detailed documentaries of declining mental health in American literature. Scott heroically persevered against this deterioration in *The Gravestones Wept;* one has only to compare her letters of the same period to the poetry to measure her line-by-line victory. She kept her lonely post, in spite of these struggles, and sought integration even as an antitotalitarian who managed to isolate herself nearly completely.

Except that she was not alone. Evelyn Scott was a part of a small community of women writers who were unified by a determination to apply their minds and energies to being artists within, and sometimes against, the idioms of modernism. By paying tribute to each other, responding to each other's work, and most of all believing in each other, these writers created space for the work and enabled each other as artists. Their will to create—collectively and individually—shaped their subjects, marked their writing, and forged their friendships.

APPENDIX

The Book of Cincinnati

Kay Boyle

This previously unpublished poem is copyright Kay Boyle, published by permission of the Estate of Kay Boyle. The text is taken from a typescript copy Kay Boyle sent to Lola Ridge in 1923, now located in the Lola Ridge Papers, Sophia Smith Collection, Smith College.

I

Cincinnati browsing in the bronze of hot autumn, through the gone smoke of heaped twilight fires, steps upon brittle winter, a plough horse on fine glass. Beneath road trees, beer bottles empty-mouthed suck summer within them.

River body in a wide soft bed, close crowded with roofed faces like a mother pressed with blank mouths, I have not shattered you with the weight of my body. At night, shaken old chains in movement of rested water, wounded with slow loveliness of light's latent crimson, intangible rhythm when I stooped to curve you cupped in my palms.

Cincinnati river, grey pencil stroke on curl-edged paper, clear water cooling the long dry throat of the land. Dancing beside I met a drunken man whose hands pursued each other through the stars. Arm-linked our shadows passed on the wet grass. Our fat untidy voices rolled against the stars. Drunk, brother, we sang, and the soul of Cincinnati is sober.

II

Spring on the impotent hill. Empty womb of the hill shall be filled. Life shall be given here. Roots to spread hill-wards, earth-wards, rain-wards.

Blue-shirted man with a wide smile and a woman forever pregnant say: There are to be trees. Grass will grow. We can sit here.

Woman swings suede feet: "The committee . . . beautifying the city . . . it will be lovely here." Hours are yawning mouths she covers with her white-throated fingers.

Summer, the young hill bearing giant grass, golden-headed like candles; beetle-backs on green tubes, straight in the swayed wind. Old rose moon a dull peach hanging silence on the downward river. Stooped in the tall grass, three for the favors of one woman, white in a blue dress.

Cool blue dress.

Beating the bushes, a bent woman: My old man's after the girls again somewhere in the long grass.

III

Mother's underlip curls up like a fern frond. Hair, cool brown hands stroking her forehead. Feather is a blue wave breaking over her eyes.

George brings crisp Indian pipes, his fingers . . . Chinaman-yellow on their coral throats. Mother's hands fall on the moss like fresh white lace.

At night she puts kisses in my palms. I must hold them tight until morning. Grandpa makes stiff noises in the hall. When I wake up at night I hear Mother's door open: Ears have limitations. You might look under the bed . . .

Grandpa blows loudly down the hall. Close about me, Mother . . . making songs for me from an old man's words.

Grandpa's cane makes tiptoe marks in the dust: Nothing to keep her mind busy . . . reads too much . . . don't make that mistake.

Carefully I step in the places where Mother's heels have been sharp little moons in the road.

IV

Closer than pain to him, the hours nailed in coffin boxes. Suffering stretched on the dissecting table. I know this man too well . . . his hand turning . . . in the cold, his mind shrinking.

By their slim necks he holds things within me which are restless.

Brick wall passing squarely about me, beyond is nothing more free than what there is within me. Beyond, inevitably growing, hill in the high wind swinging. Palms pressed to your hard sides yielding.

Behind the wall is my swept room. Behind my father's name there is an unborn sorrow and a grey-haired pain, a man blown full with courage, sucked flat with fear. These to remain untouched by gentleness of time or thoughts that someone fingers daily.

People pass and read my father's name, black and white on brick wall's red. Eyes do not lift to the strong strange hill, but pass . . .

V

I, an old man grown to dusk-weed in a meadow.

My mother's memory makes me full with hatred.

At school in England, studied for the priesthood. Dogma that I could not take within me, nor stomach after taking.

My wife, long since beneath staid Pennsylvania grasses, at sixteen left her family faith to worship through conviction as a Presbyterian. Spirited child I first saw washing dishes, cheeks hard autumn apples . . . in the kitchen of my uncle. Jennie was my cousin.

My wife . . . a strong will and liver trouble.

My son's wife and two children are my roots to shade in summer, to protect in winter. Janet in a red hood finding waves beneath the boardwalk. Katherine without teeth in front, smiling. Keep pain from them, keep from them always pain. Put them behind this wall and set my back against it. My son is not man enough.

But we have come through.

Here then, switchboard of lights and buttons. Two black fists hit on the ears. When there is the sound of flies sleepy in a summer orchard, quickly green cord gold mouthed into the hole sharply, making white sparks blue-haloed.

Below, the silky sound of lithe machinery. Below, men known as numbers. Through sweet pasture air the flies crescendo . . . plug one or two or three.

One two and three will sign the Debs petition, smiling goldly. Sure. The war's over.

The old man grown to dusk-weed in his closed office: Sign? I think no, my dear . . .

But, an old man, Debs . . . in prison . . .

Rising rage through the office stepping.

Goose-step, goose-step,
Stomach flops flip-flop
If Debs had been president
There'd be a German General
In every maiden-lady's bed.

VI

Richard is a gold beach.
Feet of waves run printless across him.

His eyelids
Are smooth shells
Curved beneath his forehead.

His eyes,
The sharp elbows of his mind
Through his threadbare face,

Rain swirls about legs,
An unruly skirt.
Richard walks with rain over his shoulders
Like a loose mantle.

VII

Small ways like crooked fingers from the straight palms of broad hands beckoning. Below many-fingered trees are roots spreading, thin fingers of a wide hand groping, into fresh earth hungering.

Lawyer Klein offers ice-cream on paper spoons and heads the relay races. Lawyer Klein, father of sticky babies. Every Thursday night for seven years he has simplified Marx to comrades who for seven years have listened.

From the tree-stump: There will be talks from Comrades Lune and Feldhaus.

Lune who walked ten miles to carry literature because the law forbade it in a vehicle. Feldhaus, a Christmas tree in sunlight, sentence to serve under the Espionage.

Beneath August trees, children hot on the trod grass, children to come heavy beneath warm skirts clinging. Veins of hot life leaping in unspent revolution.

On the stump, Mary D. Brite, body closed like a fist about the sharp blade of her voice. Sorrow is a throat parched against words . . . speech brims in her hands . . .

Speech . . . through Cincinnati streets walk feet of Child Crusaders, tight bitter words through a loose mouth.

Children's Crusade . . . Elbertine's hands are curled-up leaves blown in your eyes. When she sees the river her hands cry sharply together.

Sun tumbles in the grass. Why do you not run, children, carrying the field high in your arms? Children's eyes fumble among your words. Legs stand erect like sprigged dry heather.

Progress to Washington . . . President Harding: They may play on the White House lawns.

Grass can be new-washed skin on your palms and forehead. But Elbertine stands like a candle at the gate, black letters on the white banner:

My father is in prison for expressing his opinion.

VIII

House with raised eyebrows, surprised against restless trees. In its lap, held by green-hedge arms, curls the shiny-faced garden.

Sunday evenings, windows open on the grass push fragile hands against the moonlight. Voices swing like stars in tree boughs. Hours leave foot-prints in cigaret ashes.

Duane Swift speaks, conscientious objector . . . face an open door:

Leavenworth nights, a long chain linked closer than hot bodies. Days rise bent-backed, bed-rocks to be broken under the sun. Pick lifts into the sky, drops a thin finger pointing earthward. Flat clang of stone against stone, square-headed hammer falls numb on shrill bones. Castrated of response, bodies surrendered upon life.

Set tables are rows of teeth bared in the great room. Hours stretched in the sun breed hunger. Thin soup and one slice of bread . . . heads swing dully . . . Bread . . . hardly uttered . . . Bread . . . wooden spoons lift, sound on the table . . . Bread . . . knocks louder . . . Bread . . . articulate . . . Bread . . . beating seconds . . . Bread . . . more than a hundred more than a thousand voices rising.

Duane Swift, kitchen foreman, passes the false order: One slice each again, once around. Dry tongues move words like withered leaves over the bare floor of night.

Railroad Union Local. Duane Swift speaks in a room summer-night filled:

Democrats have a press, Republicans a press, but the Labor party... Now that we're putting it over, comrades, we count on you. Think... Russia...

Eyes drift. Tobacco shifts. Russia.

"Only worker's government in the world..."

Shoulders shift the slumped air.

"The Federated Press means... What does the public remember? Thaw shooting Stanford White ten years ago. Last week, five Union Miners shot to death in West Virginia. The public to remember that... we ask your support..."

"Time's up, buddy. Step outside, we'll take a vote."

Door behind punctuates thoughts between. Wooden slide window hole and two eyes dwindling: "Sorry. The local can't take anything on just now."

Inward voice rising: "Look here, fellows, we gotta have another cooler in this hang-out..."

"Sure... all in favor?... put it through. Pass the hat and let's get out of this hot hole and have a game of ball."

IX

Golden Rule is a grey cat dragging dirtily across unclean backyards. Soft cat's paws on the bruises of blue beaten fences. Arched cat's back under fingers stroking...

The A. Nash Tailoring Company... Arthur Nash... when curled lashes lay on his cheeks and each day a rounded life-time, watched men and women passing to shops and workrooms against life closing.

Evening across his window. By the wide fire reading, her calm hair parting above her eyes, joining curved hands again behind her head... mother...

"Little son, heed. The Lord hath said, 'Do thou unto others...'"

Words turn soil for later growing. "The Bible Text That Worked a Business Miracle"... someday, my factory, my shop!

Hair, a quiet crown he wears so that the feel of thorns comes to the listeners, Golden Rule Nash before the Rotary Club speaks softly:

"What I have learned at the knee of her... who nursed me, can I forget?" Suppliant hands. "The years have brought an heritage of peace . . . for with the Golden Rule there is no need of organized labor."

Ann Craton, small foot forced in the closing door: "That is not true. I have been turned away." Words carried around other corners, pass almost unheard. "Policemen keep questions from the workers. Through early mornings I have walked pavements to the factory, home on them at evening. To reach the shop at day-break, cloth-cutters ride the owl car. Golden Rule Nash for longest hours pays the lowest wages."

Bishop Jones is stirred in protest: "Disadvantages in the absence of amalgamated labor, but the principle..."

Bishop without a diocese. War foamed against him, rooting him deeper. Eyes kind and puzzled. Preaching the word meant sheep within the fold. The application, going on alone.

X

In the past made lovelier by time, the boy self-educated running elevators, studying late in his unlovely room. Dr. Bigelow opens doors wide, tired hair leaning upon his forehead.

Before the war, his own church. Seats not enough to hear his eyes and his hands passing through long hair. Now public hall rears walls in his mind. Day of rest, it is the People's Church.

With the war, head thrown back under morning-pinked windows, words flung in the thinning eyes of voiceless pews, rolled uncaught on the floor's sunlight. If that wave of light reached the top of the first pew before he said "peace" again... tied to a tree with his flesh gaping.

Between his shoulder blades, long tired wounds now resting. Profile upon the beyond violin, a calm saint growing. His other, rigid upon flames built in the night, peered by faces pushing. Across country, his body naked white knife through cold, stretched for lashes, spread for tar and feathers.

His body heals, his mind sags raw wounds open. Upon the staring eyes red in his white mind, the closed lids of the middle-aged unshaken. Behind hymnals, four who are the Peace Society sing sharply.

On the platform beside, Golden Rule Nash, eyes tucked carefully in at the corners. Words, facile embroidery on the edges of Sunday napkins. Golden Rule Nash, whose principles pass unquestioned.

In the shared light, Bigelow, Bishop Jones, hold him thin against the brilliance. Outlined through him, grey figures over endless garments breaking.

XI

Election night sharp knives against faces. Feet and hands sharp in the round song of torches. Standing, hands snug beneath arm-pits, strange eyes shrill at Socialism.

Room soft with smoke and faces of men unshaven. Near the coal stove, spreading dry hands and leaning to the cuspidors, hearing William Z. Foster: Debs is in jail and the country scabs on him. Here, you an I, we're the biggest bunch of boob workers this side of hell.

Smile tight on the loose air. Now, long-legged through Michigan woods, unyielding pine.

XII

From the platform, Lincoln Steffens . . . words, footsteps of thoughts that stand tip-toe in his brain. Words, hot on the china-blue plates of his eyes. He, a close hot word thrust on the lips of life.

His footsteps in the wet earth of Russia make cradles for white northern stars.

Withered arms cling. Life sucking his spirit gaunt. Her dry hair crackles across his heart. He, tenderly . . . crooning . . . gathers close, white bones . . .

Behind the curtain, Brotherhood usher removes his Committee ribbon: If the place is raided, this official regalia. You know . . . better play safe.

XIII

Oswald Garrison Villard, Woman City Club. Beyond the door, age is an old coat hanging in tired folds. Sudden stone through a blue-lidded window. Youth is gold glass, smile flung through its torn mouth.

Shattering outer doors up the stairs rising, American Legion, stoning defenders. Protest is blood, like a thin red finger on a temple.

"We learn that differences grow less in the sympathy of our approach" . . . words calm in the room hold quivering flame static. Voices crumble against the door . . . police protection. Villard draws an unbroken current through the held waters.

XIV

In the cryless feel of night, Cincinnati clinging. Planets high on the slow beach draw upward faces of the tide, touching them with lonely fingers . . .

Cincinnati offering flat breasts to the blind teeth of stars. Acrid on the tongue, dawn thrusts down like a gold pin.

NOTES

Introduction

1. Cary Nelson, *Repression and Recovery: Modern American Poetry and Politics of Cultural Memory* (Madison: University of Wisconsin Press, 1989).

2. Allan David Bloom, *The Closing of the American Mind* (New York: Simon & Schuster, 1988); E. D. Hirsch, Joseph F. Kett, and James S. Trefil, *Cultural Literacy: What Every American Needs to Know* (New York: Vintage, 1988).

3. Poets who were social and sentimental in this time period might include Rudyard Kipling and Vachel Lindsay. Aesthetic and sentimental poetry from this period was written by poets such as William Butler Yeats, Edna St. Vincent Millay, and Oscar Wilde. The most familiar category, poets who are modern/aesthetic, includes T. S. Eliot, Marianne Moore, William Carlos Williams, and Wallace Stevens. Of course these are rough categories. Poets can be plotted at different stages of their careers with varying results, and mapping individual poems might yield different results.

4. William Drake, *The First Wave: Women Poets in America, 1915–1945* (New York: Macmillan, 1987).

5. Shari Benstock, *Women of the Left Bank: Paris, 1900–1940* (Austin: University of Texas Press, 1986); Gillian Hanscombe and Virginia Smyers, *Writing for Their Lives: The Modernist Women, 1900–1940* (London: Women's Press, 1987), 12.

6. Joseph Harrington, *Poetry and the Public: The Social Form of Modern U.S. Poetics* (Middletown, Conn.: Wesleyan University Press, 2002), 1–3.

7. Ibid.

8. Suzanne Clark, *Sentimental Modernism: Women Writers and the Revolution of the Word* (Bloomington: Indiana University Press, 1991).

9. Nancy Berke, *Women Poets on the Left: Lola Ridge, Genevieve Taggard, Margaret Walker* (Gainesville: University Press of Florida, 2001), 6.

10. Elaine Showalter, *A Jury of Her Peers: American Women Writers from Anne Bradstreet to Annie Proulx* (New York: Knopf, 2009).

11. Karen J. Winkler, "The Literary Tradition of Women," *Chronicle of Higher Education,* April 10, 2009, B12.

12. Jean Toomer, *The Letters of Jean Toomer 1919–1924,* edited by Mark Whalan (Knoxville: University of Tennessee Press, 2006).

13. Toomer to Ridge, June 24, 1921, ibid., 22. He continued, "I do not know when I have seen lines bitten in so sharply. There is economy, and not merely the strength that comes from the precise handling of one's material but also the power that arises from the certainty of knowledge."

14. Ibid., 16.

15. Cyril Kay Scott, *Sinbad* (New York: Seltzer, 1923), 7–8.

16. See Mary Wheeling White, *Fighting the Current: The Life and Work of Evelyn Scott* (Baton Rouge: Louisiana State University Press, 1998), and D. A. Callard, *Pretty Good for a Woman: The Enigmas of Evelyn Scott* (New York: Norton, 1986). Scott's autobiographies are *Escapade* (1923) and *Background in Tennessee* (1937).

17. White, *Fighting the Current,* 14.

18. Ibid., 16.

19. Evelyn Scott, *Escapade* (New York: Seltzer, 1923); Cyril Kay Scott, *Life Is Too Short: An Autobiography* (Philadelphia: Lippincott, 1943). A third retelling of this episode exists in their son's unpublished autobiography: Creighton Scott, "Confessions of an American Boy," Henry E. Turlington Papers, series III: Scott Family Papers 1931–82, box 9, folder 6, Harry Ransom Humanities Research Center, University of Texas at Austin.

20. Lola Ridge, "Evelyn Scott," *Playboy: A Portfolio of Art and Satire* (1919/1920): 24.

21. Scott to Davy Lawson, January 11, 1948, Lola Ridge Papers, Sophia Smith Collection, Smith College.

22. Kay Boyle, *Process,* edited by Sandra Spanier (Urbana: University of Illinois Press, 2001). The manuscript for this novel, completed in 1925, was lost until Spanier discovered it in the New York Public Library. It was first published in 2001, edited with an introduction by Spanier.

23. See Sandra Spanier, *Kay Boyle: Artist and Activist* (Carbondale: Southern Illinois University Press, 1986), and Joan Mellen, *Kay Boyle: Author of Herself* (New York: Farrar, Straus & Giroux, 1994).

24. Boyle to Spanier, November 19, 1984, quoted in Spanier, *Kay Boyle,* 10. Copyright Kay Boyle. Reprinted by permission of the Estate of Kay Boyle.

25. Charlotte Wilder to Ridge, April 15, 1935, Lola Ridge Papers, Sophia Smith Collection, Smith College.

26. Versions of Scott's unpublished novels are in the Evelyn Scott Collection at the Harry Ransom Humanities Research Center, University of Texas at Austin, and the Evelyn Scott Collection at the University of Tennessee Libraries, Special Collections, Knoxville. Scott's poetry was collected and published in Evelyn Scott, *The Collected Poems of Evelyn Scott,* edited by Caroline Maun (Orono, Maine: National Poetry Foundation, 2005).

27. Introduction to *Women Poets on Mentorship: Efforts and Affections,* edited by Arielle Greenberg and Rachel Zucker (Iowa City: University of Iowa Press, 2008), xiv.

Chapter 1. Imagism, Socially Engaged Poetry, and Lola Ridge

1. Michele Leggott, "The First Life: A Chronology of Lola Ridge's Australasian Years," Bluff '06: A Poetry Symposium in Southland, http://www.nzepc.auckland.ac.nz/features/bluff06/leggott.asp (accessed October 5, 2009); Cary Nelson, *Revolutionary Memory: Recovering the Poetry of the American Left* (New York: Routledge, 2003), 51; Lola Ridge, *Light in Hand: Selected Early Poems of Lola Ridge,* edited by Daniel Tobin (Williamsburg, Mass.: Quayle Press, 2007), vii.

2. There have been objections to Ridge's use of archaisms in syntax and diction in her later poetry (*Firehead* and *Dance of Fire*). Lola Ridge, *Firehead* (New York: Payson & Clarke, 1929) and *Dance of Fire* (New York: Smith & Haas, 1935).

3. Kay Boyle, preface to *The Autobiography of Emanuel Carnevali* (New York: Horizon Press, 1967), 10. Copyright Kay Boyle. Reprinted by permission of the Estate of Kay Boyle.

4. Alfred Kreymborg, *Our Singing Strength: An Outline of American Poetry (1620–1930)* (New York: Coward-McCann, 1929), 484.

5. Paul Avrich, *The Modern School Movement: Anarchism and Education in the United States* (Oakland, Calif.: AK Press, 2006), 88.

6. Emanuel Carnevali, *The Autobiography of Emanuel Carnevali,* 117.

7. Ibid., 117–18. Kay Boyle, who edited (and made many embellishments to) Carnevali's autobiography after his death, included "My Speech at Lola's," which the younger poet Carnevali intended as a wake-up call to the group of artists that included Ridge, Williams, Alfred Kreymborg, Maxwell Bodenheim, and William Saphier. Carnevali criticized this group for becoming comfortable and for taking shelter in their shop talk about modernist techniques. Most of these writers (Saphier was also a sketch artist and illustrator) were at the heart of the American modernist movement in poetics. In his introduction, written some years after he gave the talk in 1919, Carnevali indicated that he might have gotten carried away, but he did not want these writers to become cynical or desensitized. The talk is of great interest because it reveals something of the social circle in which Ridge was a central figure.

8. William Carlos Williams, *The Autobiography of William Carlos Williams* (New York: New Directions, 1967), 136.

9. Robert McAlmon, *Post-Adolescence,* edited by Edward N. S. Lorusso (Albuquerque: University of New Mexico Press, 1991), 37.

10. Unpublished diary, December 8, 1940, Lola Ridge Papers, Sophia Smith Collection. Quoted in Drake, *The First Wave,* 3.

11. Gaston Bachelard, *The Poetics of Space* (Boston: Beacon Press, 1994), 6.

12. Ridge gave her birthday as December 12; In "The First Life," Leggott lists Ridge's birth date as December 19, 1873, from the birth registration. On a questionnaire found in the A. G. Stephens papers at the Mitchell Library, New South Wales, Ridge reported her birth date as December 12, 1876, and later she told people that her birth year was 1883.

13. Quoted in Drake, *The First Wave,* 188.

14. Ibid., 189.

15. Katherine Anne Porter, *The Never-Ending Wrong* (London: Secker & Warburg, 1977), 44.

16. See also Berke, *Women Poets on the Left*, 52ff., for a discussion of Ridge's contribution to the Sacco-Vanzetti cultural phenomenon.

17. In this argument Ridge foreshadowed arguments made effectively in Jared Diamond's *Guns, Germs, and Steel: The Fates of Human Societies* (New York: Norton, 2005).

18. See Berke, *Women Poets on the Left*, 58ff., for an excellent discussion of the role of horses in this episode and for the discussion of "Three Men Die" in general.

19. Of particular value has been "The First Life," the Internet-published documentary timeline by New Zealand poet and scholar Michele Leggott. Also of great value is the story of Ridge's life told in several chapters of William Drake's *The First Wave*.

20. Unpublished letter, Rosa Webster to A. G. Stephens, January 27, 1904, Mitchell Library, New South Wales.

21. Unpublished diary, May 2, 1940, Lola Ridge Papers, Sophia Smith Collection, Smith College.

22. *New York Times*, May 21, 1941. Paul Avrich gives her death age as seventy-seven instead of sixty-seven, doing the math in the other direction. See *The Modern School*, 358.

23. This typescript is in the A. G. Stephens Collection at the State Library of New South Wales.

24. Ridge's misspelling, although it may be traditional. Also spelled "Lake Kaniere."

25. For instance "The Martyrs of Hell," *Mother Earth* 4 (April 1909): 33, which was republished as "A Toast" in *The Ghetto and Other Poems* (New York: Huebsch, 1918).

26. The one Australian poem from the "Verses by Lola Ridge" typescript that was included in *The Ghetto and Other Poems* was the lyric "Under-Song." Originally titled "Voices of the Bush: Under-Song," the poem was extensively revised for *The Ghetto and Other Poems* (1918). It was earlier published in *Overland Monthly* 6 (June 1908): 540, with only minor revisions from the version in the typescript.

27. Francisco Ferrer (January 10, 1859–October 13, 1909), a Spanish radical, was exiled in 1885. After living for a time in Paris, he returned to Spain in 1901 and opened La Escuela Moderna (The Modern School). He was arrested in 1906 and released from jail in 1908. After his release, he wrote *The Origins and Ideals of the Modern School*, which appeared in English in 1913. In 1909 he was arrested again and executed by a firing squad.

28. Avrich, *The Modern School Movement*, 146. "Libertarian" in this case connotes a society characterized by freedom rather than the specific right-wing meanings it has gathered in our present political landscape.

29. Ridge to Mrs. Bartlett, May 28, 1935, Lola Ridge Papers, Sophia Smith Collection, Smith College.

30. William Butler Yeats, "Anima Hominis," *Essays* (New York: Macmillan, 1924), 492.

31. W. H. Auden, "In Memory of W. B. Yeats," *Collected Poems*, edited by Edward Mendelson (New York: Vintage, 1976), 248.

32. Cleanth Brooks, *The Well Wrought Urn: Studies in the Structure of Poetry* (New York: Harcourt, Brace, 1947), 17.

33. Harold Loeb, *The Way It Was* (New York: Criterion, 1959), 112.

34. Ibid., 121.

35. Ibid.

36. Peter Quartermain, "Lola Ridge," *Dictionary of Literary Biography,* vol. 54: *American Poets, 1880–1945,* edited by Quartermain, 3rd series, part 2: N–Z (Detroit: Gale Research, 1987), 358.

37. Loeb to Ridge, in *The Way It Was,* 122.

38. Loeb reported in *The Way It Was* that, when Ridge suggested publishing an essay by Scott, they had an immediate conflict:

> Our other difficulties were more specific. Lola had stated in a letter:
>
> > Evelyn Scott has written to me about an article on American Esthetics and she asked me to send it on. She is perhaps the most brilliant critic in America.
>
> I knew what was going to happen. I attempted to be tactful. Risking insincerity, I answered, "I like Evelyn Scott's poetry," feeling that it was no worse than a lot of other poetry; "I probably would like her novel which I have not read, but I dislike her criticisms. They seem to be hollow, erudite obscurities . . ." a discussion which continued back and forth for many months (124).

39. Ridge to Loeb, July 11, 1922, ibid., 223.

40. Ibid., November 15, 1922, ibid., 42.

41. Matthew Josephson, *Life among the Surrealists: A Memoir* (New York: Holt, Rinehart & Winston, 1962), 246.

42. Ridge, *Light in Hand.*

43. Michael Arend Rozendal, "On the Line: A Reconsideration of 1930s Modernist and Proletarian Radicalism" (Ph.D. diss., State University of New York at Buffalo, 2006).

44. Quartermain, "Lola Ridge."

45. See also Berke, *Women Poets on the Left,* 52ff., for a discussion of Ridge's contribution to the Sacco-Vanzetti culture.

46. Representative reviews of *The Ghetto and Other Poems* include: D.L.M., *Boston Transcript* (January 15, 1919): 6; *Catholic World* 108 (February 1919): 694; Conrad Aiken, *Dial* 66 (January 25, 1919): 83–84; F.H. [Francis Hackett], *New Republic* 17 (November 16, 1918): 76–77; and Louis Untermeyer, *New York Evening Post* (February 1, 1919): 1.

47. Drake, *The First Wave,* 186.

Chapter 2. "Unwieldy with enormous births"

1. Ridge to Harrison Smith and Robert Haas, December 7, 1937, Lola Ridge Papers, Sophia Smith Collection, Smith College. Quoted in Lola Ridge, "Woman and the Creative Will," edited by Elaine Sproat, Michigan Occasional Paper no. 18 (Spring 1981): 2.

2. Unpublished diary, Lola Ridge Papers, Sophia Smith Collection, quoted in Sproat, n8.

3. Ridge, "Woman and the Creative Will," 4.

4. Alfred Kreymborg, *Troubadour* (New York: Sagamore Press, 1957), 258.

5. Ibid, 11.

6. Ridge, "Woman and the Creative Will," 10.

7. Ibid., 12.

8. Ibid., 18.

9. Helene Cixous, "The Laugh of the Medusa," *Signs* 1 (Summer, 1976): 875–93.

10. Ridge, review of *Precipitations*, by Evelyn Scott, *Poetry* 17 (March 1921): 334–37.

11. Scott suffered from paranoid personality disorder with symptoms manifesting themselves as early as the late 1920s. This mental disability affected her work and wreaked havoc with her interpersonal relationships. She was generally unable to conduct professional relationships with those in the publishing industry who might have helped her career. She alienated agents, publishers, and friends. See White, *Fighting the Current*, and Callard, *Pretty Good for a Woman*, for extensive discussions.

12. There are a few letters from Ridge to Scott at the Harry Ransom Humanities Research Center, University of Texas at Austin, and several surviving carbon copies of Ridge's letters to Scott in the Sophia Smith Collection at Smith College.

13. Ridge to Scott [1919], Evelyn Scott Papers, Harry Ransom Humanities Research Center, University of Texas at Austin.

14. Padriac Colum, "Two Women Poets," review of *Precipitations, New Republic* 29 (November 2, 1921): 304–5.

15. Mark Van Doren, "Sapphics," review of *Precipitations, Nation* 112 (January 5, 1921): 20.

16. Ridge, review of *Precipitations*.

17. Robert Welker, "Evelyn Scott: A Literary Biography" (Ph.D. diss., Vanderbilt University, 1958), 149.

18. Mina Loy, "Love Songs," *Others* 1 (July 1915): 6.

19. Robert McAlmon and Kay Boyle, *Being Geniuses Together, 1920–1930* (San Francisco: North Point Press, 1984), 152. Copyright Kay Boyle. Reprinted by permission of the Estate of Kay Boyle.

20. Scott, *The Collected Poems*.

21. White, *Fighting the Current*, 30–32.

22. Scott to Ridge [1919], Lola Ridge Papers, Sophia Smith Collection, Smith College.

23. Ibid.

24. Ibid. [1920], Lola Ridge Papers, Sophia Smith Collection, Smith College.

25. Ibid. [Spring 1922], Lola Ridge Papers, Sophia Smith Collection, Smith College.

26. Ibid. [1920], Lola Ridge Papers, Sophia Smith Collection, Smith College.

Chapter 3. "Women with shining secrets in their eyes"

1. There are two biographies of Kay Boyle, both of which treat some aspects of her relationships to Lola Ridge and Evelyn Scott. See Spanier, *Kay Boyle*, and Mellen, *Kay Boyle*.

2. Boyle, "Report from Lock-Up," in *Words That Must Somehow Be Said: Selected Essays of Kay Boyle, 1927–1984,* edited by Elizabeth S. Bell (San Francisco: North Point Press, 1985).

3. McAlmon and Boyle, *Being Geniuses Together,* 17. Copyright Kay Boyle. Reprinted by permission of the Estate of Kay Boyle.

4. Boyle to Ridge [Fall 1923], Lola Ridge Papers, Sophia Smith Collection, Smith College. Copyright Kay Boyle. Reprinted by permission of the Estate of Kay Boyle.

5. Malcolm Cowley, *Exile's Return* (New York: Penguin Classics, 1976), 179.

6. Boyle to Cowley, July 26, 1981, quoted in Sandra Spanier, "'Paris Wasn't Like That': Kay Boyle and the Last of the Lost Generation," in *Lives Out of Letters: Essays on American Literary Biography and Documentation in Honor of Robert N. Hudspeth,* edited by Robert D. Habich, 182 (Madison, N. J.: Fairleigh Dickinson University Press, 2004). Copyright Kay Boyle. Reprinted by permission of the Estate of Kay Boyle. Spanier also noted that Jack Seltzer told this story in *Kenneth Burke in Greenwich Village: Conversing with the Moderns, 1915–1931* (Madison: Wisconsin University Press, 1996), 108–114. See also Cowley, *Exile's Return,* 179. There was a lapse in publication between April and July 1923, and the periodical ceased publication with the January 1924 number.

7. Boyle to Ridge [Fall 1923], Lola Ridge Papers, Sophia Smith Collection, Smith College. Copyright Kay Boyle. Reprinted by permission of the Estate of Kay Boyle.

8. Russell Murphy, "Alfred Kreymborg," in *Dictionary of Literary Biography,* vol. 54: *American Poets, 1880–1945,* edited by Peter Quartermain, 3rd series, part 1: A–M (Detroit: Gale Research. 1987), 198.

9. Elaine Sproat, e-mail to author, January 24, 2010.

10. McAlmon and Boyle, *Being Geniuses Together,* 15. Copyright Kay Boyle. Reprinted by permission of the Estate of Kay Boyle.

11. Ibid., 15. Copyright Kay Boyle. Reprinted by permission of the Estate of Kay Boyle.

12. Ibid., 17. Copyright Kay Boyle. Reprinted by permission of the Estate of Kay Boyle.

13. Boyle, *Words That Must Somehow Be Said,* 38. Copyright Kay Boyle. Reprinted by permission of the Estate of Kay Boyle.

14. McAlmon and Boyle, *Being Geniuses Together,* 217. Copyright Kay Boyle. Reprinted by permission of the Estate of Kay Boyle.

15. Ibid., 285. Copyright Kay Boyle. Reprinted by permission of the Estate of Kay Boyle.

16. Author's interview with Elaine Sproat, Northampton, Massachusetts, September 9, 2009.

17. Boyle to Ridge, November 29, 1927, Lola Ridge Papers, Sophia Smith Collection, Smith College. Copyright Kay Boyle. Reprinted by permission of the Estate of Kay Boyle.

18. Eugene Jolas, "Proclamation," *transition* 16–17(June 1929): 13.

19. Spanier, *Kay Boyle,* 25–26; see also Clark, "Revolution, the Woman, and the Word," in her *Sentimental Modernism,* 127–52.

20. McAlmon and Boyle, *Being Geniuses Together,* 43. Copyright Kay Boyle. Reprinted by permission of the Estate of Kay Boyle.

21. Spanier tells the story of the *Process* manuscript in her introduction to Kay Boyle, *Process.*

22. McAlmon and Boyle, *Being Geniuses Together,* 22. Copyright Kay Boyle. Reprinted by permission of the Estate of Kay Boyle.

23. See particularly Mellen, *Kay Boyle.*

24. McAlmon and Boyle, *Being Geniuses Together,* 23. Copyright Kay Boyle. Reprinted by permission of the Estate of Kay Boyle.

25. Boyle to Ridge, January 26, 1923, Lola Ridge Papers, Sophia Smith Collection, Smith College. Copyright Kay Boyle. Reprinted by permission of the Estate of Kay Boyle.

26. Ibid. Copyright Kay Boyle. Reprinted by permission of the Estate of Kay Boyle.

27. Ibid., August 20, 1923, Lola Ridge Papers, Sophia Smith Collection, Smith College. Copyright Kay Boyle. Reprinted by permission of the Estate of Kay Boyle.

28. Spanier, introduction to Boyle, *Process,* xxvii.

29. Gloria Garrett Samson, *The American Fund for Public Service: Charles Garland and Radical Philanthropy, 1922–1941* (Westport, Conn.: Greenwood, 1996), 83.

30. Ibid., xxvi.

31. Ibid.

32. Boyle, "The Book of Cincinnati," Lola Ridge Papers, Sophia Smith Collection, Smith College. Copyright Kay Boyle. Reprinted by permission of the Estate of Kay Boyle.

33. See "The Children's Crusade for Amnesty," in *The Children's Crusade* (pamphlet). *National Rip-Saw,* March 10, 1922, Frank P. O'Hare Collection, box 12, folder 18, Missouri Historical Society, St. Louis, http://womhist.alexanderstreet.com/kro/doc016.htm (accessed February 13, 2012).

34. Boyle to Ridge, December 31, 1923, Lola Ridge Papers, Sophia Smith Collection, Smith College.

35. "Increases Wages, Cuts Working Week," *New York Times,* January 3, 1922.

36. "Pacifist Whipped in Kuklux Style," *New York Times,* October 30, 1917, 3.

37. "Cincinnati Women Object to Villard," *New York Times,* February 4, 1921, 3.

38. Quoted in Spanier, introduction to Boyle, *Process,* xxvi.

39. Boyle to Ridge, August 20, 1923, Lola Ridge Papers, Sophia Smith Collection, Smith College. Copyright Kay Boyle. Reprinted by permission of the Estate of Kay Boyle.

Chapter 4. Important Gifts

1. Scott to Ridge [December 1921], Lola Ridge Papers, Sophia Smith Collection, Smith College.

2. Garland later became the Scotts' patron for a time, providing them with a monthly income from February 1922 through October 1928 with some lapses—see White, *Fighting the Current,* 84, 102, and 112.

3. Marilyn Elkins, "'Another Facet of Herself': The Complicated Case of Evelyn Scott and Kay Boyle," in *Evelyn Scott: Recovering a Lost Modernist,* edited by Dorothy M. Scura and Paul C. Jones, 69 (Knoxville: University of Tennessee Press, 2001).

4. Scott to Ridge, February 24, 1923, Lola Ridge Papers, Sophia Smith Collection, Smith College.

5. Ibid.

6. ibid.

7. Ibid. [May 13, 1923], Lola Ridge Papers, Sophia Smith Collection, Smith College.

8. Ibid. [1923], Lola Ridge Papers, Sophia Smith Collection, Smith College.

9. Ibid. [January 1923], Lola Ridge Papers, Sophia Smith Collection, Smith College.

10. McAlmon and Boyle, *Being Geniuses Together,* 155. Copyright Kay Boyle. Reprinted by permission of the Estate of Kay Boyle.

11. Ibid., 152. Copyright Kay Boyle. Reprinted by permission of the Estate of Kay Boyle.

12. Ibid., 153. Copyright Kay Boyle. Reprinted by permission of the Estate of Kay Boyle.

13. See the biographies of Scott by Callard and White, who document some of Scott's later struggles with mental illness. Perhaps her most detrimental and poignant obsessive enterprise was the intense and years-long struggle to reestablish normal relations with her son, Creighton Scott, who maintained minimal contact with her after a visit in 1949. Creighton and his wife, Paula, kept Scott informed about major events in their lives, but her tendency to write to postmasters and employers in an effort to enforce contact was damaging to their personal and professional lives.

14. McAlmon and Boyle, *Being Geniuses Together,* 153. Copyright Kay Boyle. Reprinted by permission of the Estate of Kay Boyle.

15. Ibid., 152. Copyright Kay Boyle. Reprinted by permission of the Estate of Kay Boyle.

16. Ridge to Scott [1919], Evelyn Scott Collection, Harry Ransom Humanities Research Center, University of Texas at Austin.

17. Scott to Ridge [1924], Lola Ridge Papers, Sophia Smith Collection, Smith College.

18. Ibid.

19. Ibid.

20. Boyle to Ridge, June 20, 1923, Lola Ridge Papers, Sophia Smith Collection, Smith College.

21. Ibid., December 31, 1923, Lola Ridge Papers, Sophia Smith Collection, Smith College. Copyright Kay Boyle. Reprinted by permission of the Estate of Kay Boyle.

22. McAlmon and Boyle, *Being Geniuses Together,* 150. Copyright Kay Boyle. Reprinted by permission of the Estate of Kay Boyle.

23. Ibid., 151. Copyright Kay Boyle. Reprinted by permission of the Estate of Kay Boyle.

24. Scott to Ridge [1923], Lola Ridge Papers, Sophia Smith Collection, Smith College.

25. Ibid. [1924], Lola Ridge Papers, Sophia Smith Collection, Smith College.

26. Ibid.

27. Boyle to Scott, August 11, 1924, Evelyn Scott Collection, Harry Ransom Humanities Research Center, University of Texas at Austin. Copyright Kay Boyle. Reprinted by permission of the Estate of Kay Boyle.

28. Dorothy Scura, afterword to Evelyn Scott, *Escapade* (Charlottesville: University Press of Virginia, 1995), 313–15.

29. Boyle to Ridge, August 11, 1924, Lola Ridge Papers, Sophia Smith Collection, Smith College. Copyright Kay Boyle. Reprinted by permission of the Estate of Kay Boyle.

30. Ibid. Copyright Kay Boyle. Reprinted by permission of the Estate of Kay Boyle.

31. Scott to Ridge, October 15, 1924, Lola Ridge Papers, Sophia Smith Collection, Smith College.

32. The original letter from Scott to Boyle has not survived. Scott is quoted in Boyle to Ridge, December 15, 1924, Lola Ridge Papers, Sophia Smith Collection, Smith College. Copyright Kay Boyle. Reprinted by permission of the Estate of Kay Boyle."The Book of Cincinnati" is published for the first time in an appendix to this book. Copyright Kay Boyle. Published by permission of the Estate of Kay Boyle.

33. Ibid. Copyright Kay Boyle. Reprinted by permission of the Estate of Kay Boyle.

34. Ibid. Copyright Kay Boyle. Reprinted by permission of the Estate of Kay Boyle.

35. Ibid. Copyright Kay Boyle. Reprinted by permission of the Estate of Kay Boyle.

36. Boyle to Ridge, April 1, 1925, Lola Ridge Papers, Sophia Smith Collection, Smith College. Copyright Kay Boyle. Reprinted by permission of the Estate of Kay Boyle.

37. Ibid. Copyright Kay Boyle. Reprinted by permission of the Estate of Kay Boyle.

38. White, *Fighting the Current*, 103.

39. Boyle to Ridge, October 21, 1925, Lola Ridge Papers, Sophia Smith Collection, Smith College.

40. Ibid., March 24, 1926, Lola Ridge Papers, Sophia Smith Collection, Smith College. Copyright Kay Boyle. Reprinted by permission of the Estate of Kay Boyle.

41. Ibid., November 5, 1926, Evelyn Scott Papers, Harry Ransom Humanities Research Center, University of Texas at Austin. Copyright Kay Boyle. Reprinted by permission of the Estate of Kay Boyle.

42. Ibid. Copyright Kay Boyle. Reprinted by permission of the Estate of Kay Boyle.

43. Scholars disagree about the actual nature of Ethel Moorhead's relationship with Ernest Walsh. The two main biographies of Boyle, by Spanier and Mellen, diverge in their interpretation of the situation. It is true that Ethel Moorhead was twenty-six years older than Walsh. The fictionalized version of their relationship in Boyle's novel *Year before Last* represents the two as nephew and aunt, but in most respects the aunt behaves as a jealous lover. Until more evidence surfaces, scholars will be unable to decide on the fine details. Certainly the emotional dynamic with Boyle, Walsh, and Moorhead was of a romantic triangle.

44. Boyle to Ridge, January 12, 1927, Lola Ridge Papers, Sophia Smith Collection, Smith College. Copyright Kay Boyle. Reprinted by permission of the Estate of Kay Boyle.

45. Boyle to Scott, March 18, 1927, Evelyn Scott Collection, Harry Ransom Humanities Research Center, University of Texas at Austin. Copyright Kay Boyle. Reprinted by permission of the Estate of Kay Boyle.

46. McAlmon to Williams, 1921, quoted in McAlmon and Boyle, *Being Geniuses Together,* 23. Copyright Kay Boyle. Reprinted by permission of the Estate of Kay Boyle.

47. McAlmon and Boyle, *Being Geniuses Together,* 202. Copyright Kay Boyle. Reprinted by permission of the Estate of Kay Boyle.

48. Boyle to Scott, October 22, 1927, Evelyn Scott Papers, Harry Ransom Humanities Research Center, University of Texas At Austin.

49. Ibid. Copyright Kay Boyle. Reprinted by permission of the Estate of Kay Boyle.

50. Boyle to Ridge, November 29, 1927, Lola Ridge Papers, Sophia Smith Collection, Smith College. Copyright Kay Boyle. Reprinted by permission of the Estate of Kay Boyle.

51. "What Evelyn Scott sent me of her report to the Guggenheim," Kay Boyle Papers, Morris Library, Southern Illinois University. Copyright Kay Boyle. Reprinted by permission of the Estate of Kay Boyle.

52. McAlmon and Boyle, *Being Geniuses Together,* 151. Copyright Kay Boyle. Reprinted by permission of the Estate of Kay Boyle.

53. Callard, *Pretty Good for a Woman,* 6.

54. Ibid., 5.

55. Scott, "Selected Letters of Evelyn Scott," *Southern Quarterly* 28 (Summer 1990): 72.

56. Scott created new names for the principal characters in the book and recast her mother and father as aunt and uncle, in part to shield her parents' identities. It is truer to the relationships the book portrays to acknowledge the actual ties, especially the one between Evelyn and her mother. In my discussions of *Escapade* "Aunt Nannette" is referred to as Evelyn's mother; "John" is referred to as Cyril; "Uncle Alec" is referred to as Evelyn's father; and "Jackie" is referred to as her son, Creighton Scott.

57. Scott, *Escapade* (New York: Seltzer, 1923), 214.

58. The basic biographical material summarized here found its way into subsequent fiction and autobiography written by Evelyn Scott and Cyril Kay Scott. Maude Dunn reappears as Mrs. Farley in *The Narrow House* and *Narcissus* by Evelyn Scott and in Cyril Kay Scott's novel *Blind Mice* and his autobiography, *Life Is Too Short.*

59. White, *Fighting the Current,* 208–9.

60. Cyril Kay Scott, *Life Is Too Short,* 168.

61. Boyle to Ridge, December 31, 1923, Lola Ridge Papers, Sophia Smith Collection, Smith College. Copyright Kay Boyle. Reprinted by permission of the Estate of Kay Boyle.

62. Boyle, *Process: A Novel,* edited by Sandra Spanier (Urbana: University of Illinois Press, 2001), 2. Copyright Kay Boyle. Reprinted by permission of the Estate of Kay Boyle.

63. Ibid., 7. Copyright Kay Boyle. Reprinted by permission of the Estate of Kay Boyle.

64. Ibid., 1. Copyright Kay Boyle. Reprinted by permission of the Estate of Kay Boyle.

65. Ibid., 2. Copyright Kay Boyle. Reprinted by permission of the Estate of Kay Boyle.

66. Ibid., 18. Copyright Kay Boyle. Reprinted by permission of the Estate of Kay Boyle.

67. Ibid., 19. Copyright Kay Boyle. Reprinted by permission of the Estate of Kay Boyle.

68. Ibid., 68. Copyright Kay Boyle. Reprinted by permission of the Estate of Kay Boyle.

69. Ibid., 33. Copyright Kay Boyle. Reprinted by permission of the Estate of Kay Boyle.

70. Ibid. Copyright Kay Boyle. Reprinted by permission of the Estate of Kay Boyle.

71. Ibid., 54. Copyright Kay Boyle. Reprinted by permission of the Estate of Kay Boyle.

72. Ibid., 86. Copyright Kay Boyle. Reprinted by permission of the Estate of Kay Boyle.

73. Ibid., 87. Copyright Kay Boyle. Reprinted by permission of the Estate of Kay Boyle.

74. Elkins, "'Another Facet of Herself,'" 80.

75. Boyle, *Process,* 62. Copyright Kay Boyle. Reprinted by permission of the Estate of Kay Boyle.

76. Ibid., 95. Copyright Kay Boyle. Reprinted by permission of the Estate of Kay Boyle.

Chapter 5. "The mind spins from the mind"

1. Gilbert Harrison, *The Enthusiast: A Life of Thornton Wilder* (New Haven, Conn.: Ticknor & Fields, 1983), 246–49; Thornton Wilder, *The Selected Letters of Thornton Wilder,* edited by Robin G. Wilder and Jackson R. Bryer (New York: HarperCollins, 2008). Currently the biographical materials in *Selected Letters* are the most reliable for information about Charlotte Wilder. Available information about her will expand with the publication of Penelope Niven's *Thornton Wilder: A Life* (HarperCollins) in autumn 2012); White, *Fighting the Current,* particularly 226–27; Callard, *Pretty Good for a Woman,* 164, 177; Katherine H. Adams, *A Group of Their Own: College Writing Courses and American Women Writers, 1880–1940* (Albany, N.Y.: SUNY Press, 2001), 148–49.

2. Letters from Charlotte Wilder to Evelyn Scott begin in July of 1932 (Wilder to Scott, July 14, 1932, Evelyn Scott Family Archive). Wilder and Scott resided in separate quarters at Yaddo in July 1931 and September 1933; in a letter written to poet Louise Bogan after Scott's death, Wilder remembered meeting Scott and her husband, John Metcalfe, in 1930 (Wilder to Bogan, January 29, 1964. Louise Bogan Papers, Archives and Special Collections, Amherst College Library).

3. Amos Niven Wilder, *Spiritual Aspects of the New Poetry* (New York: Harper, 1940), 138–39. This study also briefly discusses Scott's novel *A Calendar of Sin,* 176.

4. Scott to Amos Niven Wilder, April 16, 1939, transcribed by Amos Niven Wilder, Amos Niven Wilder Papers, Yale Collection of American Literature, Beinecke Rare Book and Manuscript Library, Yale University.

5. For instance Charlotte Wilder provided a critique of Scott's 1937 novel *Bread and a Sword* while it was still in manuscript. Wilder to Scott [1934], Evelyn Scott Family Archive.

6. Thornton Wilder, *The Selected Letters of Thornton Wilder*, 118.

7. *Llamarada 1919*, Mount Holyoke College, 154; Leslie Fields, Mount Holyoke College Electronic Records Archivist, e-mail to author, June 1, 2011.

8. Charlotte Wilder's contributions to the *Mount Holyoke Monthly* include "The Tile," 28 (June 1918): 70–71; "The Farmerette Trolleys," 28 (November 1918): 91–94; "Fabre: Poet and Scientist," 28 (December 1918): 114–16; "My Monarch Visible," 28 (March 1919): 236–38; and "Storm. A Story," 28 (April 1919): 261–69.

9. Micheline Letendre, Mount Holyoke College, e-mail to author, May 26, 2011.

10. Thornton Wilder, *The Selected Letters of Thornton Wilder*, 125.

11. Ibid., 153.

12. Ibid., 159.

13. Amos Niven Wilder, "Wilder Records," 2. Amos N. Wilder Papers, Yale Collection of American Literature, Beinecke Rare Book and Manuscript Library, Yale University.

14. Zephorene L. Stickney, college archivist and special collections curator, Wheaton College, e-mail to author, June 2, 2011.

15. John Salmond, *Gastonia 1929: The Story of the Loray Mill Strike* (Chapel Hill: University of North Carolina Press, 1995), 76.

16. *New York City Guide* (New York: Random House, 1939). Wilder noted in a letter to her brother Amos Niven Wilder that she contributed to the chapter covering Central Park. Charlotte Wilder to Amos Niven Wilder, February 21, 1938, "Wilder Records," 8–9, Amos Niven Wilder Papers, Yale Collection of American Literature, Beinecke Rare Book and Manuscript Library, Yale University.

17. Letters document some of this financial activity. Charlotte Wilder to Amos Niven Wilder [summer 1932], "Wilder Records," 3, Amos Niven Wilder Papers, Yale Collection of American Literature, Beinecke Rare Book and Manuscript Library, Yale University; Charlotte Wilder to Thornton Wilder, March 20, 1939, Thornton Wilder Papers, Yale Collection of American Literature, Beinecke Rare Book and Manuscript Library, Yale University; Charlotte Wilder to Evelyn Scott [early 1941], Scott Family Archive. In this late letter to Scott, Wilder showed her willingness to loan Scott money borrowed from another friend—possibly demonstrating one more aspect of the crises she faced at that time.

18. Reviews of *Phases of the Moon* include: William Rose Benét, "The Phoenix Nest," *Saturday Review of Literature* 14 (June 6, 1936): 16; William Lyon Phelps, "As I Like It," *Scribner's Magazine* 103 (September 1936): 187–88. Eda Lou Walton, "Two New Books of Poetry," *New York Times Book Review*, April 19, 1936, 21; Morton Dauwen Zabel, "Poets of Five Decades," *Southern Review* 2 (Summer 1936): 160–77.

19. Wilder to Ridge, April 15, 1935, Lola Ridge Papers, Sophia Smith Collection, Smith College. Ridge wrote a letter supporting Wilder for the Houghton-Mifflin Fellowship, which Wilder did not receive.

20. Wilder to Ridge [1935], Lola Ridge Papers, Sophia Smith Collection, Smith College.

21. "Isolation," *Nation* 138 (May 23, 1934): 595; "After Anger," *Saturday Review of Literature* 11 (April 27, 1935): 646; "Song For Her," *Voices* 83(Autumn 1935): 29; "To Beauty," *Poetry* 47 (January 1936): 198.

22. The nineteen previously published poems collected in *Mortal Sequence* are "Disarrangement," *New York Herald Tribune Books,* September 21, 1930, 4; "Apprenticed," *New York Herald Tribune Books,* October 19, 1930, 4; "Of Persons Not Alive." *Poetry* 39 (March 1932): 303; "Requiem," *Saturday Review of Literature* 9 (July 23, 1932): 1; "Sculptured," *Nation* 138 (January 24, 1934): 105; "Ferns," *Saturday Review of Literature* 11 (August 25, 1934): 66; "Of the Chase," *Saturday Review of Literature* 11 (August 25, 1934): 66; "Spider View," *Voices* 83(Autumn 1935): 30; "From Winter...," *Voices* 83(Autumn 1935): 30; "Evensong," *Voices* 83(Autumn 1935): 31; "City Streets," *Poetry* 47 (January 1936): 198; "Self-Knowledge," *Saturday Review of Literature* 16 (October 2, 1937): 4; "Loew's Sheridan," *Nation* 146 (June 18, 1938): 703; "Sanctuary," *Poetry* 52 (July 1938): 202; "Sober Dance," *Voices* 95 (Autumn 1938): 35; "Alas the World," *Voices* 95 (Autumn 1938): 35; "Arid Land," *Voices* 95 (Autumn 1938): 36; "New Gods," *Voices* 95 (Autumn 1938): 37; "The Boughs of Love," *Saturday Review of Literature* 20 (June 17, 1939): 4.

23. Charlotte Wilder to Thornton Wilder, July 8, 1967, Thornton Wilder Papers, Yale Collection of American Literature, Beinecke Rare Book and Manuscript Library, Yale University; Charlotte Wilder to Elizabeth Ames, August 18, 1928, Yaddo Records, 1870–1980, Manuscripts and Archives, New York Public Library.

24. Charlotte Wilder to Thornton Wilder, January 5, 1935, Thornton Wilder Papers, Yale Collection of American Literature, Beinecke Rare Book and Manuscript Library, Yale University.

25. Charlotte Wilder, "Words of Annotation," *Phases of the Moon* (New York: Coward-McCann, 1936), 89.

26. Ibid., 87–88.

27. Charlotte Wilder to Amos Niven Wilder [early 1939], "Wilder Records," Amos Niven Wilder Papers, Yale Collection of American Literature, Beinecke Rare Book and Manuscript Library, Yale University.

28. For instance in Herman Rubin's *Eugenics and Sex Harmony* (New York: Publishers Guild, 1933), the idea of abstinence as a cause of nervous disorders is broadly accepted. Rubin followed Freud in saying "the repression of the normal sexual instinct is directly traceable [in] practically all cases of hysteria, and a good proportion of nervous, mental, and physical disorders that afflict womankind," 154.

29. Charlotte Wilder to Isabella Wilder [1935], Thornton Wilder Papers, Yale Collection of American Literature, Beinecke Rare Book and Manuscript Library, Yale University.

30. Saxe Commins to Scott, April 18, 1935, Amos Niven Wilder Papers, Yale Collection of American Literature, Beinecke Rare Book and Manuscript Library, Yale University.

31. Thomas Wentworth Higginson, "The Horizon Line," *Century* 46 (September 1893): 736.

32. Wilder, "Words of Annotation," *Phases of the Moon*, 88.

33. Thornton Niven Wilder to Charlotte Wilder [telegram], March 23, 1936, Thornton Wilder Papers, Yale Collection of American Literature, Beinecke Rare Book and Manuscript Library, Yale University.

34. Charlotte Wilder, *Phases of the Moon*, 89.

35. Louise Bogan, "The Season's Verse," *New Yorker*, May 23, 1936, 80.

36. Wilder to Bogan, May 31, 1936, Louise Bogan Papers, Archives and Special Collections, Amherst College Library.

37. Bogan to May Sarton, October 22, 1955, in *What the Woman Lived: Selected Letters of Louise Bogan, 1920–1970*, edited by Ruth Limmer, 300–301 (New York: Harcourt Brace Jovanovich, 1973).

38. This episode is recounted in White, *Fighting the Current*, 231.

39. Wilder to Bogan [October 1937], Louise Bogan Papers, Archives and Special Collections, Amherst College Library.

40. A group of Charlotte Wilder's unpublished poems is preserved in the Beinecke Rare Book and Manuscript Library, Yale University.

41. Wilder to Rollo Brown, October 15, 1939, "Wilder Records," 16, Amos Niven Wilder Papers, Yale Collection of American Literature, Beinecke Rare Book and Manuscript Library, Yale University.

42. Boyle to Scott, December 29, 1933, Evelyn Scott Collection, Harry Ransom Humanities Research Center, University of Texas at Austin.

43. Amos Niven Wilder, "Wilder Records" and "Concerning Charlotte Wilder Running from 1932 to 1961," Amos Niven Wilder Papers, Yale Collection of American Literature, Beinecke Rare Book and Manuscript Library, Yale University.

44. Charlotte Wilder to Amos Niven Wilder [December 1940], transcribed by Amos Niven Wilder in "Concerning Charlotte Wilder," 4–8, Amos Niven Wilder Papers, Yale Collection of American Literature, Beinecke Rare Book and Manuscript Library, Yale University.

45. Scott to Amos Niven Wilder, December 5, 1940, transcribed by Amos Niven Wilder, Amos Niven Wilder Papers, Yale Collection of American Literature, Beinecke Rare Book and Manuscript Library, Yale University.

46. Scott's correspondence with Emma Goldman spans from 1925 until November 1939, a few months before Goldman's death in May 1940. The Emma Goldman Papers were published on microfilm, and copies are held in various research libraries: *The Emma Goldman Papers: A Microfilm Edition*, 69 reels (Cambridge, U.K.: Chadwyck-Healey, 1991).

47. Scott to Dreiser, April 30, 1939, Theodore Dreiser Papers, Annenberg Rare Book and Manuscript Library, University of Pennsylvania.

48. Callard, *Pretty Good for a Woman*, 164–65.

49. Ibid, 167.

50. Scott to Amos Niven Wilder, December 5, 1940, transcribed by Amos Niven Wilder, Amos Niven Wilder Papers, Yale Collection of American Literature, Beinecke Rare Book and Manuscript Library, Yale University.

51. Ibid.

52. Charlotte Wilder to Amos Niven Wilder [December 1940], transcribed by Amos Niven Wilder, Amos Niven Wilder Papers, Yale Collection of American Literature, Beinecke Rare Book and Manuscript Library, Yale University.

53. Charlotte Wilder to Scott [early 1941], Scott Family Archive.

54. Isabella Wilder to Amos Niven Wilder, March 1, 1941, "Wilder Records," 20–21, Amos Niven Wilder Papers, Yale Collection of American Literature, Beinecke Rare Book and Manuscript Library, Yale University.

55. Thornton Wilder, *The Selected Letters*, 358.

56. Ibid., 497.

57. Thornton Wilder to Amos Niven and Catherine Wilder, September 10, 1953, ibid., 514.

58. Charlotte Wilder, autobiographical fragment, Wilder Family Papers, Yale Collection of American Literature, Beinecke Rare Book and Manuscript Library, Yale University. While—according to family members—there was an extant copy of Wilder's autobiography, it can no longer be found (author's interviews with Tappan Wilder, October 12, 2009, and July 8, 2011). It is not clear from the remaining fragment how much of this work she completed or if this surviving fragment is a part of the original autobiography she titled "I Remember."

59. Charlotte Wilder, autobiographical fragment, Wilder Family Papers, Yale Collection of American Literature, Beinecke Rare Book and Manuscript Library, Yale University.

60. Isabella Wilder to Amos Niven Wilder, March 2, 1941, "Wilder Records," 21–22, Amos Niven Wilder Papers, Yale Collection of American Literature, Beinecke Rare Book and Manuscript Library, Yale University.

61. Charlotte Wilder to Scott, November 9, 1945, "Concerning Charlotte Wilder Running from 1932 to 1961," 15–16, Amos Niven Wilder Papers, Yale Collection of American Literature, Beinecke Rare Book and Manuscript Library, Yale University.

62. Charlotte Wilder to Thornton Wilder [1941], Wilder Family Papers, Yale Collection of American Literature, Beinecke Rare Book and Manuscript Library; Charlotte Wilder to Amos Niven Wilder, March 9, 1946, Amos Niven Wilder Papers, Yale Collection of American Literature, Beinecke Rare Book and Manuscript Library; Charlotte Wilder to Amos Niven Wilder, March 30, 1946, Amos Niven Wilder Papers, Yale Collection of American Literature, Beinecke Rare Book and Manuscript Library, Yale University.

63. Charlotte Wilder to Scott, October 20, 1945, Amos Niven Wilder Papers, Yale Collection of American Literature, Beinecke Rare Book and Manuscript Library, Yale University.

64. Ibid.

65. Ibid.

66. White, *Fighting the Current,* 227.

67. Scott to Charlotte Wilder, May 31, 1946, transcribed by Amos Niven Wilder, Amos Niven Wilder Papers, Yale Collection of American Literature, Beinecke Rare Book and Manuscript Library, Yale University.

68. Scott to Amos Wilder, March 3, 1948, transcribed by Amos Niven Wilder, Amos Niven Wilder Papers, Yale Collection of American Literature, Beinecke Rare Book and Manuscript Library, Yale University.

69. Thornton Wilder to Scott, July 28, 1944, in *The Selected Letters of Thornton Wilder,* 422–23.

70. Charlotte Wilder to Scott, September 23, 1951, Evelyn Scott Collection, University of Tennessee Libraries, Special Collections, Knoxville.

71. Charlotte Wilder to Scott, September 28, 1951, Evelyn Scott Collection, Library, University of Tennessee Libraries, Special Collections, Knoxville.

72. Charlotte Wilder, unpublished poem, Wilder Family Papers, Yale Collection of American Literature, Beinecke Rare Book and Manuscript Library, Yale University.

Chapter 6. "Reflecting bright pain"

1. Showalter, *A Jury of Her Peers,* xiii.

2. For bibliographical information on Scott, see Peggy Bach, "Evelyn Scott, 1920–1988," *Bulletin of Bibliography* 46, no. 2 (1989): 76–91; Will Brantley, "Evelyn Scott's Reflections on Modernism: The Nonfiction Prose," in *Evelyn Scott: Recovering a Lost Modernist,* 201–21; and Paul Jones, "Evelyn Scott's Nonfiction Prose: A Supplemental Bibliography," *Mississippi Quarterly* 59 (Fall 2006): 627–39. To date there are two biographies of Scott, each chronicling the vicissitudes of her career: Callard, *Pretty Good for a Woman* and White, *Fighting the Current.* Callard treats the poetry lightly; White gives more attention to both *Precipitations* and *The Winter Alone,* but does not treat *The Gravestones Wept,* which was only in manuscript at the time she completed her study.

3. Scott, *The Collected Poems. The Gravestones Wept* was first published in the 2005 edition of *The Collected Poems.*

4. Early versions of many poems in *The Gravestones Wept* were composed within a framework of Scott's conversion, which was brief. She later edited out evidence of a specifically Catholic inspiration. For a discussion of this process, see *The Collected Poems,* 211–34.

5. The manuscript history and background of *The Gravestones Wept* are discussed in the introduction to *The Collected Poems of Evelyn Scott.*

6. There is a brief mention of *The Winter Alone* in William Soskin, "Other Notable Books," *New York Evening Post,* March 26 and 27, 1930, 15. Other reviews of *The Winter Alone* include *Boston Transcript,* May 24, 1930, 2; *New York World,* March 30, 1930, 10; Dudley Fitts, "The Verse of Evelyn Scott," *Poetry: A Magazine of Verse* 36 (September 1930): 338–43 (Fitts's reading loses some of its power because he misquoted a key line he was explicating from "Low Tide"). Babette Deutsch, "A Seeing Eye," *New York*

Herald Tribune Books, April 27, 1930, 20; Eda Lou Walton, "The Poetry of a Novelist," *Nation* 131 (July 23, 1930): 100–101.

7. John Metcalfe, *Sally: The Story of a Foster-Girl* (New York: Scribners, 1936).

8. McAlmon and Boyle, *Being Geniuses Together*, 151. Copyright Kay Boyle. Reprinted by permission of the Estate of Kay Boyle.

9. Some of Scott's editorial changes to revise or "erase" the conversion experience from her text (specifically in a poem titled "Many Mansions") are documented in Caroline Maun, "Erasing Grace: A Revised Conversion Experience in Evelyn Scott's *The Gravestones Wept*," *Mississippi Quarterly* 59 (Fall 2006):613–26.

10. David Gelernter, *1939: The Lost World of the Fair* (New York: Free Press, 1995), 67.

11. Scott, preface to the novel "Escape into Living," 12–14, Evelyn Scott Collection, University of Tennessee Libraries, Special Collections, Knoxville.

BIBLIOGRAPHY

Manuscript Collections

Louise Bogan Papers, Archives and Special Collections, Amherst College Library.

Kay Boyle Papers, Morris Library, Southern Illinois University.

Theodore Dreiser Papers, Annenberg Rare Book and Manuscript Library, University of Pennsylvania.

Lola Ridge Papers, Sophia Smith Collection, Smith College.

Evelyn Scott Collection, Harry Ransom Humanities Research Center, University of Texas at Austin.

Evelyn Scott Collection, including "Escape into Living," University of Tennessee Libraries, Special Collections, Knoxville.

Evelyn Scott Family Archive, Seaford, U.K.

A. G. Stephens Collection, State Library of New South Wales.

Amos Niven Wilder Papers and Thornton Wilder Papers, Yale Collection of American Literature, Beinecke Rare Book and Manuscript Library, Yale University.

Yaddo Records, 1870–1980, Manuscripts and Archives, New York Public Library.

Published Sources

Adams, Katherine H. *A Group of Their Own: College Writing Courses and American Women Writers, 1880–1940.* Albany, N.Y.: SUNY Press, 2001.

Auden, W. H. *Collected Poems.* Edited by Edward Mendelson. New York: Vintage, 1976.

Avrich, Paul. *The Modern School Movement: Anarchism and Education in the United States.* Oakland, Calif.: AK Press, 2006.

Bach, Peggy. "Evelyn Scott, 1920–1988." *Bulletin of Bibliography* 46, no.2 (1989): 76–91.

Bachelard, Gaston. *The Poetics of Space.* Boston: Beacon Press, 1994.

Benstock, Shari. *Women of the Left Bank: Paris, 1900–1940.* Austin: University of Texas Press, 1986.

Berke, Nancy. *Women Poets on the Left: Lola Ridge, Genevieve Taggard, Margaret Walker.* Gainesville: University Press of Florida, 2001.

Bloom, Allan David. *The Closing of the American Mind.* New York: Simon & Schuster, 1988.

Bogan, Louise. *What the Woman Lived: Selected Letters of Louise Bogan, 1920–1970.* Edited by Ruth Limmer. New York: Harcourt Brace Jovanovich, 1973.

Boyle, Kay. *Process.* Edited by Sandra Spanier. Urbana: University of Illinois Press, 2001.

———. *Words That Must Somehow Be Said: Selected Essays of Kay Boyle, 1927–1984.* Edited by Elizabeth S. Bell. San Francisco: North Point Press, 1985.

Boyle, Kay, and Robert McAlmon. *Being Geniuses Together, 1920–1930.* San Francisco: North Point Press, 1984.

Brantley, Will. "Evelyn Scott's Reflections on Modernism: The Nonfiction Prose." In *Evelyn Scott: Recovering a Lost Modernist,* edited by Dorothy Scura and Paul Jones, 201–21. Knoxville: University of Tennessee Press, 2001.

Brooks, Cleanth. *The Well Wrought Urn: Studies in the Structure of Poetry.* New York: Harcourt, Brace, 1947.

Callard, D. A. *Pretty Good for a Woman: The Enigmas of Evelyn Scott.* New York: Norton, 1986.

Carnevali, Emanuel. *The Autobiography of Emanuel Carnevali.* Edited, with a preface, by Kay Boyle. New York: Horizon Press, 1967.

"The Children's Crusade for Amnesty." In *The Children's Crusade* (pamphlet). St. Louis: *National Rip-Saw,* March 10, 1922, Frank P. O'Hare Collection, box 12, folder 18, Missouri Historical Society, St. Louis. Reprinted in Lubna Alam, "Kate Richards O'Hare and Peace Activism," Saint Louis University, http://womhist.alexanderstreet.com/kro/doc016.htm (accessed February 13, 2012).

Cixous, Helene. "The Laugh of the Medusa." *Signs* 1 (Summer 1976): 875–93.

Clark, Suzanne. *Sentimental Modernism: Women Writers and the Revolution of the Word.* Bloomington: Indiana University Press, 1991.

Cowley, Malcolm. *Exile's Return.* New York: Penguin Classics, 1976.

Diamond, Jared. *Guns, Germs, and Steel: The Fates of Human Societies.* New York: Norton, 2005.

Drake, William. *The First Wave: Women Poets in America, 1915–1945.* New York: Macmillan, 1987.

Elkins, Marilyn. "'Another Facet of Herself': The Complicated Case of Evelyn Scott and Kay Boyle." In *Evelyn Scott: Recovering a Lost Modernist,* edited by Dorothy M. Scura and Paul C. Jones, 69–84. Knoxville: University of Tennessee Press, 2001.

Gelernter, David. *1939: The Lost World of the Fair.* New York: Free Press, 1995.

Goldman, Emma. *The Emma Goldman Papers: A Microfilm Edition.* 69 reels. Cambridge, U.K.: Chadwyck-Healey, 1991.

Greenberg, Arielle, and Rachel Zucker, eds. *Women Poets on Mentorship: Efforts and Affections.* Iowa City: University of Iowa Press, 2008.

Hanscombe, Gillian, and Virginia Smyers. *Writing for Their Lives: The Modernist Women, 1900–1940.* London: Women's Press, 1987.

Harrington, Joseph. *Poetry and the Public: The Social Form of Modern U.S. Poetics.* Middletown, Conn.: Wesleyan University Press, 2002.

Harrison, Gilbert. *The Enthusiast: A Life of Thornton Wilder.* New Haven, Conn.: Ticknor & Fields, 1983.

Hirsch, E. D., Joseph F. Kett, and James S. Trefil. *Cultural Literacy: What Every American Needs to Know.* New York: Vintage, 1988.

Jolas, Eugene. "Proclamation." *transition* 16–17 (June 1929): 13.

Jones, Paul. "Evelyn Scott's Nonfiction Prose: A Supplemental Bibliography." *Mississippi Quarterly* 59 (Fall 2006): 627–39.

Josephson, Matthew. *Life among the Surrealists: A Memoir.* New York: Holt, Rinehart & Winston, 1962.

Kreymborg, Alfred. *Our Singing Strength: An Outline of American Poetry (1620–1930).* New York: Coward-McCann, 1929.

———. *Troubadour.* New York: Sagamore Press, 1957.

Leggott, Michele. "The First Life: A Chronology of Lola Ridge's Australasian Years," *Bluff '06: A Poetry Symposium in Southland, 21–24 April 2006,* http://www.nzepc.auckland.ac.nz/features/bluff06/leggott.asp (accessed October 5, 2009).

Loeb, Harold. *The Way It Was.* New York: Criterion, 1959.

Loy, Mina. "Love Songs." *Others* 1 (July 1915): 6–8.

Maun, Caroline. "Erasing Grace: A Revised Conversion Experience in Evelyn Scott's *The Gravestones Wept.*" *Mississippi Quarterly* 59 (Fall 2006): 613–26.

McAlmon, Robert. *Post-Adolescence.* Edited by Edward N. S. Lorusso. Albuquerque: University of New Mexico Press, 1991.

McAlmon, Robert, and Kay Boyle. *Being Geniuses Together, 1920–1930.* San Francisco: North Point Press, 1984.

Mellen, Joan. *Kay Boyle: Author of Herself.* New York: Farrar, Straus & Giroux, 1994.

Metcalfe, John. *Sally: The Story of a Foster-Girl.* New York: Scribners, 1936.

Murphy, Russell. "Alfred Kreymborg." In *Dictionary of Literary Biography.* Vol. 54: *American Poets, 1880–1945.* 3rd series, part 1: A–M. Detroit: Gale Research, 1987.

Nelson, Cary. *Repression and Recovery: Modern American Poetry and Politics of Cultural Memory.* Madison: University of Wisconsin Press, 1989.

———. *Revolutionary Memory: Recovering the Poetry of the American Left.* New York: Routledge, 2003.

New York City Guide. New York: Random House, 1939.

Porter, Katherine Anne. *The Never-Ending Wrong.* London : Secker & Warburg, 1977.

Quartermain, Peter. "Lola Ridge." In *Dictionary of Literary Biography.* Vol. 54: *American Poets, 1880–1945.* 3rd series, part 2: N–Z. Detroit: Gale Research, 1987.

Ridge, Lola. *Dance of Fire.* New York: Smith & Haas, 1935.

———. *Firehead.* New York: Payson & Clarke, 1929.

———. *The Ghetto and Other Poems.* New York: Huebsch, 1918.

———. *Light in Hand: Selected Early Poems of Lola Ridge.* Edited by Daniel Tobin. Williamsburg, Mass.: Quayle Press, 2007.

———. *Red Flag.* New York: Viking, 1927.

———. *Sun-Up and Other Poems.* New York: Huebsch, 1920.

———. "Woman and the Creative Will." Edited by Elaine Sproat. Michigan Occasional Paper no. 18 (Spring 1981).

Rozendal, Michael Arend. "On the Line: A Reconsideration of 1930s Modernist and Proletarian Radicalism." Ph.D. diss., State University of New York at Buffalo, 2006.

Rubin, Herman. *Eugenics and Sex Harmony.* New York: Publishers Guild, 1933.

Salmond, John. *Gastonia 1929: The Story of the Loray Mill Strike.* Chapel Hill: University of North Carolina Press, 1995.

Samson, Gloria Garrett. *The American Fund for Public Service: Charles Garland and Radical Philanthropy, 1922–1941.* Westport, Conn.: Greenwood, 1996.

Scott, Cyril Kay. *Life Is Too Short: An Autobiography.* Philadelphia: Lippincott, 1943.

———. *Sinbad.* New York: Seltzer, 1923.

Scott, Evelyn. *Background in Tennessee.* New York: McBride, 1937.

———. *Bread and a Sword.* New York: Scribners, 1937.

———. *The Collected Poems of Evelyn Scott.* Edited by Caroline Maun. Orono, Maine: National Poetry Foundation, 2005.

———. *Escapade.* New York: Seltzer, 1923.

———. *Narcissus.* New York: Harcourt Brace, 1922.

———. *The Narrow House.* New York: Boni & Liveright, 1921.

———. *The Shadow of the Hawk.* New York: Scribners, 1941.

———. "Selected Letters of Evelyn Scott." Edited by Natalie Schroeder. *Southern Quarterly* 28 (Summer 1990): 63–76.

———. *The Wave.* New York: Cape & Smith, 1929.

Scura, Dorothy. Afterword to *Escapade,* 287–321. Charlottesville: University Press of Virginia, 1995.

Scura, Dorothy, and Paul Jones, eds., *Evelyn Scott: Recovering a Lost Modernist.* Knoxville: University of Tennessee Press, 2001.

Seltzer, Jack. *Kenneth Burke in Greenwich Village: Conversing with the Moderns, 1915–1931.* Madison: Wisconsin University Press, 1996.

Showalter, Elaine. *A Jury of Her Peers: American Women Writers from Anne Bradstreet to Annie Proulx.* New York: Knopf, 2009.

Spanier, Sandra. *Kay Boyle: Artist and Activist.* Carbondale: Southern Illinois University Press, 1986.

———. "'Paris Wasn't Like That': Kay Boyle and the Last of the Lost Generation." In *Lives Out of Letters: Essays on American Literary Biography and Documentation in Honor of Robert N. Hudspeth.* Edited by Robert D. Habich, 169–88. Madison, N.J.: Fairleigh Dickinson University Press, 2004.

Tompkins, Jane. *Sensational Designs: The Cultural Work of American Fiction, 1790–1860.* New York: Oxford University Press, 1985.

Toomer, Jean. *The Letters of Jean Toomer 1919–1924.* Edited by Mark Whalan. Knoxville: University of Tennessee Press, 2006.

Welker, Robert. "Evelyn Scott: A Literary Biography." Ph.D. diss., Vanderbilt University, 1958.

White, Mary Wheeling. *Fighting the Current: The Life and Work of Evelyn Scott.* Baton Rouge: Louisiana State University Press, 1998.

Wilder, Amos Niven. *Spiritual Aspects of the New Poetry.* New York: Harper, 1940.

Wilder, Charlotte. "Fabre: Poet and Scientist." *Mount Holyoke Monthly* 28 (December 1918): 114–16.

———. "The Farmerette Trolleys." *Mount Holyoke Monthly* 28 (November 1918): 91–94.

———. "My Monarch Visible." *Mount Holyoke Monthly* 28 (March 1919): 236–38.

———. *Mortal Sequence.* New York: Coward-McCann, 1939.

———. *Phases of the Moon.* New York: Coward-McCann, 1936.

———. "Storm. A Story." *Mount Holyoke Monthly* 28 (April 1919): 261–69.

———. "The Tile." *Mount Holyoke Monthly* 28 (June 1918): 70–71.

Wilder, Thornton. *The Selected Letters of Thornton Wilder.* Edited by Robin G. Wilder and Jackson R. Bryer. New York: HarperCollins, 2008.

Williams, William Carlos. *The Autobiography of William Carlos Williams.* New York: New Directions, 1967.

Yeats, William Butler. *Essays.* New York: Macmillan, 1924.

Index

www.ingramcontent.com/pod-product-compliance
Lightning Source LLC
LaVergne TN
LVHW050153080826
844660LV00002B/186

* 9 7 8 1 6 1 1 1 7 0 8 6 3 *